Management
in
International
Perspective

ADMINISTRATION SERIES
Eugene E. Jennings, *Editor*

Edited by

S. BENJAMIN PRASAD
University of Nevada

Management
in
International
Perspective

New York

APPLETON - CENTURY - CROFTS
Division of Meredith Publishing Company

To Michael David Prasad

Preface

In the field of industrial management and economics the influence of international events, since World War II, has been significant. The study of comparative economic systems and of developmental economics is now recognized in most parts of the world as an integral and growing field in economics. If one were to identify the basic problem of economic development as one permeated by the problem of industrial development, then management is clearly important to economic growth. The diversity of the problems of management at a comparative level is of considerable interest not only to students of management but also to students of economic development strategy.

There is neither a paucity of articles and books in management literature nor is there a lack of definitions of management. Management literature contains definitions and usages applying the term "management" to a process, to a set of functions, to a type of skill and ability, to a class of people. Most of these definitions and usages are culture-oriented and they are legitimately so. One fruitful endeavor to employ the term management in the context of a sociocultural framework and of economic change is that of Clark Kerr, John Dunlop, Frederick Harbison, and Charles Myers in their *Industrialism and Industrial Man*.

To reflect for a moment, when we consider "management" it is in terms of the values and the ends to which we are accustomed, and also as it relates to the conduct of business enterprises as we see them in North America. The American economy is an archetype of what is loosely known as the Western world. But to consider management simply as it is known in the Western world is a rather restricted conception, for, outside the United States, there exist different types and sets of managerial problems especially as these problems are related to industrial development. Moreover, the existing managerial organization theories which attempt to explain, predict, and influence industrial organization behavior have limitations in terms of their orientation, applicability, and usefulness in different cultures with differing industrial structural patterns. Modern management is chiefly bred in the Western world, and despite its aspiration toward universality it bears the stamp of Western issues and institutions.

The idea of collecting papers which converge on the general theme of comparative management appears fruitful especially in terms of manifesting the sociocultural orientation of management theories and practices in various parts of the world. The pioneering effort in this direction was made some years ago by Frederick Harbison and Charles Myers. From a review of literature in "management in a world perspective" two complementary but somewhat distinct approaches can be delineated. The first, *international business* or *international business management,* focusses its attention on the strategies of multinational corporations in a world-market situation. The second, *comparative management,* centers its attention on national corporations, both public and private, in terms of their strategic role in the country's industrial development. This approach, of course, essentially entails the comparative method.

The purpose of this volume, in which the general theme is comparative managerialism rather than international business management, is threefold:

1. To illustrate, particularly to the student in economics and business studies, that management as we identify it and the managerial tools and techniques as we apply them are not the same in all countries although some similarities prevail.

2. To bring together a small number of selected materials, published in the United States and abroad, which articulate the theme of comparative managerialism, so that the volume could usefully serve as supplementary reading material for such courses as Comparative Economic Systems, Comparative Management, International Business, Management of Economic Development, and for graduate level seminars in business, economics, and allied social sciences.

3. To augment the scope of teaching and research interest in the area of comparative management. It is an area of study which

is just beginning to secure a permanent academic position, just as developmental economics did some years ago. A few graduate schools of business have, in recent years, launched such courses as *comparative management, comparative management systems,* and *management of economic development.* Part III is especially meant to serve this objective.

The editor expresses his gratitude to the following persons who have, in some important way, been of help to him in the preparation of this volume. They are Professor Paul Gordon of Indiana University, Professor Evsei Liberman of Kharkov University (USSR), Professor Anant Negandhi of UCLA, Mr. Otto Nowotny of Hoffman-La Roche & Company (Basle, Switzerland) and Dean Robert C. Weems of the College of Business Administration, University of Nevada.

Acknowledgment is made to the following institutions and organizations which granted permission to reproduce the editor's and other articles as well as selected materials: Academy of Management, Administrative Management Society, Harvard Business School, Joint Economic Committee of the Congress of the United States, The Institute of Industrial Relations of the University of California at Berkeley, International University Contact for Management Education (The Netherlands), Graduate School of Business Administration of the University of Michigan, McGraw-Hill Book Company, Inc., New York University Press, School of Business Administration of Seton Hall University, and the Regents of the University of California.

S.B.P.

Contributing Authors

Joseph Berliner
Brandeis University

J. Boddewyn
New York University

Keith Davis
Arizona State University

Milton Derber
University of Illinois

Bernard D. Estafen
*University of California,
Los Angeles*

Richard Farmer
Indiana University

Joseph Froomkin
Economist, I.B.M. Corporation

Frederick Harbison
Princeton University

Eugene C. McCann
Louisiana State University

John F. Mee
Indiana University

Charles Myers
*Massachusetts Institute of
Technology*

Anant R. Negandhi
*University of California,
Los Angeles*

E. Schmidt Nestley

Otto Nowotny
*Hoffman-La Roche & Co.,
Basle, Switzerland*

S. Benjamin Prasad
University of Nevada

Barry Richman
*University of California,
Los Angeles*

Narendra Sethi
*St. John's University,
Jamaica, N. Y.*

Raymond Vuerings
*Lovanium University,
Léopoldville*

Contents

II. MANAGERIALISM IN ADVANCED
AND DEVELOPING COUNTRIES

III. MANAGERIAL MODELS IN
WORLD PERSPECTIVE

Introduction

This volume is divided into three parts. Part I, *Comparative Management Philosophy and Development* (papers 1-6), deals with some comparative studies of managerial philosophy in the United States, Europe, and Latin America as well as the prospects of managerial philosophy in developing countries. It also deals with the logic of managerial development on an international scale. Part II, *Managerialism in Advanced and Developing Countries*, encompasses management, organization, and decision-making as they are affected by the goals of enterprises and economies. Papers 7-14 deal with such advanced countries as Switzerland, Japan, United States, Soviet Russia, and with emerging countries in Africa, Asia, and the Middle East. Part III, *Managerial Models in World Perspective* (papers 15-19), presents some theoretical structures in the area of comparative management. The subject dealt with here is still in its infancy and one can recognize the importance of theoretical models which are imperative for empirical work.

The contributors of these papers represent many nationalities and manifold backgrounds and experiences. Some are Americans who have had considerable field experience in the analysis of managerial problems as they relate to countries other than the United States. Some are nationals of other countries who are well informed about the economic and managerial problems in their own countries. Others are or were nationals of other countries, who are now in the United States, and who have incorporated their knowledge and experience of more than one geographical entity in their presentations. It is interesting to bear in mind the backgrounds and experiences of the contributors when examining their essays. The following is a brief introduction to each of the selections. A conclusion based upon these papers is provided at the end of the book.

1. American versus European Management Philosophy. Otto Nowotny compares and contrasts managerial philosophy as professed and practiced in the United States and Western Europe. He is primarily concerned with delineating the differences between these philosophies and he does so by exploring several concepts which influence and account for these differences. The author endeavors, first, to demonstrate the relative importance of "facts" to "values" in the case of top-level managerial decision-making, and then examines the essential differences between American and European management philosophies. This analysis permits Nowotny to hypothesize that "the basic characteristics of American and European managerial philosophies are so strikingly complementary that a combination of what is best in both must lead to an improvement in the conduct of Euro-American free enterprise economies." This is rather a unique notion about two regions which manifest ample cultural semblance.

2. An Aspect of Management Philosophy in the United States and Latin America. In this paper, Eugene McCann deals with an aspect of managerial philosophy in the North American and South American regions where cultural semblance may be said to be minimal. It is the decision-making aspect of the managerial philosophy with which the author is concerned. He discusses the question of why, in Latin American countries, the scientific method of inquiry-analysis and problem-solving is almost conspicuous by its absence. He ascribes this phenomenon to the cultural and personality characteristics of the population in general and the business managers in particular. McCann makes the important point that the implication and consequences of whether management is more philosophy, art, or science, or some combination thereof, can be of great import in approaching management in diverse cultural settings.

3. Comment: Decision-Making in Latin American Business. This is an extension of McCann's hypothesis. Employing McCann's observation on the comparative decision-making aspect between American and Latin American management philosophy, S. Benjamin Prasad has provided a more comprehensive framework within which the significance of McCann's hypothesis could be recognized. Drawing primarily from literature on Latin America, he develops a framework which permits him to deduce a major hypothesis which may have validity in other areas of emerging economies as well.

4. Future Management Philosophy: A Synthesis. John F. Mee discusses the emerging stage of management thought and the future management philosophy as an integral part of the broad question: "If our dynamic economy is to continue through another century, what must be done to develop further a management philosophy that will augment economic growth and social satisfactions?" Emphasizing that management philosophy for the future will evolve to accommodate the decisions and actions of managers to a changing economic, social, political, and technological environment, Mee identifies four stages in the evolution of management thought. This selection pertains to the stage of synthesis—a treatment of the possible elements of future management philosophy in world perspective.

5. Logic of Management Development. The concept of industrial management since the days of Frederick Winslow Taylor has been broadened in scope with the introduction of new perspectives by several scholars such as Follet, Barnard, Drucker, and Simon. Based upon studies of eighteen countries, Frederick Harbison and Charles Myers infer that there is a logic of management development in advanced as well as in emerging countries. They expound this concept by means of a threefold concept of management as *an economic resource, a system of authority,* and *a class.*

6. International Search for Managerial Talent. The initial premise of S. Benjamin Prasad is that the paucity of managerial talent in many of the developing nations has slowed the tempo of industrialization. He emphasizes that modern management is an integral part of modern technology. From the point of view of effectively executing industrialization programs, the basic problem, as the author sees it, is the lack of managerial talent and the problems of seeking it. Within the context of India, he explores the problem of the lack of opportunity in terms of the impediments to entry into the managerial class. Potential managerial talent may not be scarce in many countries but what is certainly scarce is the opportunity to exercise or develop such talent.

7. Management and Management Teaching in Switzerland.

E. Schmidt Nestley, a Swiss professor, precedes his discussion by a brief review of the Swiss economy. Within this context, he then explores the premise that in developing and formulating general principles and methods of management, national conditions and attitudes strongly influence both the thinking and acting of the manager in various parts of the world. For example, concerning the thinking and acting upon enterprise goals, Nestley points out that the only criterion in Switzerland is the monetary profit. This author also tries to dovetail the problems and prospects of management education in Switzerland.

   8. *Management and Organization in Japan.* Drawing from his experiences emanating from his business trips to Japan, Joseph Froomkin discusses the vital question, How does Japanese management practice make a high rate of economic growth possible, when it is generally characterized by little formal organization, little delegation of authority, and little reliance on staff functions? The discerning reader should explore the question, What lessons can enterprises in emerging countries learn from the management style in a traditional society such as Japan?

   9. *Managerial Incentives and Decision-Making: A Comparison of the United States and the Soviet Union.* Joseph Berliner deals, on a comparative basis, with such issues as education and career choice, competition among careers, material incentives for managers, and the nature of production, procurement, and investment decisions in the Soviet economic system. A major conclusion of this Joint Economic Committee inquiry was that since American managers operate in a different environment, their problems and practices differ from those of the Soviet managers. But in those aspects of economic life in which the American economy approximates the operating conditions of the Soviet economy, American managers develop forms of behavior similar to those of the Soviet enterprise managers.

   10. *New Managerialism in Czechoslovakia and the Soviet Union.* While neocapitalism is spreading in Western Europe there has emerged a set of changes in Eastern Europe which Prasad refers to as the *new managerialism.* He explores the new managerialism with reference to two countries: Czechoslovakia and the USSR. The paper highlights the most recent managerial changes. Plausible implications are also explored. The general tenor of this analysis is

that Comecon countries are likely to open their economic systems to some Western influence but they can do this only in a political context which is acceptable to them.

11. Managing Productivity in Developing Countries. Improvement in productivity is a universal goal of enterprises. Keith Davis examines the "managing of productivity" as an international managerial problem situation in which a blending of various cultures and new adjustment by all persons involved are imperative. The useful insights which this author provides concerning effective overseas management stem from his personal observations in several countries. His conclusion is that if management in underdeveloped countries is approached with the view of integrating modern technology and management with the cultural patterns, then increased industrial productivity is sure to follow.

12. Some Managerial Aspects of the African Economic Problem. Dealing with Africa as one region, Prasad discusses the duality of the African economy, the necessary classification of business enterprises, and the duality of the African managerial problem. His concern is with two vital questions, namely, how to minimize the continued dependence upon foreign high-level manpower, and how to augment managerialism among indigenous Africans. He hypothesizes that "small business management" has a vital role to play in African managerialism and economic development.

13. Problems of Industrial Management in Developing Countries. Raymond Vuerings discusses the problems encountered in the newly independent African countries from the point of view of how firms and foreign investors react when the countries are not disposed to leave development to the control of private enterprise. After examining the factors which dominate the new environment in the African countries, the author deals with the attitude of free enterprise in regard to 1. investment, 2. African public authorities, and 3. the Africanization of staff. The theme of aligning the objectives of the private firms to those of the new African states permeates his discussion.

14. Some Aspects of Management in Israel. Despite its small population (about 2.5 million people) and the recency of its industrialization, Israel provides an interesting scene for a study of "management." Milton Derber bases the analysis of worker participation in management on his field studies of large Israeli enterprises. In many industrializing countries one recognizes two sectors —public and private. In Israel there are three—public, private, and histadrut (labor). The author explores the extent of worker participation in management in these three sectors of Israel's economy, and raises some intriguing questions about management and organizational behavior in general: 1. Does the management process limit worker participation? 2. Can workers serve as co-managers? 3. Does "industrial democracy" call for participation?

15. The Comparative Approach to the Study of Business Administration. J. Boddewyn addresses himself to three questions fundamental to a clear understanding of the comparative approach. These are: "Compared to What?" "Compared as to What?" and "Compared for What?" The author deals with the methodological problems which are inherent but not insurmountable in comparative studies in management.

16. International Management. Within an interdisciplinary frame of reference, Narendra Sethi examines the current constituents and future trends of international management systems by 1. analyzing the values comprising the totality of internationalization, and 2. interpreting the broad essential themes of international management from the viewpoint of industrial development.

17. A Model for Research in Comparative Management. Richard Farmer and Barry Richman develop a theoretical approach to study managerial efficiency at a comparative level. The authors focus on the external constraints and their effect on management and develop a new conceptual framework for comparative studies.

18. An Appraisal of the Farmer-Richman Model in Comparative Management. This is an evaluation by S. Benjamin Prasad of the above model. He rearranges the structure of the Farmer-Richman model, and discusses the merits and demerits of the methodology and approach of Farmer and Richman.

19. A Research Model to Determine the Applicability of American Management Know-How in Differing Cultures and/or Environments. Anant Negandhi suggests a research approach in which three major variables—management philosophy, process, and effectiveness—serve as the pillars for the structure of the model. He has developed a method for studying enterprises in truly comparable situations with a view to ascertaining what aspects of American management are transferable to an alien culture.

I

Comparative Managerial Philosophy and Development

1

American Versus European Management Philosophy *

OTTO NOWOTNY

Most top executives develop and practice their own management philosophy. Obviously, then, there is nothing so clear-cut as a single managerial style which is uniformly adhered to by all American or all European business leaders. Yet underlying the behavior and attitudes of these two different groups of executives are certain general characteristics or common denominators which can be identified. In this article I will attempt to deal in a systematic manner with some of the major aspects of American and European management philosophies, hoping to show where and why these philosophies differ and what we can learn from these differences.

Naturally, I am conscious of the controversial nature of attempts to generalize on such a vast subject, and I partly share the apprehensions of those who believe that all generalizations are false. Thus, what will be said in this article should be taken as a finger pointing in the direction of truth rather than the truth itself.

FACTS AND VALUE

Oscar Wilde's well-known saying, "a cynic is a man who knows the price of everything and the value of nothing," is a poet's re-

* Reprinted with permission from the *Harvard Business Review* (March-April, 1964), and the author. Otto Nowotny is with F. Hoffmann-La Roche & Co. Ltd. Basle, Switzerland.

minder that we tend to view everything in life in quantifiable "fact" and/or nonquantifiable "value" terms. We have done so since the beginnings of human history, and it is improbable that this dual way of looking at things will ever be replaced by a purely factual approach which eliminates all value judgments. Therefore, top executives—like all other people—will continue to base their decisions on so-called facts, on the one hand, and subjective values, commonly referred to as management or business philosophy, on the other.

The relative importance of "facts" to "values" in top-level decision-making will naturally vary with each particular business situation. However, it is significant that top managers often make decisions because they value certain ways of action—in spite of the price they must pay. Yet rarely, if ever, will they do something they do not value just because the cost is low. Mere common sense, therefore, indicates that value judgments will usually have priority over purely factual considerations in making vital business decisions.

This seemingly trite conclusion is interesting, however, because it contradicts the popular and, I fear, growing belief that increasing complexity in business—necessitating a large staff of specialists and expensive data processing equipment—will make top managers proportionately more dependent on "facts" for their decision-making. It is, of course, highly probable that the vast amount of available information will tempt many business leaders to use "facts" as an escape from the freedom (and burden) of choosing the proper "values." But if business is to be led with creative imagination instead of being merely administered bureaucratically, more rather than less management philosophy will be required in the future.

Because scientific progress will force middle managers to spend more time in keeping up with the many technical developments in their areas of responsibility, top managers, to counterbalance this increasing specialization, will have to concentrate more on the fundamentals of management philosophy if they do not want to descend, gradually but surely, to the level of mere coordinators. To express it differently: "doing" will require more "knowing" by middle managers, and more "maturity" by top executives. And there is hardly a better way for top managers to become more mature than to try to understand and, if necessary, to assimilate the values and beliefs of others which are different from their own. Let us, therefore, investigate the essential differences between European and American outlooks first and then analyze some of the differences in management philosophy.

PAST VERSUS FUTURE

The most striking difference between the outlooks of Europeans and Americans lies in their orientation toward time. It is as if they were standing back to back, with the European inclined to look to the past and present, and the American seeing the present and the future. The European's attachment to the past accounts for his respect for such characteristics as wisdom, stability, convention, necessity, quality, and diversity. The American's more futuristic outlook leads him to respect vitality, mobility, informality, abundance, quantity, and organization. But unless Europeans abandon some of their excessive attachment to the past and Americans their more or less profound disregard for it, little change can be expected. I certainly do not share the optimism of businessmen who believe that what is best in the American and European management philosophies will automatically find its way from one continent to the other by a kind of effortless "osmosis." A brief analogy may clarify my point:

If we connect two steel tanks, one containing high-pressure cold air and the other low-pressure hot air, we will inevitably end up with a tepid and rather pressureless mixture in both vessels, unless the lack of pressure in one and the lack of heat in the other are compensated for by supplying the required energy from the outside. In other words, an effort has to be made if the specifically high energy levels of each tank are to be maintained after having been connected to one another.

In management philosophy, as well, an effort has to be made, unless we want to run the risk of having the typically American and European qualities simply meet at the level of the lowest common denominator.

WISDOM VERSUS VITALITY

There is hardly a better way to illustrate the meanings of vitality and wisdom, and to show how differently these two qualities are

valued in America and Europe, than by briefly comparing some of
the typical traits of a man who is in his twenties with those of a
man who is in his sixties.

The young man, impatient to apply his overflowing energy
(and wasting a lot of it in the process), is mainly interested in the
"here and now," the practical side of life. His preoccupations are
essentially short range, and he frequently ignores the side effects
that his actions are likely to produce in the future. There is always
a halo of naïveté around him, which his youth does not allow him
to get rid of. His most positive characteristic, conditioning all his
others, is certainly vitality. But this greater urge for expansion, distinguishing the vital from the nonvital person, when combined with
his youthful experience of life, keeps him swinging dangerously
from one extreme to another and makes him correspondingly superficial.

The older man, whose vital energies have calmed down considerably since the heydays of his youth, has developed a certain
amount of moderation. To him one can apply the words of the
dean of a California law school, who, in defending his school's
policy of hiring only professors aged sixty-seven and above, said:
"Most bad habits are out of their system. If they weren't, they'd be
dead by now." Life has taught the older man to be skeptical and to
prefer slow, organic growth to rapid change. He thinks a little more
about the long-range effects of his actions and, appreciating the
contemplative side of life, has lost some of his former gregarious-
ness. His most positive characteristic can be called wisdom, although
this quality may also make him less mobile and less enterprising.

Though neither continent can claim to have a monopoly on
vitality or wisdom, it is reasonably true to say that American management philosophy is, in general, more vital than wise, while
Europe's is more wise than vital. Here is an example:

One of the most rigorous belt-tightening operations by a major corporation was undertaken by Chrysler Corporation in 1961. It fired 7,000 of
36,000 white collar employees, from secretaries to high-ranking executives.
The action helped lower Chrysler's break-even point to 725,000 cars and
trucks from a million units. President Lynn A. Townsend says the cutback didn't impair efficiency.[1]

---

[1] "White Collar Cutback," *The Wall Street Journal* (January 3, 1963), p. 19.

Obviously, some very superfluous things must have been allowed to happen in the past, or else the company could not have cut its white collar work force by twenty percent without a loss of efficiency. Vitality (the urge to expand) not moderated by wisdom, had resulted in an extremely uneconomic situation which only equally extreme countermeasures could correct. But—and this again is proof of vitality—the necessary measures were taken.

Slow Growth

In Europe the moderating influence of wisdom (that is, top management's preference for slow, organic growth) has admittedly prevented many production and clerical jobs from being mechanized a long time ago. But at the middle-management level and, even more, at the top-management level, in comparison with American, understaffing rather than overstaffing seems to be the rule. Important decisions are still made by single individuals or at least by a much smaller group of top executives than in the United States.

With most of the strategic decisions concentrated at the top, there is also a pronounced tendency not to communicate the reasoning behind these decisions to those at lower management levels. Obviously, European top executives try to save a part of the time American executives spend on communications, though they do so somewhat at the expense of middle-management "learning." This fact, indeed, is reflected by the smaller percentage of key positions in European businesses held by executives aged 40 or less. The theory that a good wine requires many years of aging in the dark, coolish cellar has been extended to the business executive and seems to have become an integral part of European management philosophy. To complete the analogy, it must be added that no one pretending to know about wines and being responsible for their quality would think much of changing promising bottles from one wine cellar to another.

This particular way of thinking, I believe, explains the relatively small interest European top executives still show for training their potential managers in American or American-style business schools. In addition, they are convinced, though they will rarely admit it in public, that only the more technical aspects, and not the essence or the style of executive leadership, can be learned there.

They would certainly agree with a comment recently made in *The Wall Street Journal* that "the individual manager's style will probably be decisive in the end, in terms of executive success, failure, or mediocrity. *Style* is the secret plus or minus." [2] Or as the French scientist and writer Georges-Louis de Buffon has put it even more briefly: *"Le style est l'homme même."*

As a result of this attitude, climbing up the corporate ladder in Europe takes the aspiring executive, generally speaking, more time than in North America. But once he reaches the top, the risk of his coming down again is also much lower. Anyone who would go to the trouble of counting the number of executives who have been displaced from the top of their pyramid would probably find this percentage to be considerably higher in America than in Europe.

Combining the Advantages

Many examples, of course, could be cited to reveal how wisdom and vitality are given different weights in the American and European management philosophies. But they would all lead us to the same conclusion: to optimize our business performance it is necessary to combine the advantages of both characteristics. How can this be done?

In Europe large reserves of vital energy could certainly be released by dropping some of the most outdated conventions. For example, those that require most decisions to be made at the top rather than at the lowest possible level in the organization, or those that hold an executive responsible to his superior but do not require the superior to bother about actively developing his subordinate's capacities. Many of these conventions need close questioning so that the weight given presently to different values can be redistributed more logically.

In American business an increase in wisdom could probably be achieved if top executives would try to keep in mind wisdom's most basic definition—"Avoiding the unnecessary." Or as the Chinese philosopher Chuang Tzu put it nearly 25 centuries ago: "If one wants to act sanely one must do but the inevitable. To stick to the inevitable is the way of the wise." Pointing in exactly the same

2 *Ibid.* (July 24, 1963), p. 12.

direction, but of more recent origin, are the famous three laws of Parkinson:

> An official wants to multiply subordinates, not rivals.
>
> Officials make work for each other.
>
> Expansion means complexity, and complexity decay.[3]

All three of these laws are nothing else than a warning to top management to do only that which is absolutely necessary and to avoid "futile busy-ness." To put a conscious break between stimulus and reaction—as Napoleon is said to have done when he once decided to leave his mail unopened for a certain time, only to find that at the end of it most of the letters had taken care of themselves and so did not have to be answered—is one of the particular privileges and duties of which top management must make more liberal use.

For wisdom requires deliberation and deliberation requires time. The late Speaker of the House, Sam Rayburn, is reported to have said that one of the greatest statements ever made by anybody was *"Just a minute."* He was pointing out the catalytic effect of time in the legislative process. The same is important in the judicial process and in life in general.

STABILITY VERSUS MOBILITY

After what has already been said, it is certainly not surprising to find stability and mobility two other typical opposing characteristics of our respective management philosophies.

Accordingly, intercompany job changes in the higher echelons are much less frequent in Europe than in America. In part this is a matter of language and geographical barriers; but it is also the result of Europeans being more skeptical about human nature than Americans. They prefer to let several years of observation pass before giving high-level responsibility to a new member of management, who, by the time he gets it, is of course no longer new. Switching companies at a frequency customary in America would

[3] C. Northcote Parkinson, *Parkinson's Law* (Boston: Houghton Mifflin Company, 1957), p. 4; and C. Northcote Parkinson, *Inlaws and Outlaws* (Boston: Houghton Mifflin Company, 1962), p. 233.

normally lead to an intolerable loss of time in the career of a European executive.

Similarly, changing jobs within companies in the sense of job rotation has never been as fully accepted by big business in Europe as it has been in America. This is partly due to the fact that specialization on lower- and middle-management levels has not been pushed as far ahead as in America; thus, job rotation seems less urgent. It is also due partly to top management's belief that rotating people through various jobs is costly and can lead to situations where a great number of employees have had experience in a lot of areas but lack solid competence in any one. With all strategic and many tactical decisions still being made at or at least close to the top, there is also less need for vision on the lower levels. There is, however, more demand for highly competent "spade-work" on which European top management can solidly build its decisions without having to resort to double- and triple-checking through extensive committee work. Committees are, therefore, far less important in the European than they are in the American management process.

Another illustration of stability and mobility can be found in the area of job titles. Business on the European continent uses, in general, a very limited number of official titles—much as the military forces do in employing a relatively small number of different ranks. Thus, knowing a European executive's title and the size of the company he works for makes it fairly easy to estimate his responsibility as well as his earnings. The latter are rarely, if ever, spoken of openly, contrary to the practice in America where knowing the earnings of an executive is often the only way to measure his responsibility—the number of titles being so great as to make quick orientation a rather hopeless affair.

"If the deserving employee is hungry for a title, the good manager gives him one, even if it turns out to be but Third Assistant to the Head of Sub-Assembly Department No. 3," is a typical bit of reasoning by the American manager which would find little acceptance in Europe. European top executives believe that the widespread use of custom-tailored titles to compensate for a lack of job satisfaction is a short-range expedient which merely starts a vicious circle, forcing top management to dole out ever more status symbols and leading ultimately to the highly sophisticated and eventually costly kind of human relations being practiced by large corporations in America. Indeed, by comparison, human relations in European business still have a kind of rustic simplicity.

CONVENTION VERSUS INFORMALITY

Although an open-door policy and a first-name basis are both widely accepted practices in American business, they are but two exterior signs of how American management philosophy has given preference to informality, where numerous conventions are still strictly adhered to. But the roots of our different convictions go much deeper, and it seems as if in the eternal dilemma of all executives—having to exercise authority and trying to be liked—European top management has constantly preferred to put more weight on the former and American top management more on the latter quality.

Thus, American managers seem to feel that human relations in Europe have an authoritarian and paternalistic flavor, and consider the social distance between individuals a remnant from feudal times. Europeans, in turn, believe America to be guilty of promoting excessive egalitarianism and status stripping which, in their eyes, is not only naïve and unrealistic, but must inevitably destroy management effectiveness in the long run.[4] The results of these different attitudes are interesting.

Whereas human relations in European business lack the outer nonchalance and friendliness found in America, they do not seem to share the inner tensions which are often apparent on the other side of the Atlantic. American tensions stem, it seems, largely from trying to adhere to the overly idealistic point of view that one must be like everybody or, if that cannot be done, at least pretend to do so. Though the former is impossible except for those approaching sainthood, the latter—because of the pretense involved—creates all kinds of nervous tensions, feelings of guilt and frustration, which any ordinary person can easily detect.

---

[4] See, for example, Abraham Zalensnik, "The Human Dilemmas of Leadership," *Harvard Business Review* (July-August, 1963), p. 51. For a contrary point of view see Robert N. McMurry, "The Case for Benevolent Autocracy," *Harvard Business Review* (January-February, 1958), p. 82.

But between the extremes of bullying or loving people there is ample room for the less spectacular but more effective way of simply respecting them. It will always depend on the maturity of the individual top executive how good a balance he can finally strike between convention and informality. However, no progress will be possible unless top executives give up the idea that only the American or the European brand of human relations is correct, and will admit that both have severely suffered from inbreeding the same ideas for many decades. Success will come only to the extent top executives learn to live with open minds.

NECESSITY VERSUS ABUNDANCE

The relative lack of natural resources in Europe and their abundance in America has not been without profound impact on the management philosophies of our two continents. Thus, the tendency toward thrift and the desire to avoid waste are only too evident in the thinking of European executives, to whom the concept of planned obsolescence still seems to be as foreign as ever.

Nowhere can this important aspect of managerial philosophy be observed any better than in various types of automobiles produced in Europe and America. The differences in horsepower, in body design and finish, in fuel consumption, and in size, for example, all serve to illustrate the same point: Europe has been, and still is, subject to the law of necessity and cannot afford to conduct its business with American generosity and disregard for seemingly less important details. Cars such as a Volkswagen, a Citroën, or a Mercedes are the definite reflection of an entirely different management philosophy than are a Chevrolet, a Ford, or a Cadillac.

United States military strategy, to use another example, has also been based on the country's abundance of resources. This is evidenced by the American way of fighting World War II, namely, to concentrate large masses of troops and to act fast. This is, of course, the logical military application of Newton's Law: Net Force = Mass × Acceleration. But Europe, not having the same resources (mass), had to build its strategy mainly on flexibility (acceleration) and surprise. It was Churchill who said that "the good-luck charm of success in war is surprise," thus stating the typically European approach. Surprise and particularly its cause, secrecy, are therefore a natural part of European management philosophy.

American executives and financial analysts often complain about the rudimentary information given by European companies in their balance sheets and profit and loss statements. But the smaller amount of information published is in strict accordance with local government rules. And if no voluntary supplements are handed out to the general public, it is only partly to seek additional protection from foreign competition behind the smoke screen of secrecy. It is also caused by the general conviction that the more information a company releases, the more explanations it has to give. The tendency toward thrift and the desire to avoid what is not really necessary are, therefore, two important reasons why European business seems to be playing its cards close to its chest.

QUALITY VERSUS QUANTITY

With economic necessity being such an important factor in European management philosophy, business in Europe has always found it necessary to stress quality much more than quantity. How else—to cite an extreme example—could a small country like Switzerland, with hardly any natural resources, have become a prosperous nation than by simply doing a few things better than anybody else would do them? Quality, not quantity, is, therefore, the outstanding characteristic of European management philosophy and explains many facets of the way European executives think.

A very typical facet is the fairly general tendency of Europeans to think before trying. As a leading European businessman once said: "We are not in the habit of increasing through wastefulness the chance of a random hit."

And so, the technique of "brainstorming," which has been given much publicity in America, has never really been accepted in Europe. Preference has always been given to high-quality, individual thinking rather than to group thinking which explains, as already mentioned, why the managements of European companies seem to be relatively understaffed in comparison with American firms. The following quotation reflects this difference.

Europeans have learned by tradition to get along with less personnel, especially less university-trained personnel. I have been told that, after the war, United States and British industrialists could not understand how so important a drug as antimalarial quinacrine could have been developed by researchers operating in three small rooms, since in the United States several hundred scientists were employed to test all possible variations of the basic formula and, in the end, came up with the same compound.[5]

Another technique which has never made much impression in Europe is "speed reading." Although the quantity of reading matter has increased as much for the European as it has for the American executive, the former has in general refused the speed solution, believing that it necessarily leads to an accent on quantity at the expense of quality. He has relied more on selectivity to solve his reading problems.

He has also applied this same principle in his community and public activities, which seem to be but an infinite fraction of what many American executives have accepted. The reason behind this consistent refusal to get too involved outside the immediate sphere of work is the European conviction that each individual should, above all, concentrate on his job, because nobody aiming at top performance can afford to dissipate his energies. Top performance in any field requires a multiple effort in comparison with merely average performance.

I am assuming, as does the European, that outside activities inhibit on-the-job performance, a fact which many Americans vigorously would deny. Thus, by preferring quality to quantity (sometimes without regard to economic realities, to the extent of worshipping quality as an end in itself), European management is forced necessarily to favor selectivity and a concentration of efforts.

But by saying *yes* to quantity, one cannot say *no* to standardization, because these two characteristics of managerial philosophy are linked like Siamese twins. Quantity *per se* is certainly not bad. On the contrary, it has considerable social benefits, such as the increase in the standard of living resulting from mass production. But there are always the attendant dangers of excessive standardization trailing in its wake and of overorganization stifling individual initiative.

[5] Paul de Haen, "European Pharmaceutical Research," *Drug & Cosmetic Industry* (January 1961), p. 44.

DIVERSITY VERSUS ORGANIZATION

Overorganization, the European believes, is a particularly threatening consequence. The ideal of all our national economics and individual businesses is, of course, to arrive at a proper balance between organized, controlled activity and that which offers an incentive for a freer use of individual initiative. The European achieves order through definite status levels in his organization, but he does not try to organize man's every effort as do many American firms.

No doubt, there can be too little organization, that is, too much diversity. And in many instances European business performance could be improved if there were more of it. But top executives must be aware of the fact that aiming at good organization is like trying to keep a small ball balanced on top of a big one. Good organization is always—although we do not seem to be conscious of it—in a state of unstable equilibrium, needing slight but constant corrective action from the top. The goal is to strike a proper balance between European and American attitudes toward organization, with resulting higher performance.

Reaching this happy compromise is not easy and requires more wisdom than seems to be generally available. Here are the reasons.

The more vital energy we have, the more we want to do and the more we, therefore, favor organization, because organizing means doing things. There is a natural trend toward organization which is extremely difficult to resist, because organizational measures are not only easily set down on paper and made communicable (and "file-able!"), but also leave one with the exhilarating feeling that something has been done with apparently immediate results. Sometimes the result is much like that where an inoffensively weak virus is transferred from patient to patient and in the process becomes more virulent. So also can overorganization reach a dangerous stage.

Those who propose organizational measures to stimulate individual incentive are actually in a fairly weak logical position because the best incentive-building measure they often end up advocating is not to take any measure at all. This attitude lies at the root of one of our valuable educational tools, the case method, and is the basis of our free enterprise democracy. All three start out from the same principle—that individual incentive is best developed by the individual himself, with a minimum of order imposed from the outside.

CONCLUSION

The basic characteristics of American and European management philosophies are so strikingly complementary that a combination of what is best in both must lead to an improvement in the conduct of our Euro-American free enterprise economies. Of course, the crucial question is how to bring about this desirable change.

Surely no success whatsoever is to be expected of large-scale attempts to have top executives hold special international meetings in order to discuss some of the important topics of managerial philosophy. With "publicity" hanging over their heads like a sword of Damocles, few top executives, if any, would take the risk of seeing their statements misinterpreted. They would speak only in the most cautious terms—so cautious, indeed, that the essence of their statements would seldom be more than an agglomeration of euphemistic platitudes.

Although the written word is a wonderful medium for conveying "facts" to a larger public, we forget too easily that, in discussing "values," oral communication within a small group of individuals is by far the most preferable and practically the only way to avoid either banality or confusion.

Thus, the present trend in politics toward a more personal and secret diplomacy might well portend the direction in which top executives will have to move if they want to make a synthesis of what is best in American and European management philosophies.

2

An Aspect of Management Philosophy in the United States and Latin America *

EUGENE C. McCANN

The question of whether management is more philosophy, art, science, or some combination is frequently regarded as little more than useless academic debate. The position taken, however, has considerable bearing for research, education, and practice in the field. The implications and consequences of that starting position can be profound in approaching management in diverse cultural settings. In these days of aroused interest in Latin American exchanges involving programs of public and business administration, one of the relatively neglected points is the contrast between North Americans and Latin Americans in appraising scientific components of management.

MANAGEMENT: ART AND/OR SCIENCE

If management contains no guides, laws, principles, or any of the other elements of a science, then it must be an art. If it is truly an art, then everything which has ever been written about manage-

* Reprinted with permission from the *Academy of Management Journal* (June, 1964).

ment is of little or no use. All those who profess to teach management are either *estupidos* or frauds. Whether art can be codified and taught is not a settled matter. Art is skillful performance which comes from within a person and which can be learned only through practice and experience. Expression of an art is an individual matter. What can be taught, however, is science—truths, principles, laws. This aspect of management philosophy, therefore, must satisfy the question of whether management is an art, a science, or a combination.

For the most part, US business practitioners and business academicians agree that management is partly a science and partly an art. Businessmen and scholars have not always held this position. For instance, in the United States, before about 1880, management was considered solely an art:

A "manager" was born or was made so in the hot crucible of experience. He thus relied upon intuitive guidance when faced with a decision. . . . So in a sense he learned nothing from previous generations and could pass nothing on to succeeding generations as far as management skills were concerned.[1]

Frederick Taylor, Henri Fayol, Henry Gantt, Frank and Lillian Gilbreth and others, however, were not convinced. They felt that somewhere in management there is logic, that management embodies basic principles and relationships which can be set down, codified, and communicated. The search for management principles carried on since the turn of the century has uncovered many. Admittedly, certain areas of management, for the moment, must remain in the realm of art. Nevertheless, modern US businessmen and others who are concerned with group coordination believe that management does contain a science.

Management generally is considered an art in Latin America. Several indications tend to support this statement. Only rarely does one encounter a book or an article which deals with management in Latin America from a Latin American viewpoint. Furthermore, only rarely is management taught in Latin American colleges and universities. The major emphasis is on liberal arts.

[1] Michael J. Jucius and William Schlender, *Elements of Managerial Action* (Homewood, Ill.: Richard D. Irwin, Inc., 1960), p. 20.

Another indication which lends support to the notion that management is considered an art in Latin America is the sparing use of scientific method in Latin American business operations. Since Frederick Taylor popularized the use of scientific method as an aid to managerial decision-making, it has become basic to American management philosophy. Though the scientific method has been stated many times in many ways, Ralph C. Davis explains it probably as well as any. "The term 'scientific method' may refer to any orderly method that seeks to apply the logic of effective thinking to the solution of some type of problem." [2]

In American culture the utilization of this approach is widespread and not limited to business management. Scientific method meshes nicely with cultural attitudes that encourage an analytical approach to all types of decision-making activities. As a result, scientific method is the most used of any of the "tools" of American management. The lack of utilization of such a concept undoubtedly hampers Latin American decision-makers. Why they make little or no use of it warrants discussion.

CAUSES FOR IGNORING SCIENTIFIC METHOD

The effective utilization of scientific method requires patient, careful, orderly thinking and the ability to see reality objectively. The Latin American, however, tends to be impatient, impulsive, emotional and to disregard objectivity.[3]

Basing action on emotion is accepted, expected, and desired among Latin Americans because giving immediate expression to one's feeling is accepted, expected, and desired. Latin Americans are men of passion. In writing about the Spanish influence on Latin America and specifically on using emotion and intuition as the basis for determining action, William Schurz noted: "So that he may not do things according to reason or logic or cold calculation, for his mind is not orderly or systematic, but according to the light of intuition and the urge of strong feeling. He may even do some-

2 Ralph C. Davis, *Industrial Organization and Management,* 3rd ed. (New York: Harper & Row, 1957), p. 61.

3 Harry Stark, *Modern Latin America* (Coral Gables, Florida: University of Miami Press, 1957), p. 70.

thing for no good reason at all, but only by the prompting of caprice." [4]

Latin Americans are not so interested in results as are Anglo-Americans.[5] Action is important to a Latin American but not from a results point of view. The utility of results is relatively unimportant. Since he is a man of passion, action becomes more important than results because it allows the free expression of inner feelings. This is the important element—spontaneous expression. In fact, passion opposes logic. Logical action requires that expression can be subordinated to the will; logical action reflects a deliberate speed and a predetermined direction. Passion reflects spontaneity of action at whatever speed and direction the emotion of the moment generates.[6]

DECISION-MAKING—LATIN AMERICAN STYLE

The Latin American relies heavily upon intuition, the passion of the intellect, to point out the solutions to problems. Thought proceeds in a series of direct revelations or perceptions of "truths" concerning the object being contemplated. These perceptions are independent of any demonstrated reasoning process and, therefore, neither verifiable nor repeatable. The tendency is toward action which appears improvised. This characteristic frequently leads Latin Americans to act without planning, at least without conscious planning. Salvador de Madariaga touches this notion using the Spanish as examples:

Intuition also excludes any possibility of establishing a method beforehand. And in fact, method is far from being a typical feature of Spanish thought. A method, we have said, is a road for the mind. It is difficult to imagine how a road towards knowledge could be traced by people who find themselves in knowledge before they set foot on the road. . . . Spanish thought has a method of its own which is certainly not the road-schedule. . . .[7]

4 William L. Schurz, *This New World* (New York: E. P. Dutton & Co., 1954), p. 82.

5 John Fayerweather, *The Executive Overseas* (Syracuse: Syracuse University Press, 1959), p. 63.

6 Salvador de Madariaga, *Englishmen, Frenchmen, Spaniards* (London: Oxford University Press, 1931), p. 42.

7 *Ibid.*, p. 78.

While emotion, as a basis for action, may often lead to unsound decisions, improvisations, and ineffective results, attempts have been made to justify it—to explain logically the use of emotion as a basis for action. Those who attempt to justify it argue that man has been a reasoning being for, at most, a few thousand years. Before that, man survived by following his instincts and impulses. "The Latin could, therefore, advance good support for the assertion that those impulses that have survived the great sieve of evolution must be those best suited to man's survival and continued development." [8]

The proponents of this theory claim that the urgings of man's heart might spring from the sifted and stored-up wisdom of all that man has learned throughout time. By comparison, recorded knowledge must appear rather insignificant. As one philosopher put it:

> It is not wisdom to be only wise
> And on the inward vision close the eyes
> But it is wisdom to believe the heart.[9]

In discussing thought in a man of passion, de Madariaga explains that he contemplates and waits in apparent passivity for the object of the contemplation to reveal itself:

He lets the continuous stream of life pass through him, until such time as a flash of perception or intuition moves him. Until he experiences inspiration, and because cold logic and result-oriented action have little appeal, he tends to do things in the manner which involves the least risk and effort. If he faces a situation requiring action about which he has no intense feelings, the manner which involves the least risk and effort is to conform to some existing pattern.[10]

If he follows the rules there will be no complaints, he will not have to make a mental effort, and the situation will be taken care of.[11]

But how did this characteristic become ingrained in the psychological make-up of the Latin American?

8 Stark, *op. cit.*, p. 63.
9 From a poem, "O World, Thou Choosest Not," by George Santayana, and quoted in Stark, *op. cit.*, p. 63.
10 Madariaga, *op. cit.*, p. 74.
11 Fayerweather, *op. cit.*, p. 64.

THE OLD WORLD'S BEQUEST

The great emphasis on science and utilization of scientific method resulted from the scientific revolution which swept Europe in the 1500's. This revolution was, in large measure, a result of the Renaissance and the Reformation. Before this time, Europeans patterned their lives and thoughts according to the dogma prescribed by authorities. These authorities were Church officials, political officials (frequently the same), or monarchs. For hundreds of years, people were told what to do and how to think about practically every aspect of their lives. They were accustomed to authoritarian leadership, expected it, and, perhaps, even demanded it. The Renaissance and the Reformation represented change. Man was expected to think independently and to reach his own conclusions about worldly and religious matters.

The Renaissance eventually spread into Spain, but the Spanish scholars directed their efforts not to revolt but to attempts at purification and maintenance of the Church. The Reformation, however, never reached Spain. Thus, the attitude of independent, analytical thinking was not emphasized and never became an important part of the approach to decision-making and problem solution. This characteristic became part of the New World's legacy.

SUMMARY

The aspect of management philosophy considered in this article has been North American versus Latin American inclusion of scientific thinking in approaching management.

In the US, management is considered to contain scientific components. In Latin America, management generally is considered solely an art. The very heart of the American approach to business management—scientific method—is ignored and denied in Latin America because of cultural and personality characteristics which lead persons to rely upon intuition as a basis for decision-making.

Because Latin Americans are not strongly result-oriented, management by objectives is not so common in Latin America as it is in the United States. Rather, Latin Americans regard action not in terms of how it aids in achieving desired goals, but as an end in itself.

These characteristics—regarding management as an art, viewing action as an expression of inner feelings rather than as a calculated means to an end, and ignoring scientific method as a decision-making tool—pose challenges among Americans interested in better management.

3

Comment: Decision-Making in Latin American Business *

An Extension of McCann's Hypothesis

S. BENJAMIN PRASAD

During the last century even in the United States management was considered solely as an art. Now it is regarded as a "science." [1] Eugene McCann, in contrasting some aspects of management philosophy in the United States and Latin America, pointed out that management is generally regarded as an art even today in Latin American countries.[2] He ascribed such a managerial philosophy among Latin American managers to the sparing use of the scientific method. An understanding of what "scientific method" and "science" are will augment an understanding of the broader problems of technology, management, and economic development in Latin America.

* Reprinted with permission from the *Academy of Management Journal* (December, 1965).

1 See *Business Week* (December 28, 1963), pp. 44-51, for an informative discussion of a research study relating to the question of how big corporations in the United States are embracing new scientific techniques to run their businesses. The Harvard group which made the study gave "Management Science" a broad definition encompassing all the sciences that can aid managers. This was broader than the traditional definition used by scientists and engineers to describe the application of mathematics and model-building techniques to operating problems.

2 See Eugene McCann, "An Aspect of Management Philosophy in the United States and Latin America," Ch. 2 in this volume.

The purpose of this paper is to provide additional details, and to develop a more comprehensive framework for the Latin American region in which Eugene McCann's observations can be more fully understood. A brief characterization of Latin America will be followed by a discussion of how scientific method and science may be construed with a view to facilitating the adaptation of technology with the aid of management philosophy.

SOME FEATURES OF LATIN AMERICA

Victor Urquidi has argued that despite a growing tendency to the contrary, it is advisable to consider the twenty republics of Latin America—Argentina, Bolivia, Brazil, Chile, Colombia, Costa Rica, Cuba, Dominican Republic, Ecuador, El Salvador, Guatemala, Haiti, Honduras, Mexico, Nicaragua, Panama, Paraguay, Peru, Uruguay, and Venezuela—as a single region because there exist circumstances and characteristics typical of the region as a whole. The ensuing data are based upon his book.

There is a numerical preponderance of Brazilians and Mexicans in the Latin American region. In 1962, there were 69 million Brazilians and 37 million Mexicans who accounted for half the inhabitants of Latin America. Based upon the trend of birth rates, Mexico and Brazil are likely to account for a progressively higher proportion of the total Latin American population.

Of these twenty republics, seven countries—Brazil, Chile, Colombia, Mexico, Peru, and Venezuela—contain 81 percent of the population and contribute 87 percent of the total Latin American domestic product. Bearing in mind the preeminence of these seven countries, Latin America's total gross product may be broken down into the following components:

Manufacturing	24 percent
Agriculture & Livestock	20 percent
Mining & Petroleum	6 percent
Transportation, trade, finance & government service	47 percent
Construction	3 percent

From 1951 to 1960, the average annual growth rate of the Latin American region was 4.5 percent; population grew at 2.5 percent;

and per capita product went up, on the average, by 1.95 percent. Economic growth in Latin America has not only been considered as slow but also as unevenly distributed. Industrialization has been concentrated in five or six of the most populous countries, and has not been uniform. The Latin American economy is not autonomous. As Urquidi puts it, "it always has been and will continue to be linked to the rest of the world, especially to countries that traditionally have imported primary products from Latin America in order to transform them into finished goods." [3] With these few data on the Latin America region, the two key concepts of scientific method and science will be elucidated to develop the frame of reference to examine McCann's hypothesis.

SCIENTIFIC METHOD

Scientific method is a particular style of inquiry which the scientist has developed, although the term itself is a misnomer, in that it is not a method—a formal procedure—but rather an attitude and a philosophy providing guidance by which dependable overall concepts can be extracted.[4] Amitai Etzioni and Eva Etzioni refer to the process of deliberate innovation, which includes inventions in science and thought, as the "scientific method." [5] What Wilbert Moore refers to as "institutionalized rationality" approximates scientific method as identified above. He terms it a "problem solving orientation and a dedication to deliberate change which is rather a general characteristic of the fully developed industrial societies." [6]

Whether one regards "scientific method" as an attitude or a process or institutionalized rationality, it is quite relevant in terms of McCann's observation that "the very heart of the U.S. approach to business management—scientific method—is ignored and denied

3 Victor Urquidi, *The Challenge of Development in Latin America* (New York: Frederick A. Praeger, Inc., 1964), p. 14.

4 Henry Margenau and David Bergamini, "The Scientific Method," *Fortune* (December 1964), p. 100.

5 *Social Change*, Amitai Etzioni and Eva Etzioni, eds. (New York: Basic Books, Inc., 1964), pp. 427-428.

6 Wilbert Moore, *Social Change* (Englewood Cliffs, N.J.: Prentice-Hall, Inc., 1963), p. 96.

in Latin America because of cultural and personality characteristics which lead persons to rely upon intuition as a basis for decision-making." [7]

A further understanding of McCann's observation may be gained by looking at Bernard Barber's view of science. According to Barber, science is not a randomly collected assortment of elements and activities but a coherent structure in which parts have functionally interdependent relations. He suggests that a systematic comprehension of science can be obtained by considering it first and fundamentally as a social activity.[8] By so viewing, one can:

1. see the determinate connections that it has with different parts of a society; for example, with political authority, with the occupational system, with the structure of industry and class stratification, and with cultural ideals and values;
2. see how its products—its inventions and discoveries—are the products of a process that has essentially social characteristics; and,
3. direct one's attention more fruitfully to some of the social problems of science as well as the social control of science.

Science viewed as a social activity and as a special kind of thought and behavior which takes place in different ways and degree in different societies may shed additional light on the scientific attitude which prevails in American industry and the lack of it in Latin America, or for that matter in most of the less-developed nations.

SCIENCE AND TECHNOLOGICAL PROGRESS

Science is an evolution in thought and behavior. The Western-type technology expedites the evolution but not without surmounting the multifarious obstacles. The greatest single distinguishing feature of the modern age is technological advancement. Yet such advancement is not novel. What is new and unique about the modern era is the rapidity, depth, and constancy of the flow of

---

[7] Eugene McCann, *op. cit.*

[8] Bernard Barber, *Science and the Social Order* (New York: Collier Books, 1962), p. 26.

technology. Technological progress in the modern sense is dependent upon applied science, and ultimately upon pure science. However, the progress of applied science is dependent upon the resources which are available and applied to scientific endeavor as well as the interrelated scientific attitude which prevails in a society. For example, consider education. Education is generally regarded as one way of diffusing the scientific attitude and scientific outlook by breaking those traditional beliefs which remain impediments to scientific and subsequent economic progress. In the Latin American region, education is as much an economic problem as a social problem.

Accepting the typology recently developed by Frederick Harbison and Charles Myers,[9] one can say that the Latin American countries occupy level III. In terms of the composite index of human resource development, this suggests that they are semi-advanced countries.[10] Even so, the majority of the population in Latin America has had no educational training. According to a UNESCO study,[11] in 1950, almost one half of the Latin Americans aged fifteen years or older had never attended school or had dropped out before finishing the first grade; 44 percent had some primary instruction; and only 8 percent had completed primary school education.

The modern economist would rightly assert that, to accelerate economic development, minimal critical investments are imperative in capital goods, and that the labor force must increase in size as well as in skill and competence level. Thus, one can see that education is an economic problem although it is often presented as a social one. Education and economic development must be dealt with jointly; otherwise there is likely to be only a tenuous and indirect link between the two. As Urquidi suggests, "if education is to be treated as a high-priority productive investment, those re-

[9] Frederick Harbison and Charles Myers, *Education, Manpower and Economic Growth* (New York: McGraw-Hill Book Company, 1964).

[10] The composite index used by Harbison and Myers to slot seventy-five countries into four levels is the arithmetic sum of 1. enrollment at secondary level of education as a percentage of the age group 15 to 19, adjusted for length of schooling, and 2. enrollment at the third level of education as a percentage of the age group, multiplied by a weight of 5.

[11] UNESCO, *Social Aspects of Economic Development in Latin America*, Vol. 1 (Paris, 1962).

sponsible for preparing and promoting economic development programs in Latin America must make allocations of resources to education contingent upon adaptation of the educational systems to the needs of the developmental programs." [12]

Of course there are higher institutions of learning in most of the Latin American countries. But the intellectual environment they have so far created does not appear to be very conducive to the augmentation of the scientific attitude. As George Blanksten has stated, "the higher educational systems in Latin America reflect Spanish as well as French university influence, with the intellectual environment far more humanistic and artistic than scientific." [13]

The underdeveloped world is a complex one. If one were to arbitrarily dichotomize it into the new and the old countries, Latin America would fall under the latter category while the Asian and African countries would come under the former category. Yet there are many characteristics which are similar in both categories.

The implications of the question whether management is more philosophy, art, or science or some combination, as Eugene McCann noted, can be profound in approaching management and management decision-making in diverse cultural settings among the old and new states. The profundity of these implications can be further seen in John Mee's observation that "if there can be established a logical relationship among management concepts and a scale of values of management decisions with a given historical perspective of environmental conditions, such an intellectual discovery can have several values." [14]

Among the values of management philosophy in a dynamic economy, Professor Mee emphasized the value to developing countries. One can safely extend it to the Latin American region and subscribe to the point of view of Urquidi who argues that "if economic development in Latin America requires that an increasing amount of modern technology be assimilated to achieve gains in productivity . . . Latin American countries should have to

12 Urquidi, *op. cit.*, p. 79.
13 George Blanksten, "The Politics in Latin America," in Almond and Coleman, eds., *The Politics of Development Areas* (Princeton, N.J.: Princeton University Press, 1960), p. 471.
14 John F. Mee, *Management Thought in a Dynamic Economy* (New York: New York University Press, 1963), p. 22.

change radically their attitude toward scientific and technical research." [15]

CONCLUSION

A more complete comprehension of one aspect of managerial philosophy in Latin America, namely, consideration of industrial management more as an art than as a science, can be gained by further examination of such tentative hypotheses as can be deduced from discussions in this paper and Eugene McCann's article: [16]

1. Latin American managers sparingly use the scientific method in decision-making in business.
2. Lack of the use of the scientific method in decision-making may be ascribed to:
    a. Personality characteristics of the people in this region.
    b. Influence of the Spanish and French higher educational institutions.
    c. Lack of opportunities for professional education for managers.
3. Managerial philosophy, as it suits the Latin American industrial environment, has an important role to play in the process of adaptation of foreign technology including management techniques.

[15] Urquidi, *op. cit.*, pp. 107-108.
[16] McCann, *op. cit.*

4

Future Management Philosophy: A Synthesis*

JOHN F. MEE

Management thought is a product of the twentieth century. The seeds of management thought from the nineteenth century sprouted into the concepts of scientific management and the management movement early in the twentieth century. Management thought emerged in the minds of pioneering industrial managers and engineers who wanted to separate waste and inefficiency from group endeavors in a growing industrial economy. The cumulative forces of the political and economic environment resulted in the creation and development of management thought and philosophy. Once created and developed, however, management philosophy has been a stimulating and constructive influence on the maintenance of the dynamic qualities of our national economy.

Management Philosophy, as a system of thought or as an effective progress for achieving desired results and resolving problems, has not been treated as an area of study by most European institutions of higher learning or business schools. The concept of basic management functions such as planning, organizing, motivating, controlling, and innovating in business and industry has differed greatly between the United States and Europe. Dr. Herbert

* Excerpts from *Management Thought In a Dynamic Economy,* 1963, reprinted with permission from the New York University Press and Administrative Management Society.

B. Schmidt [1] concluded that the concept of management in the United States served as an argument for the higher efficiency of its economy. My own observations and experiences in Europe, Africa, and Asia support his statements. However, I would like to add the benefits to business enterprises in the United States that have come from our Constitution and our governmental climate. So long as our management processes can operate in an environment of democracy and enterprise with freedom of choice and progress, our economy can thrive and continue its dynamic growth.

If there is a relationship between the state of a nation's economy and the concept of management possessed by the nation's business and governmental leaders, then a study of the genesis and development of management thought should be of value and interest to scholars and practitioners who desire to maintain and to improve the life process of a dynamic and competitive economy.

An inquiring mind will be stimulated by such questions as:

1. What is the concept and the function of management?
2. Why does the subject of management emerge as a distinct and an identifiable discipline that can be studied, taught, learned, and practiced?
3. Who becomes aware of the values of management and the need to develop management thought or theory?
4. When does management become recognized in the historical development of a nation's economy and educational system?
5. Where is management thought most useful and for which purpose?
6. How did and do the concepts used in management thought originate and develop historically?

A meaningful approach to the study of management thought is one that relates the subject to: 1. the concepts that identify management and distinguish it from other areas or disciplines; 2. the historical perspective in which the concepts emerge and develop; and 3. the scale or standard of values by which scholars or practitioners evaluate the concepts relative to the time period of their acceptance and use.

Management thought is a product of the twentieth century.

[1] A former faculty member of the German Institute of Management.

Before the basic concepts of management emerged, there had to be developed a political and economic climate suitable for their gestation and birth. The management movement in the United States awaited this occasion.

ECONOMIC PROGRESS

The genesis of the management movement occurred in countries where economic progress was accelerated by cumulative forces generated by innovations in political, social, economic, and technological concepts. A fundamental question, which has not been answered to the satisfaction of educational and political theorists, is: Does management thought and theory originate or follow in the wake of the economic and industrial development of a national economy? An accurate answer to this question could provide an important decision-making standard for everyone interested in the improvement of the plight of the so-called underdeveloped nations of the world.

NEED FOR MANAGEMENT

Stefan H. Robock presents a point of view in his article, "Management in Underdeveloped Countries," which appeared in the January, 1962 issue of *Advanced Management and Office Executive*. Based upon his experiences as Director of International Business Studies at Indiana University and as a past Deputy Director of the Committee for Economic Development, he wrote:

If any single factor is the key for unlocking the forces for economic growth in the underdeveloped areas of the world, that factor is management. . . .

Exporting capital will not, in itself, meet these countries' needs. Many of them do need capital, both public and private, on a large scale. Some countries, however, notably in the Middle East, do not lack capital at all. What they need most are skills and better means of employing the capital they already have. And in some countries, the infusion of capital alone tends to reinforce practices, people, and regimes that must change if communism is not to become the attractive alternative to today's feudalisms.

Most of the underdeveloped countries lack both business enterprises and business managers. They seek to borrow our technology but often fail to grasp that management skills have played a vital role in our growth. Decentralized, independent, and competitive enterprises have not developed rapidly, and the power of the free market to stimulate growth has not been felt.

Some of this simply reflects the lack of development. In other cases, the new governments have kept the initiative for development in their own hands.[2]

Robock was writing primarily for those who may be planning to establish a business in a foreign country. He advised them to consider the interdependence of public and private managerial efficiency before embarking on such a venture.

The management thought streams that originated from various related disciplines during the first half of the twentieth century have developed and converged to such a degree that they can be identified and integrated with the general concept of a management process. A conceptual framework for management thought now can be constructed as a synthesis of the management concepts that have been created and expounded by scholars with diverse but related viewpoints.

The trend toward future management philosophy promises a much broader perspective which will include value concepts of the purpose of business enterprise and ethical beliefs relative to the conduct of business affairs. Thought streams and conceptual contributions from the disciplines of mathematics, psychology, physiology, sociology, and anthropology are being synthesized with the established concepts of the management process to form a conceptual framework for management thought and progress toward a general theory of management.

POSSIBLE ELEMENTS OF FUTURE MANAGEMENT PHILOSOPHY

The trend in the development of management thought indicates that there has been a logical order to the emergence of

[2] Quotation used with the permission of Administrative Management Society, Willow Grove, Pennsylvania.

management concepts in response to the changing demands of the environment. A fourth stage of management thought is forming, with a broader perspective of the conceptual framework for the future mission of management in the economy. The emerging conceptual pattern of management philosophy can be illustrated as having a structure which is composed of elements, the performance of which is a web of relationships giving a life process to the purpose of management in organized society.

Because of the surging state of conflicting concepts with so-called classical management theory, there is little certainty in any present prediction of the complete nature of management philosophy for tomorrow. For purposes of illustrations, comparisons, and criticism, one possible combination of the elements of future management philosophy is shown as a structure for a conceptual framework for management in the following diagram.

CONCLUSION

Since the advent of the twentieth century, the economy of the United States has enjoyed levels of output, efficiency, and consumer consumption that were previously beyond the comprehension of everyone except those gifted with unusual imaginative powers. Some relationship exists between the genesis and development of thought and the dynamic qualities of the economy, which has grown steadily in an environment of democracy and enterprise. Within a governmental climate which permits freedom of choice and progress, the managers of business enterprises have been able to serve society in very creative roles.

Both economic growth and the development of management philosophy have progressed in comparable stages in the same period of time. The managers in the United States have been the coalescing forces in the achievement of predetermined economic and social objectives. Furthermore, the managers have had the advantages of a developing management philosophy that has enabled the practice of management to become an art of discriminating analysis and creative synthesis for utilizing the products of technology for the benefit of organized society.

Management thought in the dynamic economy of the United

CONCEPTUAL FRAMEWORK FOR MANAGEMENT

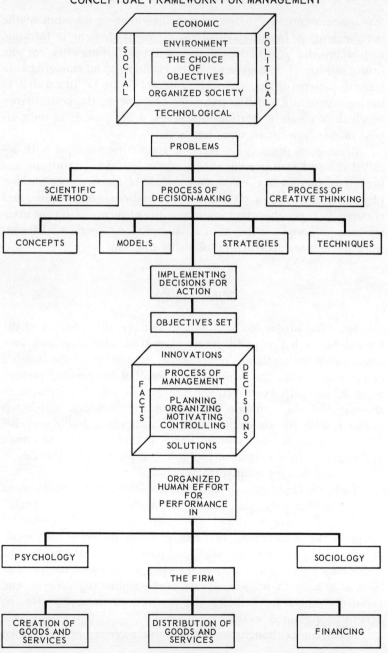

States was conceived in an unusually fertile political and economic climate. It developed to guide the distinguished destiny of managers in an environment characterized by a constant search for betterment and a willingness to accept change. Management thought has always had its identifiable channel, but it has always been fed by the tributaries of thought streams from related disciplines. The makers and developers of management thought have believed in an open system that permits the acceptance and the synthesis of applicable contributions from all sources. Consequently, the discipline of management rests upon a very broad foundation of knowledge from the arts and sciences.

The purpose of management, and a guiding management philosophy, is to provide the thought processes for the predetermination of desired results and the subsequent achievement of them by the intelligent utilization of human efforts and facilitating resources in the best-balanced interests of organized society. Management is a way of conceptual thinking for intelligent managerial actions. Progressive changes in the development of management philosophy and practices have survived resistance and doubt. The scientific management movement progressed over the objections of craft labor. Current management philosophy will continue to develop over the obstacles imposed by charismatic leadership. As the economy of the United States continues its growth, management thought and philosophy will continue to develop to guide the actions of managers in adapting the operations of their enterprises to changing environmental conditions—even though the environment expands into the dimension of space.

If the so-called scientific revolution is dividing our culture into two segments, the scientists and intellectuals, then a rational conceptual framework for management thought may serve as the bridge of understanding and integrated achievements of both. The management philosophy for tomorrow may serve this important purpose for our own economy. An understanding of the way that management thought develops in stages to combine the essential forces that generate and maintain a dynamic economy can contribute more to the advancement of the so-called underdeveloped countries than gifts of capital and premature technologies. Management thought progresses in stages in an economy. It is necessary that management philosophy be adapted to the environmental conditions of an economy instead of trying to adopt an unfamiliar one and attempt to use it as a procrustean bed. This requires constant education and research and the desire to improve the status and happiness of people in a free world which permits freedom of choice for individuals in a climate of democracy and enterprise.

5

The Logic of Management
Development: A Comparison
Among Countries *

FREDERICK HARBISON
CHARLES MYERS

Industrialism is an almost universal goal of modern nations. And the industrialization process has its set of imperatives: things which all societies must do if they have to conduct a successful march to industrialism. This is what we call the *logic* of industrialization. One of the imperatives in the logic of industrialization is the building of the requisite organizatons to combine natural resources, capital, technology, and labor for productive purposes. Organization building has its logic, too, which rests upon the development of management. And this brings us to the fundamental premise of our study: *there is a general logic of management development which has applicability both to advanced and industrializing countries in the modern world.* The major threads of the analysis should be woven into some general concepts of the development of management in industrial society.

* From *Management in the Industrial World* by Frederick Harbison and Charles Myers, pp. 117-133. Copyright 1959 by McGraw-Hill, Inc. Used by permission of McGraw-Hill Book Company.

SOME GENERAL CONCEPTS

We define *management* as the hierarchy of high-level human resources needed to perform the key functions. Management in industrial organizations (which has been our central concern) includes organization builders, top administrators, middle and supervisory management, and trained technical and professional personnel. Of these, the organization builder, naturally, is the star performer. He may be the owner of a business, a governmental appointee, or a professional administrator. He sets the tone of the organization, and he plays the central role in establishing the conditions under which the other members of the team must operate. In a sense, therefore, management is a blend of an individual and a collective personality.

We analyze management from three separate perspectives: as an economic resource or factor of production, as a system of authority, and as a class or elite group. We examine the processes of generation of managerial resources, with particular reference to the problems faced by countries which are newcomers in the march toward industrialism.

As an economic resource, management is similar in important respects to capital. If a country wants to industrialize it must accumulate the strategic human resources required for management, just as it must acquire capital for power installations, roads, bridges, communications systems, and factories. It must also find the means of channeling these strategic human resources into the most productive activities. And as in the case of the accumulation of capital, a country must generate a critical minimum quantity of productive managerial resources in order successfully to "take off" on the road to industrialization. Managerial resources, moreover, are complementary to capital. Capital-intensive industries are nearly always large consumers of managerial manpower, which means that a country's capacity to absorb capital for productive purposes is dependent upon its capacity to generate the necessary managerial resources.

As industrialization progresses, the numbers of persons in management increase both absolutely and relatively in the economy.

This is the inevitable consequence of large capital outlays, the pace of innovation, the use of more modern machinery and processes, the growth of markets, and the greater complexity of an advanced industrial society. At the same time business organizations become more complicated as they grow larger, and the effectiveness of management increasingly becomes dependent upon skill in reducing the inherent frictions and inefficiencies of complicated human organizations. Here we show that there is a direct relationship between the quality of the managerial organization and the productivity of labor, and we conclude that many plant-level labor problems stem directly or indirectly from management problems.

As a resource, therefore, management has both quantitative and qualitative dimensions; thus, successful industrialization is dependent not only upon the generation of sufficient numbers of high-talent people but also upon their proper integration into effective organization structures. For this reason, management is more intricate and, to some extent, a less tangible factor of production than either capital or natural resources.

From the second perspective, management is a system of authority within the enterprise. The functioning of this system has a direct bearing on the quality of management as a factor of production. It also affects the attitudes, aspirations and general well-being of all individuals directly involved in the industrialization process. The system of authority has two important and closely related elements; first, the exercise of authority within the managerial group and, second, the attitudes and policies of management as the rule maker in its relationships with the workers and their unions.

In looking first at the internal power structure of management, we found that the most primitive system is that of the sovereign personal rule by a single person or a single family. The most advanced is "management by objectives," where authority is based upon individual initiative, consent, persuasion, and self-direction toward agreement upon objectives. Management by sovereign rule is not viable except in small-scale operations and thus it tends to disappear in large-scale enterprise in the more advanced countries. At the other extreme, management by objectives is such a radical departure from traditional systems of authority that it is seldom, if ever, achieved in practice. It is better described as an ideal toward which some managements are striving. Between these extremes is a broad range of possible combinations of decentralized administration with central policy control. Large and even medium-sized enterprises in all industrial societies, through conscious planning or trial and error, are continuously searching for some kind of balance in this area. Almost never do they find a perfect solution, but some are more successful than others in finding arrangements which substantially reduce organizational frictions or "energy loss."

At the same time, management seeks to assert its prerogatives as the rule maker for the workers. In industrial enterprise, it displaces the head of the family, the tribal chief, or the communal leader as the authority which prescribes the duties, obligations, rewards, and punishments of the laboring class. And in this relationship, it seeks three things from workers: subordination, loyalty, and productivity. But others also seek a voice in the rule-making and rule-enforcing process. Among the principal contenders are the state, political parties, and the labor unions, as well as sometimes the military, the church, and various groups of intellectuals. They seek to limit, to regulate, or sometimes to displace the unilateral authority of management. As industrialization proceeds, management may be forced to share its rule-making power with one or more of these contenders. By legislation or by collective bargaining, governments and unions may limit management's freedom to exercise its prerogatives unilaterally. Dictatorial and paternalistic direction may give way to a kind of "constitutional" management in which wages and conditions of employment are based upon laws, contracts, or procedural agreement. And in rare cases, a system of industrial democracy may be established in which management and labor not only share in the rule-making process but also cooperate in improving efficiency and increasing output. We call this "democratic-participative" management. In a very real sense, therefore, management-labor relations may become less authoritarian and more democratic with the advance of industrialization.

From the third perspective, management may be thought of as a class or an elite group to which only selected persons may have access. The managerial elite may be patrimonial, political, or professional, or some combination of the three. In any case, the members of the managerial hierarchy constitute a group distinct from other employees of the enterprise and also distinct from other elites in the society at large. In the early stages of industrialization, management may be drawn largely from family dynasties, or, in some cases, from political parties or the government service. But technological and organizational development tends to favor professionally oriented or careerist rather than political or patrimonial management. As industrialization follows its logical course, increasingly larger numbers of trained engineers, technologists and administrators are required. As the managerial class becomes larger, it also becomes less exclusive, since of necessity the avenues of access to its ranks must become broader.

In its logical development, therefore, management at all levels becomes more of a profession than a preordained calling or "priesthood." As the industrial society continues to lay stress upon scientific discovery, technological innovation, and economic progress, patrimonial and political managements tend to be displaced by the professionals. The successful organization builders tend to become the self-conscious practitioners of the arts of leadership, direction, coordination, delegation, and control. Decision-making is no longer based upon intuitive judgment; it depends increasingly upon objective analysis, the reports of specialists, the advice of consultants, and carefully directed collective thinking. Positions within the managerial hierarchy are more precisely defined; goals are more formally established, and criteria for successful performance more explicitly stated. The strategy of management becomes based upon a set of rigidly defined principles to guide its day-to-day tactics. The organization builders who direct, coordinate, and lead the swelling cadres of "organization men" must have knowledge as well as experience; they must know a little about many things as well as a lot about some things. They must master the art of developing people as well as the simple direction of subordinates; they must know when to delegate as well as when to exercise their authority of command. Inevitably, the modern captains of industry and their associates in the managerial hierarchy become an elite of brains. They become an intelligentsia, and access to their ranks is gained increasingly through education rather than through family or political connections.

The rising professional managerial class, however, does not have the capacity, nor even, in most cases, the will to become the dominant ruling elite in modern industrial society. The increasingly intricate problems of organization and technology inherent in modern industrial enterprises consume the energies and thoughts of the members of the managerial class. Being preoccupied with the internal affairs of enterprise, they tend to become conformists rather than leaders in the affairs of state. They are servants rather than masters of the economies in which they play a vital role. And the present-day professional organization builder, unlike the old-style proprietary capitalist who is being swept aside in the march toward industrialism, does not own the means of production. He is rather the agent of a group of stockholders, a state bureaucracy, or, in some cases, a workers' council.

It follows from our threefold analysis that, in the age of modern technology, no country can expect to industrialize unless it can finance and build on a sizeable scale the particular kinds of educational institutions which an industrial society demands. In this "century of science" the outlays for scientific and technical education have become enormous in all advanced countries, and in most, great stress has been laid as well on management-training institutions to develop the administrative skills which a modern society demands. The advanced industrial economy requires an investment in a fully developed system of general education, and at the same time, it demands that its basic educational institutions become more functionally oriented to the training of skilled technicians, engineers, scientists, and administrators. But it also requires the lowering of arbitrary noneducational barriers to entry into the managerial hierarchy as well as some vertical and horizontal mobility within the managerial class itself. In some societies, the processes of generation of managerial manpower have been spearheaded by the state; in others by private initiative. As industrialization advances and even as it is being started in the presently underdeveloped countries, however, the means of generating and accumulating managerial resources is increasingly a matter for careful planning, judicious investment, and conscious effort. In the logic of industrialization with modern technology, high-talent manpower is not just naturally born. It does not grow wild; on the contrary, it requires very careful seeding and most meticulous cultivation. The generation of needed high-talent manpower, therefore, is perhaps the most difficult task facing the underdeveloped countries in their drive to industrialize.

The pillars of our concept of the development of management

have been erected, and they may be used to support three propositions which we feel have general applicability to nearly all industrial societies. In brief, they are as follows:

The general direction of management development in all advancing industrial societies is the same. In the end, management as a resource, as a system of authority, and as a class is likely to be similar in significant aspects in an advanced socialist economy, an advanced market economy, or an advanced totalitarian economy. The initial push to start the economy on the route to industrialism may be made by widely differing groups such as an existing dynastic elite in a feudal society, a rising class of proprietary capitalists in a market economy, a colonial administration, a socialist government, or a communist regime. But they all steer toward modern industrialism. And modern industrialism has a uniform prescription for management.

The pace of the march toward industrialism may be accelerated or retarded by certain factors affecting management development. Tenacious patrimonial or political managements may slow down the march or even bring it to a halt, whereas the early development of a dynamic professional element may spur it onward. Likewise, the timing, amount, and appropriateness of investments in education are crucial in determining the speed of modern industrialization. In the case of the newly industrializing countries, therefore, wise planning for development of high-level human resources may maximize the stimuli and minimize the deterrents to logical management growth. In other words, the late-comers to industrialization do not have to follow the same courses or make the same mistakes as the presently advanced countries.

There is little reason to fear that the working masses in modern industrial states will be exploited by the emerging professional managerial class. Industrialism makes possible a higher material standard of living. But at the same time, management is generally forced to share its rule-making prerogatives with agencies which directly or indirectly represent the workers' interest. Thus the odds are in favor of greater recognition of the rights and dignity of the individual worker as industrialization advances.

The threads of the general logic of management development may be traced in the essays on various countries in Part II. These essays, some of which have been prepared by different writers, are not in every respect parallel because of difficulties in securing information and somewhat different points of emphasis by those who conducted the research. In a general way, however, they are comparable, and in themselves they provide insight into the various stages of development through which these countries are passing.

COMPARISONS AMONG COUNTRIES

In each of the countries whose managerial development has been summarized in Part II, industrialization has been an important objective of national policy. In each case, moreover, the conditions generated by the process of industrialization have required increasing attention to managerial organization, attitudes, policies, and development. There are, however, significant differences among the countries both in the problems faced and in the types of reactions; these differences reflect various cultural patterns as well as variation in the stage and pace of economic development.

Cultural differences obviously have affected the growth and development of managerial resources and the nature of management as a system of authority and as an elite. In Chile, for example, the landed and traditional commercial aristocracy tended in the past to regard new entrepreneurs as social upstarts, whereas in Egypt the resurgent wave of Arab nationalism has placed high social value on efficient administrators and entrepreneurs. In Israel, the desire for higher productivity in order to achieve economic goals has brought about a recognition of the critical role of management in economic development, which is in sharp contrast to the earlier disregard for the managerial function and the glorification of manual labor. After the departure of the British, India was left with a well-established and well-trained civil service, but the bulk of the private entrepreneurs came from restricted social classes which were looked down upon by other elites in the society. These attitudes, too, have been changing under the pressure of industrialization, as government finds that public enterprises, no less than private ones, require competent professional managers.

In general, France and Italy have been characterized by a large number of small enterprises, looked on by the family as a source of personal security and conducted in an atmosphere of widespread absence of trust. In both countries there are indications that new industries, pacing the recent increase in the rate of economic development, have been directed by managements selected on the basis of qualifications and performance, rather than on the basis of family connections. In Italy, these large companies dominate the industrial scene.

The British social system, although much more flexible than it was fifty years ago, still carries over a strong feeling of the virtue of "aristocratic" values and gives high mark to the "right" background in a man. In this respect, it may be less egalitarian than that of the Swedes, although in Sweden the business elite is still drawn predominantly from a small group. Japan, among the advanced industrial countries, appears to have retained many of the precapitalistic features of an earlier period and has managed to harness many supposedly "feudal" values to the service of its economic development. The German social system has also had a strong authoritarian element, but this has been modified to some extent by the early development of organizations outside of the dominant classes and the need, in a political democracy, for the elite groups to make concessions of various sorts in order to maintain their power. For these reasons along with the pressure of an efficient educational system, the Germans have had a larger supply of technically competent personnel upon which to draw for intermediate and junior managerial positions. The Bolshevist Revolution in Russia destroyed the pre-existing social structure, but to meet the requirements of rapid industrialization, the Soviet government has consciously and forcefully set about the task of creating an administrative and managerial elite. Finally, in the United States, the social status of entrepreneurial and business groups has always been relatively high, and this has been an important factor in attracting the high-level human resources needed for our own economic development.

Management as a Resource

The depth and quality of managerial resources are clearly greater in the advanced industrial countries than in the less developed ones. The experience of firms in the United States over the past several decades shows the increasing proportion of technical and managerial personnel relative to wage earners. This has resulted from the growing complexity of technology as well as from the wider responsibilities which management is called upon to fulfill in an advanced industrial society.

The same tendency is found in Great Britain, where technology and size of firms are important factors in the postwar emphasis on more professional management. Market forces through the export trade have had an important influence on the need for better managerial resources both in Great Britain and in Sweden. The postwar resurgence of German and Japanese management, with the re-entry of these two nations into world markets, has had a similar impact on the need for improved managerial resources in these countries.

In France, modern managerial resources are growing in those private enterprises which are responding to the impact of rapid technological advances in equipment and methods, as in the automobile, chemical, rubber, oil, plastic, and electronic industries. The same is true of some of the larger public enterprises. Closer integration between all phases of production and distribution is necessary with more complex technology and wider markets, as these French firms have found. Marked competition from German firms, furthermore, has put pressure on French employers to pay greater attention to strengthening managerial resources, and this pressure may be expected to increase under the European Common Market.

In the less developed industrial countries, on the other hand, thin managerial resources continue to function with limited technology and limited markets. Perhaps the small-scale industry, family-owned and operated, will survive for many years in such countries as India, Egypt, and Chile. But even here, the impact of modern large-scale technology and wider markets, in such industries as steel, chemicals, oil refining, and fertilizer manufacture, have compelled management to add engineers, technicians, staff men of various types, and several layers of supervision. Managerial resources that were adequate for a retarded industrial society are supplanted by new skills and levels of management.

Management as a System of Authority

Many of the differences which can be discerned in the varying patterns of managerial authority are due to the different stages of industrialization of the countries studied. The economic power of labor and management both in terms of relative "scarcity" and organizational power may be affected. The stage of industrialization may also condition the way in which "the public" looks at management, and the degree to which social and economic needs can be met by alternative institutions. In short, management is likely to be most powerful and successfully authoritarian when, other things being equal, it is drawn from narrowly restricted groups which have a high degree of social prestige, when the jobs to be supervised are fairly simple, and when management is the unilateral supplier of "welfare" benefits which are urgently required by their recipients.

The process of industrialization tends, other things being equal, to limit managerial authority, both as a consequence of its direct effects on the industrial system and of its indirect effects on society as a whole. Directly, the increasing complexity and interdependence of many tasks make it necessary to elicit the cooperation of subordinates; the much larger size of establishment makes it necessary to increase the number of people in key managerial posts and makes it much more difficult to recruit them entirely from a narrow group, such as the family. Indirectly, the broadening of educational opportunities, the assumption of welfare responsibilities by governments or independent institutions and the growth of rival organizations (such as labor unions), place checks on the power of management and prompt it to seek accommodation rather than arbitrary power. These pressures also force the managerial group to base its claim for leadership on rational acceptance rather than on appeal to its status as a social elite.

Authoritarian and paternalistic managerial attitudes and practice, both within the managerial group and toward workers, are found more frequently in India and Egypt, where the pressures on management for change are still relatively weak, than in Sweden or Great Britain, where strong labor movements have forced constitutional management on an increasing number of firms. Similarly, the relative weakness of the Chilean labor movement at the plant level as well as the absence, until recently, of other similar pressures, has left much of Chilean management still comparatively authoritarian and paternalistic. Of course, the absence of community facilities, such as housing, schools, medical care, etc., in the less industrialized countries makes new industrial workers dependent upon the paternalistic policies of even enlightened employers as in India, Chile, and Egypt.

Authoritarian management is still prevalent in Egypt, where there has been little effort to enlist employee cooperation and more concern for establishing management's rule-making power, which demands first obedience and then loyalty. Governmental labor legislation in Egypt, as in India and in Chile, has limited somewhat the unilateral authority of managers, although in each country enforcement measures vary in their effectiveness. In none of the less developed industrial countries except Israel did we find "constitutional" management of the type prevalent in Sweden, England, or the United States, but labor codes (in Chile) and labor legislation and tribunals (in India) have moved managerial attitudes and practices in the direction of constitutionalism. Labor shortages, which have put pressure on management in advanced industrial countries, are inoperative in the less industrially developed countries. This has resulted in a managerial mentality of "cheap labor," as against high capital costs, and a feeling that unsatisfactory employees can be replaced—though with increasing difficulty in countries (such as India and Egypt) where discharges are subject to government approval.

Authoritarian and paternalistic practices are also common in France and Italy, despite the presence of labor movements. These, however, are politically oriented. For the most part, French and Italian unions are weak at the plant level and have been unable to force many marginal concessions. Moreover, there have been few other pressures to narrow the wide social gap that separates French and Italian owners or top managers from their employees. Centralization of control is characteristic in the French firm, as it is in the Italian or the Indian firm, for example. Despite the advanced stage of industrialization, the same pattern of authoritarian and paternalistic management seems to prevail in Japan—largely because of the social structure which, in prewar Japan, at least, emphasized the unquestioning loyalty of subordinates to their superiors, as in the Japanese family.

In each of these countries, of course, there are exceptions. Some managements, both domestic and foreign, have attempted to move toward a constitutional or even democratic-participative type of management. Foreign firms in India, for example, are generally regarded as having more enlightened managerial policies toward Indian subordinates in the management hierarchy than do most Indian firms, and their personnel policies with respect to workers are more generous. Even these firms, however, find it difficult to avoid being paternalistic in a society which places a high premium on that type of personal dependency.

Although constitutional management has developed in most advanced industrial countries, the British case points to a further development which seems likely to occur in others. British employers share their power at the industry level with trade unions through industry-wide bargaining but have as a consequence won increasing control at the plant level, where a new form of paternalism in employee relations seems to have developed. Personnel policies, including welfare programs, sports, and recreational activities, are initiated by management unilaterally or in consultation with plant or works committees which are usually separate from the union. Somewhat the same tendencies have occurred in Sweden, although the unions appear to be more active in the plant committees, which are a form of "joint consultation." The popularity of "human relations" programs among employers in all advanced industrial countries, including the United States, however, indicates that management is trying to regain some of the original control over the work force (albeit with kid gloves) which it had before the labor-union challenge to its authority. The popularity of the "organization man" in the managerial ranks is no less an indication of the control mentality of top management.

The recent assertion of managerial authority is also illustrated strikingly in the case of Israel but for a different reason. At first the ideology of the new state was, on the whole, hostile to the exercise of managerial authority, particularly as against the strong trade-union federation (Histadrut). But as industrialization has underlined the need for competent managers, especially in the public and Histadrut-owned enterprises, managerial authority has been established. Managers have been able to retrench surplus labor, despite the protests of trade-union leaders. However, as the essay on Israel points out, the environment within which Israel's economic growth is occurring has favored more democratic-participative management than that of many other comparable industrializing countries.

In contrast, despite the development of "codetermination" in some German industries by law, the authority position of German management seems now to be greater than in most other western industrial countries. The *Unternehmer* (top executive) claims total authority over subordinates as a trustee of private property, as a person with a "calling," a member of a social elite, and an individual with extraordinary powers. Although these values are not always accepted by subordinates, the peculiar circumstances of postwar Germany have minimized the conflicts which might otherwise occur in favor of a nationally oriented drive for economic rehabilitation and recognition. As a consequence, top management's authority tends to be direct and concentrated; there is delegation of only routine operations. German management is also paternalistic, making heavier investments in voluntary social services for employees than most other European countries.

Factory managerial authority in the Soviet Union seems to have increased with the era of "one-man management" which supplanted the earlier period of divided authority between the manager and the political commissar. Soviet trade unions recently appear to constitute more of a check on managerial actions than formerly, but their power is far less than that of trade unions in the advanced industrial countries of the west. Further, it would be a mistake to suppose that the objectives of communist trade unions are similar to those of noncommunist unions, and the Communists would, in their more honest moments, be the last to deny this divergence.

Management as a Class

The managerial elite in the industrializing countries is a mixture of patrimonial management in family-owned enterprises and somewhat more professional management in the public enterprises. But the variations are as striking as the similarities. In Egypt where stronger government control has been directed toward economic development since the Revolution of 1952, managers have high prestige; in some of the public enterprises, they have been drawn from the army. There is relatively little patrimonial management. In India, on the other hand, patrimonial management is entrenched in many parts of the private sector through the *managing-agency system,* and professional management is found largely in the more progressive Indian firms, the foreign companies, and in the growing number of public enterprises. Some political management is found in the latter, however, as it was in several of the public enterprises in Israel and, in an earlier period, in Soviet industrialization.

Patrimonial management, as we have stressed earlier, can absorb professionals and is not necessarily backward. But generally it has been a drag on dynamic industrial development, as illustrated in the case of management in France and Italy. The French study points out that "the nature of the family-based enterprise is not only to limit the number of persons in management, but it also tends to expand this aridness by an excessive centralization of control and the assumption of full direction of the enterprise by the head of the family without an adequate organization." In France and Italy, as in Chile and India, a newer professionally oriented managerial elite is rising to challenge the old order. The Chilean management association known as ICARE is in the forefront of this effort there, and the newer Indian Management Association is a parallel.

Although patrimonial management is still strong in Japan, access to subordinate managerial positions is almost exclusively on the basis of university affiliation and record. Similar importance is placed on the graduates of the *grandes écoles* in France and Oxford and Cambridge graduates in Great Britain. Despite the apparent exclusiveness, these managerial appointments are based as much on competence as on connection, and this is one test of professionalization of management. When the opportunities for professional training are broader, as they are in both the United States and in the Soviet Union, then access to managerial positions can increasingly be based on competence, even though "whom you know" still plays a part in both countries, as well as in the less industrialized societies.

German managers apparently tend to think of themselves not as professional managers but as engineers, lawyers, accountants, etc. The high status role of the German *Unternehmer,* many of whom are owner-executives, means that there is a gulf between the man at the top and lower managerial ranks. The top managers resist professionalization in the belief that it may threaten their formal authority position. Moreover, German top managers are organized in various associations and federations which tend to strengthen the cohesion of the German managerial class. Although works councils are imposed by law in Germany, their influence on management tends to be slight, and the basic determinant of labor-management relations is the relative power to the parties rather than specific governmental labor legislation.

With the growing professionalization of management in all industrial countries, is the managerial elite gaining so much power that it is the dominant economic and political force in each country? Our studies show clearly that the power of management is counterbalanced by strong trade unions and government in the advanced industrial countries. Management in Sweden and Britain for example, is checked by the power of the labor movement in negotiating industry-wide agreements as well as by labor's political power. Furthermore, in each country the state regulates and controls the authority of employers and of management both in economic matters and more specifically, in aspects of the labor-management relationship. Although the latter is still relatively free for negotiation between management and labor in the advanced industrial countries of Britain, Sweden, and the United States, labor codes and labor legislation are more restrictive on employers and attempt to be more protective of employees in such countries as India, Chile, Egypt, and even Japan. The role of the state in regulating the authority of management is also great in countries like France and Italy, where the power of employers through their industry and national associations is stronger than in the less developed countries.

Soviet management has clearly moved from the political to the professional type, and the Soviet manager today enjoys high status and remuneration. But speculation that this might mean superior political power for industrial managers, engineers, and technical administrators at the expense of the Communist party seems to have little foundation in recent Soviet developments. The chances for a managerial revolution displacing the party's monolithic control are dubious in the foreseeable future.

In summary, employer and managerial authority is not unchecked by rival organizations or by government in any of the countries we have studied. Although the importance and influence of management as an economic resource is rising with advancing industrialization, there is no evidence of the development of a "managerial state" or a power elite in which management is the dominant element. The German case is the nearest to the latter; but the German government has limited cartels by legislation over employer opposition, and the German trade-union movement still possesses considerable political power.

The Development of Managerial Resources

The studies of the more advanced industrial countries illustrate convincingly the relation between the competence and performance of management and the facilities for developing managerial resources. Schools of engineering and of business administration have helped staff United States firms for nearly fifty years, and postwar executive-development programs in a number of American universities are paralleled by similar programs in Great Britain and Sweden. The establishment of the Administrative Staff College in England and of executive-development programs by the Swedish Federation of Employers are evidences of the need these advanced industrial countries have for trained managerial resources. These programs are, of course, supplemented by in-plant management training programs or "staff colleges" organized by the larger firms and by short-term executive development programs at a number of universities, particularly in Great Britain.

Training for management as a profession is growing in importance in Germany, partly through conference programs such as those held annually at Baden-Baden. However, these programs also serve the purpose of developing a more uniform managerial ideology in Germany. German universities, for the most part, have not concerned themselves with management as a professional field, although university training in engineering or law is found in the backgrounds of a substantial proportion of intermediate German managers and even top executives. The same may be said of universities in France and Italy—so much so that efforts to provide facilities for management training in Italy had to be established outside the university system in a special institute sponsored by several Italian firms at Turin (known as IPSOA), and in France by the French Employers' Association. In Italy, the management training programs are not designed to prepare new entrants for management;

rather, they concentrate on courses for those who already occupy a position in the managerial hierarchy.

The university system of Japan was modified dramatically in the course of industrialization to produce engineers, technicians, and more recently, graduates of schools of commerce and business administration. Japanese employers draw heavily on the cream of the crop of leading universities for their new recruits to managerial positions. The Soviet university system has been directed even more clearly toward training scientists and engineers, and Soviet factories appear increasingly to be staffed with managers who have had university training or intensive work at one of the many correspondence or evening schools. There is no doubt that the Soviet industrial society has placed great weight on trained managerial resources.

The less developed industrial countries, in contrast, suffer from an inadequacy of institutions for generating and developing high-level managerial resources. We noted this tendency in France and Italy; it is even more pronounced in Egypt, India, Chile, and Israel, even though recent developments indicate a new trend. The Egyptian and Indian university systems were designed primarily to turn out civil servants to assist in the administration of the countries by a foreign power; they are ill-adapted to the needs of a modern industrial society. Consequently, efforts have been made to change the emphasis in some of the universities, particularly in India. The variety of general and specialized management-training programs in India since 1955 is evidence of the increasing awareness of Indian industry and government officials of the importance of generating high-level managerial resources for an expanding industrial society. Several universities in Chile have developed programs of economics and business administration. The role of the universities and technical institutes in Israel in providing trained technical and managerial manpower for Israel's expanding industries is also indicated.

In many underdeveloped countries, foreign firms play a very important role. Although there are substantial variations in policy, ranging from almost exclusive recruitment of upper-level managerial forces in the home country to sustained efforts to develop local talent, these firms almost always carry on some training. In some foreign companies, the experience gained by locally recruited managerial personnel has been sufficient to enable them to run the enterprises themselves, in an efficient manner.

The army is also a major source of administrative training in these areas, and training at foreign institutions is often encouraged. Consequently, facilities are sometimes substantially greater than would appear if we looked merely at domestic institutions. In spite of this, however, the shortage of training facilities is acute and, in many cases, may be a critical factor delaying economic growth.

In summary, the industrialization of the economically underdeveloped societies and the continued industrialization pressures in such countries as France and Italy have forced the university systems and other institutions in these countries to turn their attention more and more to the development of high-level technical and managerial resources. The road ahead has been shown by the more advanced industrial countries although even in these we have seen that training and development programs have been accentuated since the war and many new ones have been established. In these efforts, the professional management associations, no less than the leading universities, have played an important role.

The lesson which the essays on particular countries emphasize is that an industrializing country must make an increasing investment in the generation and development of technical and managerial resources if it hopes to match the achievement of the advanced industrial countries. This is one of the clear imperatives of industrialization. Although we can see the future industrial society only dimly, with the promise of computers which think and the prospect of the automatic factory,[1] the importance of high-level manpower will increase relatively, and the institutions to generate it will have to meet the challenge. The second half of the twentieth century, even more than the first half, will be an era of technical and managerial brain power in the service of an industrial society.

[1] For a provocative forecast, see Harold J. Leavitt and Thomas L. Whisler, "Management in the 1980's," *Harvard Business Review*, XXXVI, no. 6 (November-December, 1958), pp. 41-48.

6

International Search for
Managerial Talent *

S. BENJAMIN PRASAD

The scarcest factor not only in the developing nations but also in many of the mature industrialized countries is, perhaps, that of the college-trained managerial personnel. Of course, in many developing countries capital equipment, skilled labor force, and essential raw materials are scarce in relation to their needs, but the paucity of trained managerial manpower supersedes the other problems in industrialization. Pronounced as it is, this problem —despite general acknowledgment of its prevalence—did not receive adequate attention, as it should have, in the economic plans of many developing countries. It is only during the sixties, one might speculate, that there is some evidence indicating that the search for managerial talent has become a world-wide movement. Should the range of activities continue in the same direction and at an increasing rate, as they probably will, the scope of this search is likely to carry international significance.

The purpose of this paper is twofold: 1. to examine some of the patterns and prospects of this international search for managerial talent, and 2. to illustrate the case of India in the light of these patterns and prospects.

* Reprinted by permission from the January, 1965 issue of the *Michigan Business Review*, published by the Graduate School of Business Administration, The University of Michigan.

PATTERNS AND PROSPECTS OF THE SEARCH

In many of the mature countries in Europe the idyllic picture of prewar commerce and industry has been fading fast. The strain of competition has become more and more severe. The conduct of business operations has been more robust and more American-style. The following are some of the major trends which exemplify the search for managerial talent in European countries. This search has emanated from increasing demand for trained managerial personnel from commerce and industry:

1. Size of business firms is enlarging through mergers and joint ventures.
2. Production processes, methods, and techniques have been undergoing dynamic changes.
3. There has been a rush to develop and adopt American mass-marketing methods, including marketing research.
4. Business firms are seeking training for management to meet the complex operations of multinational businesses.
5. Heavy emphasis is placed on the development of middle managers and management "technicians."

In contradistinction, the demand for managerial personnel, in developing nations, stems mainly from their industrialization and development programs envisaged and executed according to their economic plans. The realization that managerial manpower is one of the key variables in industrialization programs has arisen in the developing countries. This is true of India, Pakistan, and scores of African and Latin American nations. The following are some of the general trends which can be seen in these countries:

1. There are economic plans for industrialization with priorities given mostly to heavy industries in the public sector.
2. The prevailing educational systems, although far from being adequate to meet the structural needs of the nations, are somewhat streamlined.
3. In technology, many of them have skipped one or more intermediary stages and are on the threshold of modern technology.

4. Modern management techniques are associated with modern technology.

MODEL FOR MANAGEMENT EDUCATION

One of the vital problems which confronts the seekers of modern management talent is a basic one: How to go about seeking it? In other words, the problem is related to the approach which may provide such conducive conditions as to cultivate managerial talent. The general prime condition is the educational facilities for the training and development of management personnel.

The approach, which many nations have invariably found to be effective, is the Harvard model. Sought as a model for management education, the Harvard approach—case studies and special management programs—has inspired business schools in France, Italy, Japan, Mexico, Pakistan, Spain, and Switzerland. Other American institutions have followed suit and have been instrumental in setting up educational programs in other countries. For example, Stanford University in Peru, and the Massachusetts Institute of Technology in India. In general, the influence of the American management education system has permeated greatly in such mature nations as Great Britain and France, and in such developing nations as Chile and India, to name a few.

In Great Britain, in recent years, few things have been debated more hotly than business management education.[1] The recommended graduate schools of business are now taking shape at Manchester University and the London School of Economics. The undergraduate programs in management, which are under the purview of the Ministry of Education, are offered in scores of technical colleges, some of which have been upgraded as colleges of advanced technology. There is considerable uniformity in management education at the undergraduate level since curricula are jointly drawn by the Ministry of Education and the British Institute of Management.

In France the story is different; here is the European Institute of Business Administration (INSEAD), a trilingual set-up. Its main feature is the case method. It is more like a postgraduate institute

---

[1] For details see *Business Week* (December 7, 1963), p. 84.

than a college of commerce or business. The graduates of INSEAD are greatly in demand by both American and European business firms. Many of the graduates are in the employ of IBM, du Pont, and Procter & Gamble—in overseas operations.

PROBLEMS IN DEVELOPING NATIONS

The developing nations are strongly impelled to adopt modern machinery and processes. In technology they can take long strides but to derive optimal benefits of technology they require middle- and upper middle-level managerial personnel, well trained in the art and science of modern management. This is particularly so in the public sector in many countries, for the top-level policy and decision-makers are generally chosen either from the ranks of civil service as in India, or from military service as in Egypt. The effective management of the enterprises, in terms of day-to-day operations and in terms of the predetermined objectives, then becomes a function of middle managers.

To assure a supply of these managers is not an easy task. But such managerial talent could be generated in the educational system. Unfortunately, the educational systems in many of the developing nations have placed more emphasis on such fields as Law, Philosophy, and Literature than on Engineering and Technology. Industrial management, if viewed in its true perspective, is an integral part of technology. This limitation has been repeatedly pointed out by such international observers as Gunnar Myrdal, Frederick Harbison, Charles Myers, and others. Myrdal, for instance, observed: "In addition to the literacy drive, there is need for a radical reform of higher education. I am thinking not so much of the level of higher education in most of the underdeveloped countries—low as it is—as of its direction. What these countries need is an increased output of administrators, doctors, engineers, agronomists, and all sorts of technically trained people on different levels." [2] With particular reference to management skills, Millikan and Rostow noted that "one of the most serious bottlenecks inhibiting the development of absorptive capacity in the

[2] Gunnar Myrdal, *An International Economy: Problems and Prospects* (New York: Harper & Row, 1958), p. 187.

underdeveloped countries is a shortage of managerial and administrative skills." [3]

Although lack of management talent is a high hurdle in the
industrialization programs of many developing countries, it is difficult to subscribe to the view, particularly of David who went on to
state that the "central issues of foreign economic policy cannot
be dealt with effectively . . . by mere export of capital. The
answer will be found in the massive export of managerial and entrepreneurial talent." [4] More than a massive import of these skills, an
underdeveloped country would be greatly interested, as recent evidences all over the world attest, in importing leadership skills to
develop its own programs for cultivating managerial talents. As
noted earlier, leadership in the form of the Harvard model is more
sought after than foreign managerial personnel. Perhaps, as Howe
Martyn observed, "Managerial talent is not necessarily scarce but
opportunities to exercise and develop it in modern industry have
been rare and limited mainly to advanced countries." [5]

[3] M. F. Millikan and W. W. Rostow, *A Proposal: Key to an Effective
Foreign Policy* (New York: Harper & Row, 1957), p. 61.
[4] D. K. David, *A Plan for Waging Economic War* (New York: Committee
for Economic Development, 1958), p. 7.
[5] Howe Martyn, *International Business* (New York: The Free Press of
Glencoe, 1964), p. 149.

India has been described as a state of mind, rather than a nation. Although
the 20th century has touched India in the form of rising industrial complexes,
80 percent of the people reside in villages and live in a manner that has
changed little in the past 1,000 years.

A country of great potential wealth that includes sizable desposits of iron
ore, mica, and manganese, India is burdened by problems of poverty, 75 percent
illiteracy, booming overpopulation, and an underdeveloped economy. Unlike
Red China, with is seeking to catch up with the modern industrial world by
means of totalitarian head-knocking tactics, India wants to become a self-suf-
ficient power without sacrificing the values of a free society. It is the first time
in history that a country with India's staggering problems has attempted to
solve them by democratic processes. In its development program, India prefers
government enterprise to promote a socialist pattern of society. Still, she wel-
comes private initiative and enterprises when it is felt these factors contribute
to the advancement of the economy.

India began a series of five-year plans in 1951 under which the government
decided what portion of resources should be used for capital goods and what
amount should be used for producing consumer goods. During the first five-
year plan, top priority was assigned to agriculture and to large irrigation and
power projects. Since targets were kept low, several goals were surpassed.
Emphasis was shifted from agriculture to industry under the second five-year
plan, which was twice the size of the first. Although India was forced to cut

Some of the problems of the educational system and lack of opportunities are common to most underdeveloped countries. In addition there are also special problems such as mobility barriers which will be discussed with particular reference to India.

LACK OF OPPORTUNITY IN INDIA

India has a relatively undeveloped but growing industrial sector. Economic and industrial development in India is directed through a series of five-year plans which spell out the role of the government and of private enterprise. "India has been in the forefront among underdeveloped countries in providing a variety of programs for management training and development." [6]

Large universities offer Bachelor's and Master's programs in Commerce, the core of which is accounting. The postgraduate diploma in Business Administration is a program which some universities offer but once again the scope of this is limited. Numerous organizations of businessmen, such as the local Productivity Councils and Management Associations have begun to sponsor talks, symposiums, and seminars on managerial subjects. Exposure to these avenues is limited to those already in business and industry.

Managerial positions in many Indian companies in the private sector are typically earmarked for members of the family or families controlling the enterprise. That is to say, entry into managerial positions is restricted. The extent of restriction perhaps can be surmised by noting a key conclusion of an Indian author that nine

---

back on original goals, the "hard core" of a modified program was achieved. The third plan, begun in 1961, called for $25 billion in spending, with the highest priority assigned to food production. Revision of the current plan became necessary because of the Chinese Communist invasion, which forced India to double its defense expenditures.

India's progress is evident and measurable. The framework for industry is laid, agricultural production has been increased and student enrollment is up. But India has only begun to touch the edges of poverty, disease, and social confinement.

[6] For further details, see Charles A. Myers, "Recent Development in Management Training," *Indian Journal of Public Administration* (April-June, 1958), pp. 154-164.

leading families hold nearly six hundred directorships or partner-
ships in Indian industries.[7]

Business firms generally do not visit campuses to recruit new
graduates in commerce or business administration for managerial
positions. By the same token, firms seldom have college programs
such as those found in the United States. Colleges and universities
do not have placement offices to coordinate the job-seeking activities of their graduates. A few of the commerce graduates enter business firms via newspaper advertisements and strong recommendations, only to occupy clerical positions. These practices should suggest that there is a great difference between management and
managerial development as it is known here in the United States
and as it is known in India.

To briefly characterize management in India with a view to
providing clues to the "lack of opportunity" concept, management
in the public sector is centralized by its very nature. That is, the industrial firms in the public sector are regulated and operated by
bureaucratic agencies of the central government. In the private
sector, management is highly centralized and autocratic. In fact,
if one were to succeed in examining the organizational charts of the
companies, one is likely to find several layers in the managerial
hierarchy totally absent. This is due to lack of appreciation of the
principle of delegation of authority. R. F. Pelissier in a recent article observed: "Delegation is not widely practiced. Nonetheless, in
my two months' stay in India I was asked to discuss 'Delegation of
Authority' more frequently than any other management topics." [8]

The superior-subordinate relationship is viewed among Indian
managers and executives as a competitive relationship. The subordinate is seen as a rival who might take over the superior's job.
This is in violation of one of the fundamental principles of effective management, namely, that it is part of a manager's (superior's)
job to train and improve the skills of his subordinate. This violation often results from insecurity on the part of the superiors.

No characterization of Indian management would be adequate without referring to the Managing Agency System. This was

[7] M. M. Mehta, *Structure of Indian Industry* (Bombay: Popular Book Company, 1955), p. 248.
[8] R. F. Pelissier, "Certain Aspects of Management in India," *Michigan
Business Review* (May, 1964), p. 7.

a "device through which the British would give effect to the principle of exclusiveness in business." [9] A managing agency is a business organization which has contracts to manage other companies engaged in manufacturing, mining, or trading activities. A British import, originally meant to achieve economies of production and distribution and to compensate for the shortage of managerial skills, the managing agents came to dominate Indian private enterprise. "The managing agency is an effective instrument for the tendency in Indian business to limit upper level positions to members of family, relatives, persons from the same business community, etc." [10]

CONCLUSION

The search for managerial talent all over the world is an integral part of what Gunnar Myrdal called "a living political force of immense and investible power in our contemporary world." The difficulty in acquiring the managerial skills in developing nations may be ascribed to lack of opportunity. Many nations are trying to create opportunities. In this venture many an American institution, educational and commercial, has a role to play. The best role is one of guidance.

9 *Ibid.*, p. 10.
10 *Ibid.*, p. 10.

II

Managerialism in Advanced and Developing Countries

7

Management and Management Teaching in Switzerland*

E. SCHMIDT NESTLEY

Although in the first half of this century and especially so in the last thirty years great progress has been made in developing and formulating general principles and methods governing the *art* and *science* of management, there is no doubt that local and national conditions and attitudes still strongly influence both the thinking and acting of the executive in the various economic areas of the world. It is, therefore, natural to have my talk preceded by a short review of the Swiss economy and its main criteria, in order to better understand the specific features and methods of the Swiss manager, as well as the management training systems applied in Switzerland.

SWISS ECONOMY AND ITS CRITERIA

Switzerland is not an agricultural country, nor does it draw its main income from tourism. It is, in fact, an industrial country, industrial production furnishing the greatest part of the Swiss gross

* Reprinted from *Management International,* No. 6 (1963), with permission from the International University Contact for Management Education, Rotterdam, The Netherlands. This is a slightly revised version of the original article.

national income. The structure of the Swiss economy has always been characterized by a nearly total absence of raw materials, the small size of her home market, and also by the poverty of her soil, making it impossible for agriculture to absorb the growth of the population. Swiss industry, therefore, has always had to rely upon labor-intensive production and on exports and this, in turn, necessitated precision and quality goods requiring a high percentage of skilled labor and offering special quality features justifying relatively high prices. Switzerland's industry has thus been known as the "tailoring to measure" shop of Europe. In applying this policy Switzerland has been very successful, so far, thanks to an impressive number of highly qualified workers capable of adapting themselves to the constantly changing requirements of small-batch quality production. This type of production, combined with the all-round efficiency of the Swiss craftsman, did not encourage functional organization, planning, and work study. Management's interest therefore was focused on the development of high-grade products, their quality and their sales throughout the world rather than on the organization and coordination of the business as a whole. It should also be kept in mind that Switzerland, thanks to her clever policy of neutrality, has on the whole been saved from political upheavals and losses of substance. To a certain degree this is undoubtedly due to Swiss tendency to be hesitating and careful when faced with new developments, be they of a political, technical, or financial nature, and this again has created remarkable international confidence in the Swiss political and economic system which is another source of Switzerland's wealth and high standard of living. Taking all this into account it is not surprising that until recently the general tendency was rather to perpetuate traditional beliefs and concepts and to attribute to a wise mixture of conservatism and progress Switzerland's unique prosperity.

It is also remarkable that in comparison with other countries Switzerland has a high percentage of family-owned businesses with all the advantages and disadvantages of a long tradition frequently spreading over several generations. A further characteristic of Swiss economy is the overwhelming majority of small companies. In fact, out of a number of 252,000 enterprises only 70 number more than 100 employees, which fact again explains the relatively slow development of modern management techniques, most of which grew out of the problems of the bigger businesses. Another important characteristic of the present situation is that the Swiss economy, which used to be relatively modest and well-balanced, has completely outgrown its own possibilities and resources. Due to Switzerland's enviable situation of having an intact production machinery after World War II, and due also to the uninterrupted and ever growing inflow of foreign money seeking security, the growing business possibilities could be mastered only by having recourse to foreign workers whose number now amounts to about one third of the existing labor force, but there are many plants where foreign labor even represents more than 50 percent. The problems created by this fantastic expansion have undoubtedly paved the way for a considerable change in management attitudes, at least among the younger generation, and this would probably become universal if the country had to maintain its production capacity at its rate of income without the foreign workers. At present, nobody would dare to imagine what might happen if those 650,000 foreign workers left and the country wanted to maintain its standard of living and expansion of wealth.

ELEMENTS OF MANAGEMENT

Turning now to the basic elements of management in Switzerland, practically the only generally accepted criterion for the success of an enterprise—and, therefore, for the success of its management—is the purely financial profit it can show. This, I think, is more or less the case everywhere. This profit is measured in relation to the capital invested and hardly ever in terms of the overall business potentialities.

A further general policy seems to be that in view of the past success there is a general belief that opportunities should be given time to ripen, and the practice of setting up long-term programs and objectives, and realizing them with concentrated energy, is considered inappropriate in view of past experience. He who practices such methods is rather regarded as an opportunist and troublemaker, all the more so if he is very successful. In this line of thought there is also not much interest for integrated systems of measuring performance against standards, and a common and basic opposition to organization is noted inasmuch as the Swiss individual in general does not look upon organization as a tool to free him from innumerable small decisions and preoccupations; he rather considers it a straitjacket preventing him from efficient activity. As much as the Swiss believe in democracy, which is nothing else than coordinated team cooperation in politics, as little do they practice well organized team work in everyday industrial and administrative activities. This explains why formal organizational systems derived from analytical thinking are still the exception, and the traditional system of the organization structure growing around individuals is still predominant.

One of the main features of the average Swiss is the desire to do everything himself with the greatest possible perfectionism; he therefore does not like to share responsibilities with others and hence there is difficulty in delegating. This is also illustrated by the fact that generally management receives far too much information. Consequently, executives are overburdened, and even if willingness does exist, the possibilities offered by modern planning and organization can often not be grasped because of the lack of effective relief by lower levels. In many enterprises, management is strongly rooted in the tradition of artisanal practice, and this also stems from the fact that the accent of management lies on the departmental or technical specialists and not yet on people properly prepared for overall management. The person capable of heading and coordinating the work of specialists with whose fields he is no longer familiar is mostly regarded with great scepticism. For example, the young executive who is eventually to take over his father's textile business will study textile engineering rather than business administration. On the other hand, it must be stressed that modern techniques of functional and operational management are rather widely applied all over industry and administration, and the progress made during the last 10 years is quite impressive. I am referring to fields such as time-and-work study, modern remunerations systems, factory design and layout, materials handling, costing and budgeting, office rationalization, data processing, etc. These techniques are still mainly used in what is nowadays considered their *classical* form, and only sporadically so in their *modern* form, such as integrated planning and programming systems, operations research, preparation of decisions, management accounting, etc.

However, as everywhere in Europe, Swiss management is changing in a spectacular way, but, as previously said, the evolution takes longer and is slower than elsewhere. There is another explanation for this, in that Switzerland did not find herself in a situation like most other European countries, where the aftermath of World War II simply forced managements to apply new methods and throw old ones overboard if they wanted to survive and rebuild their economy. In all those countries the introduction and application of modern management practice, as well as the training of managers in the new techniques, were strongly fostered and financially supported by the respective governments. In Switzerland, on the contrary, nobody in the whole Federal Administration has so far shown interest in fostering modern management methods on a national basis, not a single penny has been spent for this out of governmental funds, and even the big professional associations, as for instance the Federation of Swiss industries, do not hold themselves responsible for fostering and supporting the application of modern management techniques through their members, their interest being concentrated on the defense of their members against the State on the one hand, against labor on the other. Whatever has been done in this country in the field of modern management theory and practice and management training has been done thanks to the enthusiasm and idealism of a few pioneers and special groupings of interested and convinced men that were formed entirely outside the big private and governmental economic bodies and without their financial help.

The first men that were especially trained in modern management are now reaching the top ranks, and there will be many more within the next decade. So what has been said so far will probably have to be said rather differently in 1968. For the time being, however, the overwhelming majority of high management positions are still held by persons educated for their job in the traditional philosophy. This was built on the conviction that management skills and arts could be acquired only through experience gained in long years on the same job, following in the footsteps of the older successful generation. Meanwhile it has become a generally accepted fact that basic—preferably academic—training in one of the main fields, engineering, commerce, economics, or law, is a highly desirable if not indispensable prerequisite for higher management jobs.

DEVELOPMENTS

If all that has been said so far seems to prove that the general situation in this country was and still is not very favorable to incite great enthusiasm for modern management principles, techniques and training, it is all the more satisfying that at quite an early date already a number of initiatives were taken, aiming at fostering and popularizing these fields, and that some remarkable realizations were achieved at a time when bigger and less conservative countries had not even become aware of the importance of these problems. As early as 1913, I. Bally, head of the big Swiss shoe concern, became an admirer of such classical American management scientists as Taylor, Gilbreths, and Munsterberg and, as a consequence, began to foster academic and practical research and training in the field of work study and psycho-techniques, nowadays called Institutes for Applied Psychology. Another initiative came from a group of Swiss industrialists called Swiss Friends of the USA, who since 1919 promulgated American theory and practice of "rationalization" in Switzerland, which led to the formation of a permanent secretariate consulting industry in these matters.

A third move emanated from Geneva, the League of Nations and the International Labour Office which, in 1928, founded the International Institute for Rationalization. The activity of this institute and its heads, among whom were men like Lyndall Urwick, had its repercussions in Switzerland, and it was in this way that the then president of this university, Professor Rohn, recognized in 1929 the growing importance of modern industrial management. He succeeded in forming the "Forderungsgesellschaft des Betriebswissen-schaftlichen Institutes an der ETH" including among its members most leading Swiss industrialists whose objectives were to give moral and financial assistance in the establishment of an academic institute for industrial management science and a joint ordinary professorship at this School. I should like to point out that in this way a very efficient and permanently maintained cooperation between industry and university was realized in this country as early as 34 years ago. In 1932, graduate training of industrial engineers started at this university, as well as conferences, exchange of experience sessions and other activities for practicing managers and industrial personnel.

A fourth important initiative should not be forgotten here: it is personified by the St. Gall Graduate School of Economics which from the beginning aimed at the training of higher commercial personnel, as testified by the School's statutes. Following the general trend and under the influence of men like Gasser, Gsell, Motteli, and Ulrich, this School's activities have more and more developed into a comprehensive education for management in general, and its research work in this field is of very high standing.

To sum up, after World War II, there were three universities that in one form or another included elements of management training in the graduate curriculum: The Federal Institute of Technology, Berne University, and the St. Gall Graduate School of Economics. Apart from these a number of associations and institutions were dealing with management matters in the form of occasional conferences, conventions, special courses on specific topics, etc. However, special management training for postgraduates or active executives of a certain level came into existence only in the late forties and early fifties. Three moves should be particularly mentioned in this connection, two of which were initiated by big international concerns. In 1946, Aluminum Limited created CEI in Geneva, and in 1957 Nestle Alimentana established IMEDE in Lausanne. In some way or other both these ventures were inspired by American models, both schools are of distinctive international character and both became later affiliated to the local universities, namely Geneva and Lausanne, which in this way succeeded in becoming involved in academic management education, without much development of their own.

The third move, taken in 1954, endeavoured to realize a typically Swiss solution. It is the SKU sponsored by three institutions already active in the field of management education, i.e., The Federal Institute of Technology, the St. Gall Graduate School of Economics, and the Swiss Foundation for Applied Psychology.

These three ventures can be considered milestones and were undoubtedly the pacemakers for an increasing number of other moves taken during the last ten years. They can be grouped as follows. There are, first, the universities, some of which have already been mentioned. As to the others, Zurich, Fribourg, Neuchatel, and Basle are presently showing a certain initiative towards increased teaching of management subjects within their economics departments, but so far these efforts are concentrated on special fields, such as costing, data processing, and operations research. Secondly, apart from the three pacemakers mentioned, there are about six other management development programs of a regular and institutional character, varying in length and importance and mostly meant for higher personnel and top men of smaller firms, making nine in all. Of these, six are of a general character aiming at despecialization; three, while incorporating general management matters, aim at deepening knowledge in special fields. The sponsors are mainly professional or management associations, though some are companies and universities.

It can generally be said that, in spite of the obstacles mentioned before, a considerable development in management teaching has been realized, both in depth and width. It all began with personal initiatives, both in business and at some universities, which modified certain curricula to better prepare graduates for future management jobs. Later on large concerns took up the challenge and installed post-experience schools for general use. Finally, Management Associations followed suit, and some big Swiss companies developed their own in-company programs. In addition, growing interest is certified by the ever-increasing number of smaller activities of great variety. It can also be said that the general success of the whole development is undisputed. Evidence for this is threefold:

1. More and more people are interested in undergoing management training of some kind, attendance to all types of programs is steadily growing. It is most interesting to see how much higher the standard of knowledge of management problems and techniques among participants of courses is nowadays as compared with ten years ago. This is, at least partially, due to the influence of former students on the potential management personnel of their firms. The way such old-timers slowly build up complete schools of thought in their business, the members of which all undergo the same training at one time or other and layer after layer, is remarkable.

2. More and more industries become interested. At first mainly manufacturing firms of a certain size sent their people; nowadays medium and small size plants, Chemical Industries, Banks, Insurance Companies, Administration, and Trading Firms are the main clients.

3. The classical type of management training aiming only at forming future top managers is more and more—although still insufficiently—supplemented by facilities catering for lower grades. In this way, there is not only a horizontal but also vertical expansion.

In one respect, however, success is limited, with a few notable exceptions; the actual top level has not become really enthusiastic, nor have they ever taken part in a training course of some kind. As pointed out before, there are two reasons for this fact: the policy of the big industrial and patronal federations and the ever-present problem of generations. The majority of top men made their decisive careers in the years between the two wars; they cannot forget the great economic crisis of the thirties, and at the bottom of their hearts they do not really believe in the value of it all. Although in this way they will not admit that there is anything for them to learn, they do, however, let the younger generations participate. Ten years from now they will be replaced by men trained for their jobs and with them will come a still greater expansion, perhaps a bit later than in other larger European countries but none the less thorough. For one thing is certain—the relatively slow growth has considerably helped to maintain the quality of the various ventures right from the start, such as is good Swiss tradition. With very few exceptions, there were no failures; we were spared from adventurers and opportunists, and those few ventures that disappeared again after some time did no harm.

The general approach was and is a distinctly practical one; shaped by the needs and possibilities as well as by initiative a certain idealism and the information that came from over the Atlantic. Not much time was lost with theoretical considerations or questionnaires asking industry what they wanted; if, for instance, when founding the Swiss Management Courses, we had asked the opinion of the economic and industrial roof organizations they would have told us that there was no need for this type of venture and they even considered it dangerous. Apart from the schools with distinctly international character, Swiss management training facilities are pronouncedly adapted to Swiss features and conditions and offer Swiss solutions to Swiss problems. The general experience in this country is that foreign cases, examples and material should not be used without careful consideration. Good as they may be from the methodical or analytical point of view, the actual examples should be chosen from within the country. Personally I also believe that a training center should be built around one or several personalities, and a permanent staff who give it a distinct character and image; teaching teams that are replaced by others from course to course are not very favorable in this respect.

PROBLEMS OF METHODS

Turning now to the problem of methods, the Swiss solutions have followed the general trend inasmuch as active participation of the audience is as universal as the use of practical cases in one form or another. Discussions, however, have been found to give better results when adequately organized and prepared, the Swiss not being very dynamic and ready debaters. There would be too much time lost trying to let a group find its way entirely on its own. Wide use is also made of very comprehensive documentation and reading material to be perused before the courses, again in order not lose time with fundamentals and help preparing discussion contribution. Finally, Swiss employers have been found less reluctant in letting their men participate when periods of absence from business were not too long; some courses are therefore split into several parts of various length, even when residential.

These conclusions drawn from past experience form the natural basis for an outlook into the future—such as I am trying to undertake now. The following points seems to demand attention.

As I see it, the quantitative requirements for management training and management teaching in this country will continue to grow. Further graduate programs will be established, either by expansion of the existing ones, or perhaps those universities that are still in the background will come in. As to postgraduate schools, there are limitations to the number of participants so that the existing ones will either have to run parallel courses, or new ones will have to be created. There will also be a need for more specialized courses or smaller schools of a special character.

New types of training and programs have to be established. We are lacking despecialization programs for middle and lower management on the one hand, high level courses for real top executives on the other hand. As far as I know, initiatives in both directions are on the way.

Research and development work will have to be intensified. As in all fields, Switzerland will have to hold its own through the quality of its programs, the originality of the methods used and the tools employed.

Teachers and specialists of Swiss origin are needed in growing numbers; programs and facilities must be established to accelerate this process.

The last two points apply to in-company training as well; this also requires research, availability of material and preparation of suitable personnel.

As far as I can judge, and without in any way endeavoring to foster centralism and dirigism so utterly disliked by my fellow countrymen, the solution of all these future problems will require a higher degree of coordination, exchange of experience, men and material between all those involved in management training so far. Why should not others follow the example given, ten years ago, by the founders of SKU, get together and organize new types of courses or programs? Could one not tackle the problem of training and preparing future teachers as a joint venture of all those interested? Would it not be possible—in the same way—to finance and maintain a common residential center which to my mind is badly needed? In the same line of ideas, the present dispersal of support and sponsoring given by industry in the form of the various "sponsoring societies" and financial and moral assistance groups may well require some thinking over. Nowadays, it is always the same people that are asked to support half a dozen different ventures with the same basic aims; it may become necessary to find a more efficient way of exploring the total amount of existing willingness and interest which may well prove far greater still than it is already. The Belgian solution has shown the way—but even without it we management teachers and scientists might well apply one of our favorite principles and teaching topics to our own business, i.e., centralize planning and policy-making, decentralize operations and execution. In this way, perhaps, another idea could also be realized, the creation of more management training facilities for nationals of developing countries, a task for which Switzerland is ideally suited, thanks to its neutrality, its knowledge of international affairs and the fact that it never had anything to do with colonization.

CONCLUSION

To sum up, I believe we Swiss have every reason to be proud of what has been done so far under the circumstances peculiar to this country. When mentioning some of these circumstances, for instance, the lack of government interest, I may have sounded bitter. Such feelings may be excusable when looking back on many years of struggle, deception, and too slow progress. Actually there is no such bitterness because we all know that shortcomings of this kind are compensated by assets in other fields, for instance the overwhelming freedom private enterprise and initiative is enjoying in this country. It is just this which enabled us to do what we did, and I do not think anyone would like to exchange it for financial assistance and—inevitably—more control and restrictions from governmental sources. It will also help us not to become so proud and self-satisfied as to rest on our laurels. That is not the way this nation is run.

8

Management and Organization in Japanese Industry *

JOSEPH FROOMKIN

Americans who look at the organization and practice of Japanese management always have the same initial reaction: "Can this really work?"

There is little formal organization, less delegation of authority and little reliance on staff work even in the largest firms. Nevertheless Japanese industry has supported a rise in Gross National Product of 6.5 percent a year and industrial production has increased by 12 percent per annum. Management practices which make such a growth possible deserve attention from all businessmen.

The practices underlying Japanese business organization are not extensively documented. There is very little literature on the subject. The dearth of information is no accident but is due to the unwillingness of most Japanese businessmen to discuss their practices with outsiders. A Japanese corporation is a private preserve, and the internal method of operation, in the opinion of Japanese executives, is no concern to anyone outside the establishment. A definitive or detailed study of Japanese business will be done only when some top executive analyzes his organization after his retirement. The following notes gathered during a consulting trip to Japan may highlight some of the features of interest to American managers.

* Reprinted with permission from the *Academy of Management Journal*, (March, 1964).

ORGANIZATION FOLLOWS TRADITION

Despite the absence of an accepted or recorded theory of organization, most Japanese firms follow a single pattern in their organization and employment practices. This similarity reflects the impact of specific social values. Japanese society stresses the duties of leadership and assures rewards to followers. Most large Japanese firms translate these principles into the centralization of decision-making power and the no-firing rule—the so-called *permanent employment policy*. This common ground has made it possible to evolve strikingly similar practices in management.[1] Luckily for the Japanese, these practices facilitate growth and innovation.

The centralization of decision-making power varies from company to company. In some smaller companies it is so extreme that all decisions originate with the president of the company. This strong individual generally represents the ownership interest or is a major stockholder of the corporation. Companies ruled by such a dictator still exist today, but they are the exception rather than the rule.

In most of the large companies that I dealt with, strong leadership is equally evident, but it is parceled out along functional lines. The absolute power to make decisions and to give instructions is clearly vested in a single person in each different area of the business, such as the plant manager, the sales manager. Each one of these leaders possesses specific spheres of authority to the exclusion

[1] Perhaps as a corollary of the permanent employment practice in the Japanese industry is the low salaries for Japanese managers. They are believed to be the lowest paid in any industrial nation. However, top management is permitted to make the job pay off through a liberal system of expense accounts and fringe benefits. For an interesting report on this aspect, see *Business Week* (May 8, 1965), p. 100. Also, a few large Japanese corporations are adopting American managerial concepts, of course, making allowance for Japanese traditions and customs and character. Nippon Electric Company, Ltd., is reportedly making a sharp turn in its management methods. For example, the company president Kobayashi, rather than trying personally to direct all the myriad activities of the company, has set up a compact, high-powered policy-making group drawn from the board of directors, has incorporated the concept of staff-line structure in his organization which now has a single corporate administrative division, long-range planning division, and so on. For a report on Nippon Electric Company, see *Business Week* (December 11, 1965). [Editor]

of all others. In contrast to some American business practices, the committee form of organization and "touching bases" before making a decision are almost unknown.

The leaders in the various management fields are accustomed to making independent decisions, but not to working together. As numerous American businessmen who tried to reach agreements with Japanese firms have found out, it is difficult to get the leaders from different areas of the same business to agree. Japanese managers are not accustomed to interdepartmental give-and-take, and hence take an unconscionably long time to make up their minds on matters which involve more than one department.

As an American businessman who distributes the consumer electronic line for a large Japanese concern has learned, for instance, it is extremely time-consuming to have the managers of the portable and the standard radio divisions agree to a joint design for the line. It is much simpler to formalize the designs and then negotiate with the managers of the two lines separately.

COMMUNICATING CENTRALIZED DECISIONS

Many top managers of medium and large companies told me that the decision-making process had been democratized since the end of World War II. Nowadays, these managers permit their decisions to be discussed by their immediate subordinates in their own departments before such decisions are implemented. Sometimes, but not often, the subordinates' arguments are considered and the decisions reversed. This free discussion occurs most often in the marketing area, where Japanese managers have the least experience. Nevertheless, in all cases the final decision rests with the top manager.

Although decisions are generally reached rapidly in Japanese business, the democratization process requires that they be communicated and discussed slowly.

In order to preserve the dignity of fellow employees, the communication of policy-decisions takes the form of long and over-polite meetings, during which the pros and cons are discussed at great length, and the consensus demanded by the top manager is reached unanimously. This is achieved by carefully watching the important persons involved. On balance, this takes less time than most "brainstorming" or committee meetings in the US—except for the rare decisions which cross departmental lines.

NEW FUNCTIONS OFTEN LACK STATUS

A weakness of such centralized decision-making is the difficulty which Japanese firms have in adding new functions to their present organization. A box in the organization chart is not sufficient to get the operation going; it must have the backing of an important leader to be effective. Often this leader will hesitate to push the new function lest he upset the *status quo* and the working relationships with other important leaders.

Centralized product design departments or audits of market share are very uncommon in Japanese multiple-division companies, since they would introduce an unbearable outside control over the heads of the division. Adaptation to strong leadership takes precedence over the organization chart. When a new firm was formed by the merger of two companies a few years ago, for instance, an outside consultant was called in to set up the new organization. His organization chart still remains in force, but it does not describe the true power-centers of the company. In one part of the business, most important decisions are made by the head of the administrative department, and in the other, by the sales manager. All other departmental managers consult (really report to) these two men.

As often happens in Japan, the organizational chart was used here to save the prestige of a large number of employees in the merged companies. The titles on the chart did not correspond to the functions. Many employees of Japanese firms have titles such as chief of department or head of section, and even more employees are assistants to these chiefs. These titles are usually devoid of any real decision-making power; they were created to accommodate the psychological needs of employees with many years of seniority. An American can only admire this relatively painless way of keeping peace within a company.

Since the Japanese seem unable to cut up the operations of a business into relatively small and easy-to-manage functions, a strong and independent leader must be found for each important facet of the firm. On the whole, Japanese firms have succeeded in developing this type of leadership, even though the process may take considerable time.

THE TOUGH ROAD OF MARKETING— A NEW FUNCTION

In several instances, in the postwar period, marketing was neglected by large Japanese companies (it is still neglected by one of the biggest trading groups) because strong leaders could not be found within the company to head this function. The appointment of a marketing manager was not sufficient to overcome existing prejudices. Traditionally, the output of large Japanese companies is sold or consigned to an agent who distributes it to wholesalers, who, in turn, sell to retailers. Dealing directly with retailers or establishing retail locations is considered a low-status occupation—one to which, therefore, it was difficult to draw top management attention.

This lack of attention from top management precluded the appointment of men with leadership talent to handle these problems. Right after the war, a number of small, aggressive merchandisers started to eat into the traditional markets of large companies. The giants' reaction was not to make drastic changes in their organization, introduce tighter controls in marketing, or shorten the gap between the producer and the retailer. Instead, they tried to regain their share of the market by cutting prices. These price cuts generally were met by the competition. The market expanded, but the large companies did not recover their share of it. Only then did top management's attitude to marketing change. The difficult job of convincing likely candidates to accept positions in a low-status field was accomplished. By now the majority of large companies have established their own distribution outlets and have set quotas to distributors based on share of market. They are slowly introducing training schools for retailers. The traditional annual banquet or outing for agents and retailers is no longer a purely social occasion, but is increasingly taking on the aspect of an industry training school.

The past ten years' progress in this field has been very impressive. This was made clear to me by a sales call demonstration during the sales meeting of one of the largest consumer goods companies in Japan. Apart from the somewhat slower pace necessitated by the courtesy of Japanese life, the sales call could have been made in the US. It even suffered from the most general shortcoming of American sales calls—the absence of stress on the reason why the retailer should push the salesman's brand over that of competitors. I suggested that the script be amended to include references to the high quality of the company's product, which had won a prize at a trade fair, as well as reports of other retailers' success with the product. The eagerness with which these suggestions were accepted by salesmen—and later followed up at the regional sales meeting— indicated considerable flexibility in marketing techniques.

KEEPING UP MORALE IN A PERIOD OF CHANGE

How do Japanese companies carry off drastic changes in their organization and orientation without hiring outside personnel or destroying the firm's morale? The answer probably lies in their method of selecting and training managers. The characteristic attitude of management in Japanese firms is one of patient dedication. Most Japanese companies recruit young men immediately upon their graduation from a university. The best-known firms hire graduates from the equivalent of Ivy League schools, while smaller and foreign companies must content themselves with graduates of lower-ranking universities. In most cases, the first job is the only job these college graduates will ever have.

After joining the company, all college graduates go through a period of apprenticeship which lasts from ten to fifteen years. During this period they are all treated and remunerated on an equal basis. In the larger companies it is quite easy to guess a younger employee's salary by determining the number of years he has been employed. Only after this initial period are some apprentice managers advanced more speedily than others. The less able will remain in the firm until retirement and still receive minimal seniority increases.

This preservation of harmony within a firm by giving the illusion that nobody loses and everybody wins is difficult for outsiders to understand. An American sales executive complained that although the Japanese subsidiary management seemed to pay lip service to his efforts to introduce the merit system of promotion, they did nothing to bring it to life. After a particularly long lecture, which seemed to elicit agreement, he asked the local sales manager whether he would now promote an outstanding young man rather than a seasoned and mediocre older man. The Japanese sales manager replied that he was still convinced that he was obliged to promote the older man.

No Japanese manager would dare make a promotion that is blatantly out of turn—not only because it would rock the morale of the firm, but also because the apprenticeship period is valued for its "character-building" qualities. The period is spent in cementing relationships with one's contemporaries, and being observed by an important manager. A young man at this stage can have no greater joy than to perform a favor for a manager. On the other hand, the senior manager is always on the defensive against accepting such favors, lest he be morally obliged to further the young man's career. An understanding of this facet of Japanese life sheds light on the willingness of young college graduates to work as house servants or errand boys for the heads of large enterprises. The young men are investing in a personal relationship, and their behavior closely resembles that of American business school graduates who buck for the job of administrative assistant to the president of the company.

The long apprenticeship period and the systematic method of advancement have both good and bad results. While they encourage extreme devotion and loyalty to the firm, they may also lead to an atmosphere of Balkan politics within the company. Loyalty to the organization is balanced by the expectation of rewards stemming from the firm. However, loyalty to the firm may be perverted into devotion to an individual senior manager in the expectation that this devotion will be rewarded. In the final round of promotions, when leaders are chosen to head the decision centers, Japanese firms pay a great deal of attention to "noble character"—a euphemism for the broader loyalty.

The most intriguing feature of the system is the fact that accepting decisions—as well as detailed instructions for their implementation—over such a long period of time seems to further, rather than hinder, the growth of leadership. It appears to develop the ability both to make decisions and to provide guidance after promotion to a manager's job. The close contact between leaders and followers also appears to favor the promotion of the ablest to the top-level jobs, possibly more so than under our own system. By contrast, promotions to intermediate positions in Japanese business are done on a routine basis, purely according to seniority.

WHAT IS GOOD ABOUT JAPANESE PRACTICES?

The Japanese system of management development is responsible, to a large extent, for enabling Japanese industry to grow fast. The emphasis on broader loyalties and ability in choosing high-level executives gives a solid topping to the management pyramid. At the same time, clear-cut responsibilities and loyalty to the firm make Japanese top managers eager to improve operations. The important manager does not end his development as a manager when he is promoted to a decision center. On the contrary, he begins it then. Courses in executive development seldom arouse much interest among younger employees; however, older employees request them. These courses are extremely difficult to plan. Having come up the hard way, most managers are not satisfied with generalities, but are interested in specific applications of principles to their own areas. They know their operations intimately, and are exceedingly critical of superficial recommendations.

The rapid growth of the Japanese economy has required only minor modifications in the organization of the management hierarchy. Many firms which grew relatively fast in the postwar period have had to promote younger managers somewhat faster than was customary. Other firms which rose from humbler beginnings and became important have adopted the traditional practices, taking care of their older staffs, who usually remained in key positions despite the firms' high rate of growth.

It is true that impatient young men with a modern outlook now have a few avenues open to chance-taking and rebellion. A few firms, especially in the electronics industry, hire, fire, and promote employees on the American pattern. But these firms remain very much in the minority, and there are signs that with increasing maturity they, too, will conform to the modes of the Japanese business pattern.

In the meantime, to stave off raids for personnel from unconventional firms, some large companies have attempted a slight modification in their remuneration policies. Without disrupting the hierarchical ranking of employees by age, an additional dimension, that of merit, has been added to the salary structure. Raises of this type have usually occurred in new areas, such as marketing or data processing, where problems with by-passed senior personnel have been minimized.

What lessons can American enterprise learn from the Japanese experience? Probably, by far, the most important is that management development can occur very satisfactorily in an atmosphere where security predominates. Secondly, that good management can be developed well, if not better, under conditions where guidance is given, rather than by the trial-and-error method practiced by many US firms. Thirdly, that an important ingredient for fast and profitable growth is the existence of strong decision centers.

The security, the close supervision, and the close contact with strong decision-makers must be contrasted with the competitive environment, the much looser supervision, and the emphasis on committee responsibility in American business. The results of the comparison will not always favor conditions here. If risk-taking is inhibited by lack of security, and the unsuccessful innovator is heavily penalized, then the Japanese pattern is to be preferred. Also, if young managers sink or swim because of fortuitous circumstances, as authority is delegated to them without any guidelines for the implementation of their tasks, their company may find it useful to adopt some features of Japanese management practices. Finally, US businessmen should keep in mind that a strong decision-maker and manager may also make a good coordinator, and that it may be possible to have the best of both worlds.

9

Managerial Incentives and Decision-Making: A Comparison of the United States and the Soviet Union *

JOSEPH BERLINER

MANAGERIAL INCENTIVES AND RECRUITMENT

The most important decision a manager has to make is made before he ever becomes a manager—the decision to prepare for a managerial career. The factors influencing this decision are of vital importance for our industrial society. Imagine the consequences if no one aspired to become a manager, or if young people chose management only as a last resort, or if other careers were so attractive that management got only the last pickings of each year's crop of youngsters. It might therefore be appropriate to begin with some reflections on the incentives that the United States and the USSR offer their young people to choose a managerial career rather than some other.

The factors motivating young people to choose one or another

* Reprinted with permission from the Joint Economic Committee, Congress of the United States, *Comparisons of the United States and Soviet Economies*, Part I (Washington, D.C.: Joint Economic Committee of the Congress of the United States, 1959), pp. 349-76.

occupation are probably not vastly different in the two countries. Family tradition is often decisive; many a youngster chooses a career simply because he wishes to be like his father (or mother). Special talents such as those of the artist, or early-conceived deep interests, like the boy who must be a scientist, account for the career choices of some others. But most teenagers have no clear idea of what they would like to be. It is with respect to these youths that it is most interesting to speculate upon the incentive-pulls that the two systems offer for the choice of one career or another.

Education and Career Choice

The role of higher education in career choice is different in the two nations. Higher education is very much more of a prerequisite for the prestigeful and high income occupations in the USSR than in the United States. To be sure, the person with a high school education or less has an increasingly difficult time entering the managerial ladder of the large American corporation. But in such fields as trade, commerce, construction and in small business in general, the opportunities are still vast for a financially successful career. College, and education in general, is not of decisive importance. And the brute fact is that a college diploma can always be obtained somewhere in the United States, with very little effort or ability, by just about anyone who can pay the tuition and write a semiliterate paragraph. Those who don't aspire to a managerial position or who fail to make the grade can, as workingmen, nevertheless enjoy a standard of living that is the envy of the world. The point is that the young American who is not inclined toward academic work need not feel that he is out of the competition for our society's best rewards.

This is not true in the USSR. A number of conversations with young Soviet people have convinced me that to be a "worker" is something devoutly to be shunned by most young people who have reached the high school level. There are at least two reasons for this attitude, which seems so anomalous in a "worker's state." The first is the enormously high prestige that Russian (and European) culture has always placed upon the "intelligent," the learned man, the man who works with his mind instead of his hands. The Soviet regime has striven hard to make manual labor respectable, and it undoubtedly has succeeded in endowing the worker with a social position relatively much higher than before the revolution. But the young person who has reached the educational level at which he can choose between being a worker or an "intelligent" would, other things being equal, choose the latter without question.

Other things are not equal, however. In particular, the income possibilities of a worker are far smaller than those of a college graduate, and this is the second reason for the desperate, and sometimes pathetic, drive for a higher education. Of course, a person must have reached the high school level before he can even begin to think about choosing between the career of a worker or an "intelligent." The steady annual expansion in the high school population has had the effect of presenting ever-increasing numbers of young people with the choice, and few of them would freely choose to be workers. If the expansion of the school population had continued, giving more and more young people the opportunity to avoid being workers, it would have raised serious problems for the recruitment of the labor force. The radical reform of the educational system by Khrushchev was undoubtedly motivated, in part, by the wish to avoid that problem.

Thus, the undesirability of a career as a worker has intensified the desire for higher education. Add to this the fact that there is no private enterprise, no small business in which a man could pull himself out of a worker's status and reach a position of prestige and income comparable to the self-made American businessman. I do not wish to state that the door is completely closed. By dint of hard work, ability, and certain other qualities, a Soviet citizen without the college diploma can from time to time rise to an important position in some economic hierarchy. But his chances are about as good as those of an equivalent person in a progressive American corporation. And the young person evaluating the importance of higher education understands this.

Finally, the Russian teenager who decides he has to get a college diploma has very few easy ways out. He can't buy his way into college, as the American student can if he has the money. There are no private colleges that can set whatever standards they wish. To be sure there are instances of bribery or influence, but they are certainly the exception. If the Soviet student wants a college diploma very badly, he has to work hard to gain admission and to be graduated. The very intensity of the drive for education, and the competition of many applicants for the limited number of admissions, permits the high schools and colleges to maintain high standards of performance. Moreover the colleges are financially independent of student tuitions: not only are there no tuitions but most of the students earn stipends. The consequence is that the typical Soviet student works harder and has to meet higher standards of performance than the typical American student. The standards are different in the two countries, of course, because of differences in the philosophy of education. But there is no doubt that study is a much more serious business for the young Soviet student than for the American.

One final note on education and incentives. The quality of the managerial (and technical) manpower of a nation depends on the proportion of the population comprising the pool from which the managers are drawn. That is, if half the population were for some reason excluded from the pool, the quality of the managers would be lower than if the whole population comprised the pool. Both nations suffer in this respect from the fact that rural educational facilities are poorer than urban, which reduces the pool of the potential college group. Since the Soviet rural population is larger percentagewise than that of the United States, and since their rural educational facilities are probably relatively worse than ours, they suffer more than we from this loss. But there are other ways in which our pool is curtailed more than the Soviet. First is the fact that the private cost of education keeps a substantial portion of our talented young people in the lower-income groups out of college. I admit that this fact puzzles me. With our network of free State universities and with a fairly abundant scholarship program, I don't fully understand why any competent student who really desired it could not get a college education. It is my impression, however, that systematic studies generally show that we are losing an unfortunate number of young people to higher education for financial reasons. If this is so, we are worse off than the Soviets in this respect, for their education is absolutely free, and most students of any merit earn stipends besides. Lower-income young Soviet people may nevertheless be unable to go off to college if the family needs their earnings. A young Soviet woman told me, in reply to my question, that this was why she never went on to college. She is not a very good illustration of my point, however, for she went on to say that she really wasn't very smart anyhow.

The second group that is largely lost from America's pool of potential managerial manpower is the Negro and some other racial minorities. It may well be that the proportion of college graduates among some of the Soviet national minorities is smaller than for the Slavic nationalities; I have seen no data on this. But I would doubt that their loss from racial discrimination is as large as ours.

The third and largest group lost from our pool comprises exactly half our population—the female half. Sex discrimination certainly exists in the Soviet economy, probably more in management than in science and technology. But undoubtedly the female population enlarges the pool of technical and managerial manpower much more in the USSR than in the United States. The difference in the role of women in the two countries must, I think, enter into the balance I am trying to strike, but it is not a subject on which I would recommend that your committee consider writing corrective legislation. For one thing it is most perfectly clear which way sex discrimination works in the United States. Women discriminate against working about as much as jobs discriminate against women.

Let me summarize briefly this discussion of the relationship of education to career choice. Education, and particularly higher education, is more important in the USSR than in the United States as the gateway to a prestigeful and highly remunerative career. Competition is keener for higher education, the cost of education to the individual is less, and the standards of admission and performance are higher in the USSR. Both nations lose part of the potential pool of managerial talent; the USSR because of its large rural population, the United States because of financial burdens and racial and sex discrimination.

Competition Among Careers

How does a managerial career compare with the attractiveness of other careers in the two nations? The young American not dedicated to some particular field, but motivated by a roughly equal desire for prestige and money, might select some field such as law, medicine, business, or engineering. He would decidedly not go into education or science. An equivalent young Soviet person would make a somewhat different choice. He would certainly not select law, which has been assigned a most humble role in Soviet society. Nor would he select medicine, for while the prestige is high, the income is low. On the other hand, higher education or science would be an excellent choice. The very title of "professor" or "scientific worker" would assure him one of the highest places of honor in the society. And an outstanding career in either of those fields would assure him an income ranking in the upper 10 percent or perhaps even 5 percent (data are hard to come by) of the population. The difference in the economic and social position of the scientist and teacher in the two countries is of fundamental importance in the matter of career recruitment.

The American who decides to choose a career in the business world has a much wider range of choice than his Soviet counterpart. A great variety of fields offer roughly equivalent rewards in prestige and incomes: advertising, accounting, finance, commerce, trade, sales, light manufacturing, heavy industry. Of all these fields, it is only the latter that would exert a great pull on the Soviet young person. For forty years the government and party have hammered home the central role of heavy industry, children are instilled with an admiration of technology, and heavy industry has been endowed with an aura of glamour that exceeds even our American fascination with technology. The ideological cards are stacked, in varying degree, against all other branches of the economy. In keeping with the ideology, the prestige and income possibilities in heavy industry are decidedly greater than in the other branches.

Not only will the student be attracted to heavy industry, but he is likely to choose engineering as his path of entry into whatever branch of heavy industry he selects. He would be attracted to engineering for the educational reasons discussed above. Engineering is, moreover, the most direct line of approach to a managerial career.

The Soviet engineering graduate will find his first job opportunities rather different from those of his American counterpart. If he is at the top of his class, the best offers will come from the research institutes, with top starting salaries and opportunities for graduate work. The poorer students will find lower paying jobs in industry. In the United States the situation is quite the reverse. The most successful students will be snapped up by recruiters from the large corporations, with the best starting salary offers. Some of the top students will, to be sure, spurn the attractive job offers and go on to further graduate work, but I suspect that many of those who go immediately into graduate work are the men who didn't get the good job offers. To be sure, many of the top American students who join the corporations are put immediately into research and development, but as many of them will be working on new passenger car or dishwasher design as will be working on electronic development and automation technique. The Soviet researcher is more likely to be working on the latter than the former.

The young Soviet engineer who goes into industry starts at the bottom of the managerial ladder, as chief of a production shop, or the design or maintenance departments of the enterprise. As new job opportunities develop, he faces the choice of continuing in direct production or taking one of the staff jobs in the enterprise, such as the planning department. If he stays in production proper, his career path may lead to chief engineer of an enterprise or to one of the higher economic agencies. If he moves into staff work, his career may lead to the directorship of an enterprise or of one of the higher organs. Either career leads to the pinnacle of Soviet management.

The paths that are least likely to lead to top management are finance or sales. I would guess the proportion of top management in the United States who started in such fields as finance and sales is much larger than in the USSR. There are no colleges of business administration in the Soviet Union. The ambitious youngster who wants to work for the top of the Soviet business world studies engineering, not personnel and marketing.

Summarizing, industry in the United States has to compete with a wide variety of other branches of economic activity for its share of the best potential managerial talent. In the USSR the values and the rewards are concentrated in relatively fewer fields, and industry is far more attractive than most others. Science and higher education, which scarcely compete with industry in the United States, is a strong competitor of industry in the USSR. Among the various branches of industry, in the United States the light and consumer goods industries compete very effectively for both managerial and engineering talent. In the USSR light and consumer goods industries are much less attractive than heavy industry. And finally the nature of industrial recruitment is such that technical education is much more important as part of the training of a would-be manager in the USSR than in the United States.

My conclusion is that heavy industry, science and higher education attract, by and large, a better and more competent crop of young people in the USSR than in the United States. Moreover, the competition for education is keener in the USSR, so that they get a more rigorously trained (trained in different ways, to be sure) corps of managerial, engineering, scientific, and university personnel. On the other hand, such branches of the economy as sales, advertising, finance, trade and commerce, light industry, and law attract a much more competent group of people in the United States than in the USSR. Most of the outstanding people in these fields in the United States would, if they were Soviet citizens, have enjoyed successful careers in heavy industry, science, technology, or higher education. There is, after all, nothing startling in this conclusion. It is but another way of saying that each society gets what it pays for.

MANAGERIAL INCENTIVES AND DECISION-MAKING

Material Incentives

The incentives that attract people into management are not necessarily the same incentives that motivate managers to do their jobs and do them well. What are the goals of the manager? What are the considerations that impel him to make one decision rather than the other?

The moving force of our economic system is the pursuit of private gain. The worker chooses the higher paying job, the businessman accepts the more profitable contract, the investor buys the higher interest security. The usual exceptions must of course be made; the laws must be obeyed, public opinion may sometimes require that one decision be made rather than another, people make wrong decisions, a short-run loss may be accepted for a longer term gain. But by and large—"other things being equal," as the economist likes to say—it is private gain that determines economic decision.

The Soviets have at various times experimented with other forms of incentive, for it did not at first seem quite appropriate that a Socialist economy should stress private gain. But practicality won out over dogma, and private gain has for the last twenty-five years been the keystone of the managerial incentive system. To be sure, we still find references to various social incentives such as Communist enthusiasm. But we are also reminded that while enthusiasm is well and good, communism, as Lenin used to say, must be built "not directly on enthusiasm but with the aid of enthusiasm born out the great revolution; (communism must be built) on private interest, on personal incentive, on business-like accounting." [1] Moreover, the incentive of private gain will be with us for a long time. According to the eminent labor economist E. Manevich, it will not disappear until the day of general overabundance arrives, until the differences between country and city are eliminated, and until the differences between mental and manual labor vanish.[2] We are safe in saying that for the next several decades at least, private gain will be the central economic incentive in both economic systems.

The form that material incentives take is of some importance. For the American businessman it is clearly profit. If you ask why did he take on this contract rather than that, why did he order this machine rather than that, why did he ship by truck rather than train, the answer would normally be, "because it's cheaper that way," or what comes to the same thing, "because he would make more money that way."

For the private businessman managing his own business, profit is clearly the guide to his actions. But most American business is not managed in this way. The men who actually run the firm are salaried managers, hired by the stockholders' representative body, the board of directors. The profit of the business does not belong to the manager but to the stockholder-owners. The fact is that the private interest of the manager need not necessarily coincide with that of the stockholder. In order to bring the manager's private interest into closer coincidence with that of the owners, most corporations have instituted some kind of bonus system, on the assumption that if the manager has a direct stake in the profit of the enter-

1 *Voprosy ekonomiki*, No. 6 (1958), p. 74.
2 *Voprosy ekonomiki*, No. 1 (1959), p. 35.

prise, his decisions are more likely to be those that will earn more profit.

In fashioning an incentive system for its managers, the Soviet Government faced a problem similar to that of the American corporation. For, all Soviet enterprises are run by salaried managers. If the Soviet manager's income consisted solely of his salary, it was conceivable that his private interest would not coincide at all points with the interest of the Government. Accordingly a considerable variety of supplementary bonuses are available to the managerial staff. The bonuses are designed to motivate managers to make those decisions that the Government considers to be in its own interest.

The amount of income earned in the form of bonuses is substantial. In 1947, the last year for which detailed data are available to me, the managerial personnel of the iron and steel industry earned bonuses averaging 51.4 percent of their basic income. In the food industry at the low end, the percentage was 21 percent.[3] Since these are averages, many individual managers earned considerably more than this. Bonuses of this magnitude must be a potent incentive indeed.

But incentive for what? This is surely the crucial question. For we can readily imagine an incentive which was extremely successful in motivating action, but action of an undesirable kind. The test of an incentive is therefore not only its motivating power, but the extent to which it leads to the desired kind of decision.

Before proceeding to the relationship of incentives to decision-making, let me clarify the sense in which I use the term incentive. By incentive I mean that consideration which explains why one decision was made rather than another. If a young person decides to find employment in the electrical machinery industry rather than in the furniture industry, the difference in basic salaries in the two industries may well have been the decisive consideration. In this case salary is the effective incentive. But once in the job, the salary does not vary according to whether one operating decision is made rather than another. When the manager decides to put one order into production ahead of another, or to substitute one material

---

[3] Documentation and further discussion of this Chapter's argument may be found in the author's *Factory and Manager in the U.S.S.R.* (Washington, D.C.: Howard University Press, 1957).

for another, it is not his salary he is thinking about. It is usually the size of the month's bonus that will depend on the decision taken. It is in this sense that the bonus is the principal incentive in the operational decisions of the Soviet enterprise.

Production Decisions

Two generations ago people debated the question of whether a Socialist economy could possibly work. History removed that question from agenda. The last generation changed the question to whether the Soviet economy could work at all efficiently. That question has also been answered. These hearings would not otherwise be taking place. My discussion takes for granted that the Soviet economy is reasonably efficient, and that the question at issue is how efficient.

There is little doubt that the system of managerial incentives, broadly viewed, has created a corps of managers dedicated to their work and responsive to the production demands made upon them. Like their American counterparts, they are deeply involved in their work, they worry about production quotas, they demand results from their labor force. As hired managers, they are aware that if their performance is not satisfactory, there are always other persons spoiling for a chance at their jobs. I have no way of knowing whether the intensity of managerial life is greater in the USSR than in the United States; in both countries there are variations from industry to industry. But there are two reasons why industrial life probably proceeds at a faster tempo in the USSR than here. The first is that the absence of free trade unions makes it difficult for workers to resist pressure for intense operation. The second is that industry is under constant exhortation from Government and party for ever-increasing levels of production.

But the question as indicated above is not whether management is motivated to work hard. It is rather whether the incentive system motivates them to do what the state wishes them to do; whether, in other words, they get as much mileage out of their effort as they might get.

One of the most interesting conclusions of the study of Soviet managerial incentives is that the bonus system is directly responsible for motivating management to make a variety of decisions contrary to the intent and the interests of the state. The decisions to be described go far back in the history of the Soviet economy, and have resisted countless efforts by the Government to eliminate them. Most of them have survived the great organizational changes in industrial organization of the past several years. They are clearly deeply rooted in the soil of Soviet economic organization.

First, consider the matter of the reporting of information. In a planned economy it is vital that the central planners have as accurate information as possible about the productive capacity of enterprises. The bonus system, however, acts as a prevailing motivation for managers to understate their real production capacity. The reason is that the most important of the bonuses available to managers depends on the extent to which the production target of the enterprise is overfulfilled. If the manager honestly reports his full production capacity, and if for some reason something goes wrong in the course of the month, then he and his staff will lose that month's bonus. It is safer therefore to report a smaller capacity than really exists, in order that the production target will be kept low enough to allow for emergencies. The Russians call this "insurance" or "security." The consequence is that the planners can never be sure that their plans are based on accurate figures. The Government is aware of the problem: "This is fully understandable," writes a Soviet economist, "because the lower the plan, the greater the opportunity to fulfill and overfulfill it." [4]

Because the higher state agencies cannot trust management's reporting of its productive capacity, various techniques have been fashioned for setting targets high enough to force the firms to operate as close as possible to capacity. One of these techniques is the arbitrary increase of targets over last year's production. As a prominent state planning commission economist put it, "they take as the base magnitude the level of production achieved during the preceding period and raise it by some percentage or other." [5] Sometimes this technique helps flush out the manager's "hidden reserves," but in other cases the arbitrary increase in targets leads to impossibly high tasks. Indeed, the spirit of planning is reflected in the systematic use of high targets as a device for keeping managers working at as fast a tempo as possible. In the past, targets have

4 *Voprosy ekonomiki*, No. 3 (1959), pp. 61, 67.
5 *Voprosy ekonomiki*, No. 4 (1957), p. 70.

been set so high (deliberately, one suspects) that one-third of all enterprises failed to fulfill their annual plans. There is some evidence that in the last year or two this policy of deliberate overplanning has been modified, and we are told that in the first half of 1958, 19 percent of all enterprises failed to fulfill their plans.[6] This still represents one out of five enterprises, and indicates that the high level of plan targets remains a dominant fact of life for the Soviet manager. The intense pace of plant operation has its distinct advantage from the state's point of view: it elicits from management a high level of effort that might not be forthcoming if the plans were set at a more modest level. But the price paid by the state is the manager's effort to defend his enterprise by concealing his full capacity.

When the target has been set, the manager's bonus depends on the success with which he fulfills it. Most of the firm's production does indeed follow the lines laid down in the plan. But when the end of the month rolls around and, as often happens, production is far short of meeting the month's target, then managers turn to a host of time-tested techniques of meeting—or seeming to meet— the targets. In certain types of production, such as metals, the target is expressed in tons; in such cases the manager might order his shops to curtail the production of relatively lightweight products (special and quality metals) and to throw more men and materials into the production of the heavier products.[7] In textile production we read that the practice of setting targets in "running meters" (that is, in measures of length, without regard to width) causes managers to overproduce narrow-width cloth and underproduce broad width.[8] In firms with a considerable variety of products, the production targets are expressed in value units—so many millions of rubles of production. In such cases managers tend to overproduce those products that have high fixed prices (all prices are fixed): they may deliberately use more expensive materials in order to drive up the value of production.[9] These are some of an endless variety of ways in which managers "violate the planned assortment of production," to use the official expression of disapproval.

6 *Planovoe khoziaistvo*, No. 10 (1958), p. 5.
7 *Voprosy ekonomiki*, No. 7 (1958), p. 51.
8 *Voprosy ekonomiki*, No. 6 (1958), p. 19.
9 *Voprosy ekonomiki*, No. 6 (1958), p. 129.

How widespread are these practices? We really don't know. From time to time individual managers are publicly excoriated for such practices, and figures are published to show how widely the planned assortment of production had been departed from. But these may well be extreme cases, and it would be unwise to generalize from them. Occasionally, however, the results of special studies are published, and they give us some idea of the magnitude of the problem. The State planning commission recently released the results of a survey of the production practices of 63 enterprises. Of the total production by these enterprises in excess of the plan targets, only 43 percent consisted of the basic products normally produced by them; 26.5 percent consisted of "products not included in the plan when it was originally confirmed," 20 percent consisted of "other production," and 7 percent consisted not of finished products but of an increase in semifabricated parts and goods-in-process.[10] While these data are not precisely in the form in which we would want them, they do provide a good indication of managers' tendency to produce those products that are best from their own enterprises' point of view, rather than those products that the State would most wish to have produced.

Two other consequences of the bonus system (and the pressure of high targets) should be noted. One is the simple falsification of reported production. "Thus, for example," we read in a Soviet article, "if the plan is fulfilled 99 percent, the managerial and engineering personnel receive no bonus. But if the enterprise fulfills the plan 100 percent, they receive bonuses of from 15 to 37 percent of their salary." [11] Quite a lot of money hinges on that last percentage of production, and it is no wonder that management may succumb to the temptation to "fudge" the report a bit in order to earn the bonus. Again, the techniques of covering up for falsely reported production are myriad. To cite only one, production is "borrowed" from next month and is reported as having been produced this month. If things go well next month, the "borrowed" output is "repaid"—if not, the manager may get into trouble.

More serious than falsification, however, is the deterioration of the quality of production. The poor quality of much of Soviet consumer goods production is well known. In other types of produc-

10 *Planavoe khoziaistvo*, No. 10 (1958), p. 506. The study deals only with that portion of the firm's production in excess of their planned targets.

11 *Voprosy ekonomiki*, No. 3 (1959), p. 67.

tion the danger of detection is greater, and quality standards are less readily violated. But the explanation of management's tendency to shave on quality is the same: the high production targets are so often not attainable, and the manager wants to keep his job. Much of the quality shaving is of a kind that is not easily detected: fewer stitches in the garment, fewer screws in the piece, greener lumber in the building, more impurities in the metal. But if the pressure is keen enough, more extreme forms of quality deterioration will be adopted.

Summarizing, the bonus system is an effective device for eliciting a high level of managerial effort, but in the context of excessively high production targets, it induces management to make certain types of decisions that are contrary to the intent of the State. The production of unplanned products, the concealment of production capacity, the falsification of reports, and the deterioration of quality are the unintended consequences of the system of managerial incentives.

Procurement Decisions

The high level of production targets is but half the problem facing the Soviet manager. The other half is the perpetual shortage of materials and supplies. In order to get the greatest possible production from the available stocks of materials and supplies, the State employs a variety of devices to minimize the use of materials in production and inventory. Undoubtedly these devices have served to control wasteful use of resources, and they have also helped channel the flow of resources in the direction most desired by the State. But they have been self-defeating to some extent for they have forced managers to make certain kinds of decisions which frustrate the intent of the State.

The core of the matter is that managers simply don't trust the planning system to provide them with the supplies and materials they need in the right quantity and quality, and at the right time. The recent decentralization of industrial organization may have improved matters somewhat, but the evidence we have indicates that supply problems are still the most troublesome feature of managerial life. Moreover, the reasons are similar to those we used to read about before decentralization. For all important materials the manager must still obtain an allocation order from his home office (usually the Council of the National Economy of his district), which must in turn get the allocation order from the republican or all-union planning commission.

Thus, we still read of the "existing complicated system of obtaining allocation order, under which every enterprise must submit detailed requisitions to Moscow a long time before the new planning quarter is to begin." [12] Because plans are not always finally set at the time the planning period is to begin, enterprises sometimes start with "advance allocations," that is, temporary allotments of resources designed to keep them operating until the final allocation orders are available.[13] Decentralization of the economy was supposed to have made it easier for neighboring enterprises to sell to each other without having to go through Moscow. But central purchasing agencies still exist, and agencies anywhere must find something to do. Thus the Chief Purchasing and Marketing Administration located in the republic capitals (Moscow, for example) still insist on being the middle-man in purchase and sale contracts between enterprises, even when the latter are located in the same outlying city (such as Sverdlovsk).[14] Perhaps even more serious than the complex supply planning system is the large percentage of enterprises that regularly fail to fulfill their plans, or fulfill them by producing the wrong products or substandard products. Since the production of these enterprises constitute the planned supplies of other enterprises, the supplies of the latter are delayed or simply not available. Perhaps enough has been said to explain why "managers of enterprises did not have confidence in the possibility of getting their materials on time and having them delivered to the factory by the supply depot's trucks." [15]

What does the manager do to make sure he gets his supplies? Just as he "secures" his production plan by attempting to conceal the existence of some production capacity, so he "secures" the flow of supplies in various ways. He overorders, in the hope that if he doesn't get all he ordered, he may at least get as much as he needs. He also orders excessively large amounts of some supplies in order

12 *Planovoe khoziaistvo*, No. 4 (1959), p. 58.
13 *Ibid.*, p. 65.
14 *Voprosy ekonomiki*, No. 5 (1959), p. 75.
15 *Planovoe khoziaistvo*, No. 5 (1959), p. 85.

to be able to buy directly from the producer instead of having to go through the maze of jobbing depots. A survey of fifteen Moscow enterprises showed a 10.4 percent overordering of metals for just this reason.[16] Sometimes management's boldest efforts to obtain supplies are unsuccessful: ". . . over 300,000 construction workers undergo work stoppages daily because of the absence of materials at the workplace." [17] In other cases their padded requisitions are accepted and they receive more than they need of some materials. The consequence is the piling up of hoards of supplies of all kinds, one of the most enduring problems of Soviet industrial organization. The Government has waged a longstanding war against hoarding. One of the weapons by which it attempts to hold hoarding within bounds is through the use of quotas of working capital; that is, for its annual production program the enterprise is allowed to keep on hand at any one time no more than so many tons of coal, so many board feet of lumber, so many rubles worth of inventory. These quotas must be negotiated between enterprise and government, and the enterprise's interest demands that they be set as high as possible. The mutual attempt at outguessing the other leads to a familiar bureaucratic game: ". . . enterprises try to 'justify' and obtain as large quotas of working capital as possible. The financial agencies, aware of this, strive on the other hand to reduce the quotas of working capital." [18] This kind of planning is hardly calculated to lead to the establishment of the optimal quotas. It is more likely that some quotas will be too large and some too small.

The most interesting of the techniques used by managers to "secure" their supply of materials is the employment of special supply expediters called *tolkachi,* or "pushers." The table of organization does not provide for this occupation, yet so great is the need that firms manage somehow to employ these people. The chief job of the expediter is to make sure that his enterprise gets the materials it needs and when it needs them. Accordingly he spends most of his time on the road, visiting his enterprise's suppliers, handing out little gifts here and there to assure that his orders are well-handled,[19] picking up supplies of one kind or an-

16 *Planovoe khoziaistvo,* No. 5 (1959), p. 84.
17 *Voprosy ekonomiki,* No. 8 (1957), p. 50.
18 *Voprosy ekonomiki,* No. 7 (1958), p. 120.
19 The gifts are not always very little. An expediter sent out recently to get tires for his trucking firm was given 62,000 rubles in cash for the trip. He spent 42,000 rubles for gifts. He is now in prison. *Izvestia* (April 4, 1959), p. 2.

other that his firm may be able to use or trade for other goods. Much of their activity is associated with the black market, that is, obtaining materials for which no allocation order has been issued. This may be done either by wrangling an allocation order out of a reluctant government official by one means or another, or persuading an approachable enterprise official to sell him the things he needs without an allocation order.

Some tolkachi take up permanent residence in the city in which the chief suppliers are located, and only occasionally return to their home firms for consultations. To keep the record clean, they are carried on the books as "senior buyer," or "supply agent." If they are known to be particularly adept at their jobs, they may be asked by other firms to represent them. Nothing is known of their incomes, but there is no doubt that they earn many times their base pay. And they fully earn it, both because of the vital nature of their work, and because the risks they take make them vulnerable to prosecution.

How widespread is the use of these expediters? Again, we catch only occasionally hints of their prevalence. The most recent outburst against them reports that the number of tolkachi who annually visit the typical large enterprise runs into the thousands of rubles. These, however, are only the reported expenses. More often than not their expenses are not reported as such but are concealed under such rubrics as "exchange of technical information," or "contract negotiations." Out latest informant, who is a senior investigator for the State Control Commission of the USSR, is of the opinion that despite continued official criticisms of the use of expediters, their number has actually been increasing. One of the reasons he adduces is interesting. In 1956, along with a wave of measures designed to give more freedom to plant managers, an order was issued relieving managers of the need to report in detail on all minor expenditures. Travel expenditures were among the items exempted. The measure had the unintended effect of encouraging the increased use of expediters.[20]

The economic effect of the use of expediters is difficult to assess. There is no doubt that they are of vital importance to individual enterprises, but from the national point of view much of their activity involves merely the transfer to one fortunate enterprise of resources that otherwise would have gone to another. Since the

[20] *Izvestia* (April 4, 1959), p. 2.

higher priority enterprises have less need for expediters, the chances
are that the net effect of their activity is to cause more resources to
flow to lower priority enterprises at the expense of higher priority
ones. On the credit side, however, their wide knowledge of sources
of supply, of who has what to sell, is of some importance, and they
do arrange for the movement of supplies that otherwise would have
lain idle in one plant while another had need for it. In short, the
expediter possesses a certain kind of knowledge that may be as important to economic organization as the knowledge of the engineer
or the machinist. The planning system is able to direct the bulk
of the nation's resources with reasonable effectiveness, but substantial quantities of materials and equipment elude the main
stream of planning. How to get these resources back into the system
is a problem that has exercised Soviet economists for a long time.[21]

In summary, the incentives that motivate managers to strive
for the fulfillment of their production targets are the same incentives that motivate them to evade the regulations of the planning
system. Because of the tightness of the supply system, which is
deliberately engineered by the state, managers are compelled to defend their enterprises' position by overordering supplies, by hoarding materials and equipment, and by employing expediters whose
function it is to keep the enterprise supplied with materials at all
costs, legal or otherwise. The very planning system that serves to
channel most of the nation's resources in directions desired by the
state, serves also to misdirect a substantial volume of resources toward uses that are contrary to the wishes of the state.

Investment Decisions

If one were to ask what feature of the Soviet economic system
accounts most of all for the rapid rate of growth, the answer would
undoubtedly be the high rate of capital formation. The question
at issue is whether it is as high as it might be, other things being
equal. An examination of the system of managerial incentives will
provide part, though by no means all, of the answer to this central
question.

21 Recently there have been numerous suggestions that enterprises and economic regions publish catalogs of the commodities they produce and the surplus
materials and equipment they would like to sell. The expediters are rather like
walking catalogs. *Planovoe khoziaistvo*, No. 4 (1959), pp. 64, 96.

Management has a direct interest in obtaining new capital. It adds to productive capacity, and it is good for the record to show steady increases in production. Moreover fixed capital is provided to the enterprise as a free grant by the state, with no interest charge. The problem, therefore, has not been one of inducing management to accept more machines; it has rather been one of dissuading management from ordering too many machines. Far back in Soviet economic history one can find expressions of the problem similar to that recently uttered by Khrushchev in connection with the dissolution of the agricultural machine-tractor stations:

The machine-tractor stations accept any machine whether they need it or not. They don't grow flax, but they take flax-growing equipment. They don't grow cabbage, but they take cabbage-planting machines. Consequently many machines are not used for years and hundreds of millions of rubles' worth of state resources are frozen.[22]

The reason enterprises accept any piece of equipment they can get their hands on is similar to that discussed above in connection with materials hoarding. One can never tell when he may need just that kind of machine and not be able to obtain it. If one has a chance to get it now, order it by all means. It may come in handy some day for trading in return for something one might be able to use more readily. And above all, there is no charge for holding the equipment; there is no interest payment, and if the machine is not used there is no depreciation charge either. Hence there is everything to gain and nothing to lose by holding on to as much machinery and equipment as one can obtain.

How to induce managers to take a less cavalier view of capital has been a long-standing concern of economists. They look with some nostalgia at the effectiveness of the profit motive under capitalism in this respect. An eminent Soviet economist put it this way recently:

In order to increase his profit as much as possible, the capitalist strives to use his equipment to the fullest extent possible, and in no case will he buy a machine that he doesn't need at the moment, since every surplus machine slows down the turnover of his capital and reduces his profit. For the same reason he strives to keep his inventories down to the very minimum and to market his finished products as quickly as possible.[23]

22 *Planovoe khoziaistvo*, No. 7 (1958), p. 121.
23 *Ibid.*, p. 122.

Recent economic literature contains a number of suggestions of ways in which Soviet managers might be induced to order only that amount of capital needed for production purposes. One of the more interesting is a proposal advanced by the author quoted above. He suggests that profit be calculated not as a ratio to total production cost (as has always been done), but as a ratio to value of invested capital. In this way the enterprise with too much idle capital will show a lower rate of profit, and profit is one of the principal indicators of overall performance. The suggestion is interesting because it proposes that return on capital be used as a criterion of performance, a rather "bourgeois" notion. It should not, however, be thought that the proposal envisages reliance on the "profit motive" as we know it. Profit is an important indicator of the efficiency of plant operation, but the firm does not "own" its profit, although it shares in the profit in a minor way. As a personal incentive, profit is relatively unimportant in Soviet industry, certainly by comparison with the bonus.

If the incentive system motivates managers to overorder and hoard equipment, the situation is quite the reverse with respect to technological innovation. Concern over managerial resistance to innovation is of long standing, but it has come to the fore in recent years in connection with increased emphasis on automation and modernization of plant and equipment. The reasons for managers' tendency to drag their feet in introducing new products or production techniques are well understood by Soviet economists:

The explanation is, first of all, that the introduction of new technology involves certain risks and requires a considerable expenditure of time; secondly, after new technology has been introduced, more difficult plan targets are set and consequently there is less opportunity for fulfilling them and receiving bonuses.[24]

When a manager has a well-running plant, when the workers have learned their jobs and have become experienced in using the existing equipment, he is reluctant to upset the cart by trying something new. A new production line means trouble. Production bugs have to be eliminated, workers have to be retrained, time is lost, and spoilage is high. The chances are that plans will be underfulfilled and the precious bonuses lost, particularly in view of the

[24] *Voprosy ekonomiki,* No. 1 (1959), pp. 44, 45.

tendency for plan targets to be raised to the rated capacity of the new equipment. It is courting disaster to try new things. If the old machines are wearing out, it is safer to repair or even rebuild them rather than introduce the more complicated new models. Outlays on the rebuilding of old machines often exceed the price of a new modern machine.[25]

There is another reason why managers shy away from innovation. Even if the potential gains from new technology are great, it usually takes a number of years before they are realized. But it is Soviet policy to shift managers around from plant to plant every few years. Therefore managers have a strictly short-run point of view. Why take on all the headaches of introducing a new line when one is not likely to be around to enjoy whatever benefits may eventually accrue? Capital investment policy is by its very nature a matter of long-term planning, and therefore does not commend itself to the short-run horizon of management.

How does the state combat managerial resistance to innovation? One technique is direct pressure. Pressure exerted on and by their own superiors explains much of the innovation that does occur. Enterprise managers may drag their feet for a long time, but when the direct order comes down that the new automatic line must be installed in the next six months, it is eventually acted upon. Pressure is also exerted through the Communist Party; if the party officials in the enterprise are under direct orders from Moscow that automation must be accelerated, they are in a position to force the manager to move faster than he otherwise might. Such pressures are important, although it must be noted in passing that both the manager's bosses and the local party often try to shield the enterprise from such pressures. They are as dependent for their careers upon successful plan fulfillment as are the plant managers themselves.

Direct orders from above are one way of getting management to innovate. But innovation would proceed more rapidly if managers could be made to wish to innovate, instead of waiting until they are forced into it. The literature of the past few years is full of suggestions on how this can be accomplished. It is suggested, for example, that attractively high prices be set on new machines, in order

[25] *Voprosy ekonomiki*, No. 4 (1957), p. 69.

to stimulate the producers of those machines to put them into production more rapidly.[26] While this measure might ease the financial strain on the innovating firm, it will not remove the risk that the production plan may be sacrificed. And production is much more vital to the success of the enterprise than finance.

More to the point are the suggestions that the bonus system be employed as an incentive for innovation. Soviet economists seem to have enormous confidence in bonuses as a device for getting management to wish to do what the State wishes to do. But how to adapt the bonus system to this purpose is more difficult. In the course of years a variety of special bonuses have been introduced for one purpose or another, in addition to the major bonus that comes from fulfillment of the production plan. There are special bonuses available for economizing certain critical materials, for reducing the volume of goods in process, for conserving fuel, for increasing labor productivity, for keeping the plant clean, for reducing the volume of spoilage, for operating the plant without stoppages, for winning Socialist competitions, and many others.[27]

This dilution of the bonus system may actually weaken its power as an incentive. If the special bonuses are small, they will not be very effective. If they are large they may detract effort from what is, after all, the main objective of the state: fulfillment of the production plan. It is interesting to note the evidence that the relative size of the bonus for this or that special purpose often determines the manager's decision to concentrate on this or that objective. There are two types of innovation: relatively small measures such as organizational improvements or inexpensive alterations, and the more dramatic large-scale changes in production techniques. The former are included in the overall enterprise plan each year, under the name of the plan or organizational and technical measures (*Orgtekhplan*). It happens that there are certain bonuses available for the design and introduction of the large-scale innovations, but none for the fulfillment of the Orgtekhplan. The consequence is that research and managerial personnel concentrate on the large items, and pay little attention to the small ones, even though the

---

[26] *Voprosy ekonomiki*, No. 6 (1959), p. 16.
[27] *Voprosy ekonomiki*, No. 3 (1959), p. 66. Not all these types of bonus are available to the director himself, but they are available to different groups of managerial personnel.

latter could result in great savings with relatively little cost and effort.[28] Thus the very potency of the bonus as an incentive militates against its use for too many special purposes which may compete with each other.

To conclude this discussion, the unreliability of the supply system and the absence of a charge for the use of capital motivates management to order more fixed capital than they need and to hoard machines and equipment. This tendency deflects a certain amount of currently produced capital goods from being put directly into production in their best uses. On the other hand, the incentive system discourages management from taking the risks associated with innovation. Direct orders from above lead to a substantial volume of innovation, and in many cases management may consider certain forms of innovation to be to their interest. The provision of special bonuses for innovation, if they were large enough to compete with the production plan bonus, might help provide an incentive for innovation, and much of the current discussion in the Soviet Union seems to point to this as the next phase.

SOME COMPARATIVE OBSERVATIONS

The preceding section has shown that Soviet managers are motivated to make a variety of decisions that are contrary to the interest of the State. Since the state's interest is paramount in the Soviet scheme of things, we may properly conclude that the incentive and decision-making system is "relatively inefficient," or "less than perfectly efficient." Let me caution the reader once more against inferring from this that Soviet managers do not do a good job. They do. There is no doubt that their system works well. If I have chosen to concentrate on the "pathology" of Soviet management, the purpose was not to create the impression of ineffectiveness, but to illuminate the gap that every economy shows between the actual and the ideal.

A comparison of Soviet and American management will help drive the point home. No one doubts that American management does a good job. But it would be fatuous to allege that it operates

---

28 *Voprosy ekonomiki,* No. 2 (1958), p. 136.

with perfect efficiency. An exploration of the inevitable gap between the actual and the ideal in the case of American management will help to place the corresponding gap in the USSR in proper perspective.

A comparison of Soviet and American management is difficult for a curious reason; namely, we don't know enough about the more intimate aspects of American managerial practice. A moment's thought will make the reason clear. The American firm is a private enterprise in the full sense of the word. Its internal affairs are no one's business but its own. No one has the right to pry except with special cause. To be sure, the laws of the land have, over the years, required enterprises to disclose more and more of their private affairs to public and governmental perusal. But large sectors of the enterprise's internal operations are protected from the eyes of curious outsiders.

One of the most striking differences in the conduct of American and Soviet management is precisely in this matter of privacy. The Soviet enterprise is a public enterprise in the fullest sense of the word. It has no right to conceal its operations from any officially recognized agent of the state. And a great range of such agents have been deliberately endowed by the state with the obligation of keeping close watch on management and disclosing any irregularities or sources of inefficiency that come to their attention. These agents include the "home office" of the firm (the regional economic council, or formerly the ministry), the state bank, the local governmental body, the central government's State Control Commission, the Finance Department (the tax collector), the local Communist Party boss and his staff, the party secretary of the enterprise itself, and indeed just about anyone in the enterprise who enjoys the extracurricular activity of attending meetings to discuss the affairs of the enterprise (theaktiv).

If we can imagine an American business executive suddenly placed in charge of a Soviet firm, it is this public character of the enterprise which above all would drive him to distraction. It means that any government official can at any time demand to examine any aspect of the firm's operations he wishes to, that at any time he can be called on the carpet by the local party boss to explain a charge made by an irate customer, that any member of his staff (perhaps bucking for his job) can write a letter to *Pravda* exposing him for having made an irregular deal on some supplies, that any scatterbrained worker who wants to "get his picture in the papers" can rise at a public meeting that the director is obliged to attend, and compel the director to explain why he hasn't yet installed the new assembly line. The point is that the results of this authorized prying often finds its way into the published Soviet economic and political literature, which gives us an insight into the more intimate operations of the Soviet firm that we cannot have in the case of the American firm. But in view of this committee's expressed interest in comparisons of the United States and Soviet economies, I have attempted certain comparisons below which appear to be highly suggestive.

Managers and Owners

The original form of modern business organization was the small firm in which the owner was also the manager. The owner-manager was responsible to no one but himself for his business decisions, and his interest as manager could not conflict with his interest as owner. The development of the modern giant corporation, however, had led to that separation of management and ownership first elaborated in the work of Berle and Means.[29] Under the new conditions the private interests of the hired managers (and the controlling group) need no longer coincide at all points with the interests of the stockholder-owners. This is precisely the relationship between the hired Soviet manager and the owner-state.

Berle and Means concluded from their study that "the controlling group, even if they own a large block of stock, can serve their own pockets better by profiting at the expense of the company than by making profits for it." [30] This is precisely what Soviet managers do when they produce unplanned commodities that are advantageous to their firms but not to the State, when they over-order and hoard commodities, and when they resist innovation. Because of the differences between the two economic systems, we should expect that the precise forms that the owner-manager conflict takes would be different in the USSR and the United States. In

---

[29] Adolph A. Berle, Jr., and Gardiner C. Means, *The Modern Corporation and Private Property* (New York: Macmillan, 1945).
[30] *Ibid.*, p. 122.

the United States they are to be found in such decisions as the
awarding of subcontracts, the accounting of profit in such way as to
benefit the claims of the controlling group, the awarding of bonuses
and other benefits to management, and in dividend payment policy.
As in the Soviet enterprise, the accountant is of crucial importance
in handling the books of the enterprise in such a way as to make
the best possible case for the manager; it is he, for example, who
figures out the best way to distract the state's attention from the
large expenditures on tolkachi. The accounting techniques are, of
course, different in the United States; they involve "the charging or
the failure to deduct depreciation; charging to capital expenses
which properly should be charged against income account; including nonrecurrent profits as income though their real place is in
surplus; and the creation of 'hidden reserves.' " [31]

A major difference between the Soviet firm and the American
firm is that in the last analysis profit remains the criterion of
managerial performance in the latter, whereas the Soviet manager
is evaluated by a number of criteria that are sometimes mutually
exclusive. Both systems have attempted to bring managerial interests into harmony with owner interest by some sort of profit-sharing
system. In the Soviet case, it is clear that profit plays a very minor
role, compared with bonuses, as a managerial incentive. In the
United States the manager shares directly in profit to a very limited
extent and often follows other goals in his decisions. "The executive
not infrequently tends to look upon the stockholders as outsiders
whose complaints and demand for dividends are necessary evils,"
concluded one American student of management.[32] In like fashion the Soviet manager often begins to feel like the "boss" and
resents the intrusion into "his" affairs by the state, which after all
is the owner. I have described above some of the ways in which the
Soviet manager promotes the interest of "his" enterprise by means
contrary to the interests of the owner-state. In the American corporation the forms are somewhat different. "Profits are reinvested
in the business for the sake of bigness and to protect the company, and the interests of the stockholders may be given second
place to the business leader's conception of what is best for the firm

---

[31] *Ibid.*, pp. 202-203, 335.

[32] Robert A. Gordon, *Business Leadership in the Large Corporation* (Washington, D.C.: The Brookings Institution, 1945), p. 309.

itself." Executives manifest a "general unwillingness to liquidate unsuccessful enterprises" and thus put themselves out of jobs, however consistent liquidation might be with the interests of the stockholders.[33] The dramatic growth of corporate self-financing in recent years has strengthened the power of management to expand their own enterprises without having to go through the "test of the marketplace" for capital.

It was observed earlier that the desire for "security" and for what the Russians call a "quiet life" motivates a wide variety of managerial decisions such as concealing production capacity and resisting technological innovation that might rock the boat. Students of American management have also noted the change from the adventurous business tycoons of earlier days to a more professional managerial climate in which "greater emphasis is placed on education, training, and a scientific approach, and less on rugged, venturesome, and frequently heedless individualism. The desire for security seems to have increased, and the concomitant of a growing emphasis on security is a diminishing desire for adventure for its own sake." [34] There is indeed a remarkable parallel to this development in the change in the character of Soviet managers. There would have been a great affinity between the industrial empire builders of nineteenth-century America and the Soviet directors of the first two decades of the Soviet regime. Those directors were often men of little education who came out of the romantic conflict of revolution, who dreamed great dreams of building an industrial nation and who created an ethos of bold plans and adventurous undertakings. The old Commissar of Heavy Industry, Sergei Ordzhonikidze, would have understood the spirit of the ironmonger, Andrew Carnegie, and the man who built the great ZIL automotive works (now named after him) had the drives and the dreams of the bicycle mechanic Henry Ford.

Time, and Stalin's purges, removed most of these old-timers and their place has now been taken by Soviet-educated young men born not of revolution but of bureaucracy. Organizations seem to develop "organization men" types, whether the organization happens to be communist or capitalist. An American reporter visiting with a group of communist intellectuals reports that one of them

[33] *Ibid.,* p. 309.
[34] *Ibid.,* p. 311.

had badgered him with questions about David Reisman's book, *The Lonely Crowd.* "The Communist had read Reisman's book and had been fascinated by it—not, he said, because of its application to life in the United States but because of what he maintained was its extraordinary relevance to the present conditions of life in the Soviet Union." [35] It is not, on reflection, very surprising that the job of running an industrial bureaucracy should place a common stamp on men of otherwise different backgrounds. The same would probably apply to the running of a large city or a large university.

Managers and the Laws

We have found that the Soviet manager is often compelled to evade regulations or even break laws. Part of the explanation is simply that there are so many laws. If a Chicago manufacturer fails to ship an order to a New York firm, and ships it instead to another Chicago firm, he has nothing to fear but the ire of the New York firm. But if a Kiev manufacturer fails to ship an order to a Moscow firm and ships it instead to another Kiev firm, he has injured a state enterprise and is subject to administrative action, a fine, or even criminal prosecution. If an American firm sells a substandard generator, he may lose money or his business. But if a Soviet firm sells a substandard generator, the director may go to prison. Thus, even if Soviet managers acted exactly as American managers do, we should expect to find more illegal or evasive activity in the Soviet Union than in the United States.

With the growing complexity of our society, more and more legislation is enacted to protect the public from potential abuses. With the growth of such legislation, managers find their activities more and more circumscribed by laws and regulations. The Soviet manager apparently treats such legislation rather lightly when it conflicts with the interests of his firm (and his career and pocketbook). How does American management react when confronted by a spreading web of restrictive legislation?

It is not easy to find out very much about American managerial practice in this respect. Unlike the Soviet press, which throws its pages open to reports of the irregular activities of managers in

[35] *The New Yorker* (April 6, 1959), p. 52.

order to warn others, the American press is likely to shy away from this kind of reporting. Moreover the private nature of American business keeps this sort of activity from coming to light as easily as it might in Soviet industry. Nor is it the sort of thing that businessmen are inclined to talk about very readily. If it is true that a businessman would more readily be interviewed on his private sex life than on his private business activity, then we should require the late Dr. Kinsey to help provide the answers to the extent of unlawful or quasi-lawful business activity.

Professor E. H. Sutherland, the eminent American criminologist and sociologist, made a bold attempt to investigate the phenomenon he refers to as "white collar crime." His study is based on the decisions of a limited number of courts and administrative commissions against the seventy largest industrial-type corporations in the country. In the period 1935 to 1944 these seventy corporations were convicted 585 times for such practices as restraint of trade, misrepresentation in advertising, patent and copyright infringements, unfair labor practices, granting of rebates, and a few others.[36] The average was 8.5 convictions per corporation. These data provide some idea of the extensiveness of such practices but they clearly understate the magnitude for a variety of technical reasons. Sutherland's conclusion is that a "great deal of scattered and unorganized material indicates that white collar crimes are very prevalent." [37]

The point I wish to make is that when American management finds itself in a position approximating that of Soviet management they tend to react in ways similar to those of their Soviet counterparts. Sutherland's unique study notes many aspects of American managerial practice that are astonishingly similar to those one might find in the literature on Soviet management. "These crimes are not discreet and inadvertent violations of technical regulations. They are deliberate and have a relatively consistent unity." [38] It is in precisely this way that the Soviet manager deliberately misappropriates earmarked funds or decided to shave on the quality of production. There is evidence that the Soviet manager, aware of the fact that "everybody does it" and that the investigating agencies

[36] Edwin H. Sutherland, *White Collar Crime* (New York: Holt, Rinehart and Winston, Inc., 1949), p. 26.

[37] *Ibid.*, p. 10.

[38] *Ibid.*, p. 217.

have restricted budgets, counts on the law of averages (and his own superior shrewdness) to get away with it. So a member of the Federal Trade Commission wrote that "about the only thing that keeps a businessman off the wrong end of a Federal indictment or administrative agency's complaint is the fact that, under the hit-or-miss methods of prosecution, the law of averages hasn't made him a partner to a suit," and "Samuel Insull is reported to have remarked during his trial that he had only done what all other businessmen were doing." [39]

Similarities in managerial practice are paralleled by similarities in attitude to such violations, and toward the administrative agencies enforcing the laws and regulations. The Soviet manager does not think it is "wrong" to use influence to obtain materials unlawfully, or to fudge his reports to the Government. Success is the important thing, and if you are successful you can get away with all sorts of violations. There is evidence that the Soviet manager feels contemptuous of government planners and of party hacks who try to tell him how to run his business but who themselves had "never met a payroll." Sutherland's picture of American management's attitude contains strains of the same kind.

The businessman who violates the laws which are designed to regulate business does not customarily lose status among his business associates. Although a few members of the industry may think less of him, others admire him. . . . Businessmen customarily regard government personnel as politicians and bureaucrats, and the persons authorized to investigate business practices as "snoopers." [40]

In the first section of this paper, it was pointed out that a managerial career carries a great deal of prestige in the Soviet Union and attracts a large number of the better students. These youngsters have been raised in Soviet schools and have absorbed the incessant propaganda of the communist regime. Many of them enter industry as green novices fresh from school, filled with high ideals about building the Socialist fatherland and working for the common welfare. One wonders about the process by which the naive, idealistic young *Komsomol* member is transformed into the hardheaded manager who knows all the angles for survival in the Soviet

[39] *Ibid.*, p. 218.
[40] *Ibid.*, p. 220.

business world. Numerous incidents such as the following provide a key to the answer. A young Soviet chemist had been assigned to the quality control department of his enterprise. He was quite pleased with himself when his test showed that a sample of production, which had previously been declared acceptable by his laboratory chief, turned out to contain an excess of phosphorus. He reported the error and expected to get a bonus for it. Instead, his boss obtained a new sample, gave it to an outside chemist for analysis, and submitted a report showing that the batch of production was acceptable after all. The young chemist protested, was transferred to another shop, and was finally fired on trumped-up charges.[41]

What happens to such young people? Some never quite get the point and remain ordinary engineers in the plants. Others learn to adapt themselves after a few buffetings and when they decide to play the game according to the real ground-rules, begin to rise in the managerial hierarchy.

It is interesting to note that Sutherland's interviews with American businessmen turned up accounts rather similar to that narrated above. His explanation of the process by which the naive American youngster is initiated into the business of selling used cars, settling insurance claims, covering up irregularities in clients' accounts—indeed, toning down the results of chemical analysis—helps explain the process of transformation of the young Komsomol member:

In many cases he is ordered by the manager to do things which he regards as unethical or illegal, while in other cases he learns from others who have the same rank as his own how they make a success. He learns specific techniques of violating the law, together with definitions of situations in which those techniques may be used. Also he develops a general ideology. This ideology grows in part out of the specific practices and is in the nature of generalization from concrete experiences, but in part it is transmitted as a generalization by phrases such as "we are not in business for our health," "business is business," and "no business was ever built on the beatitudes." These generalizations . . . assist the neophyte in business to accept the illegal practices and provide rationalizations for them.[42]

Summarizing, the economic world in which the Soviet manager operates compels him to engage in a variety of illegal or evasive

41 *Mashinostroenie* (February 17, 1939), p. 3.
42 *Ibid.*, p. 240.

practices. Since the Soviet business world is enmeshed in a much greater web of laws and regulations than the American, the Soviet manager finds his interest in conflict with the laws and regulations more often than his American counterpart. But when American managers' interests conflict with the laws, they too are prepared to take the chance of violating them. Both American and Soviet managers justify their actions by an attitude of contempt for governmental controls and investigating personnel, and by a hardheaded view that "business is business" and "everybody does it." Young people in both systems who wish to achieve managerial prominence have to learn to play the game according to the rules, or disqualify themselves from the tough competition for the top.

Managers and Overfull Employment

Many of the peculiarities of Soviet management spring from the fact that the economic system works under conditions of perpetual overfull employment. By "overfull" employment I mean a condition in which there are not merely as many jobs as employables (as under full employment), but the demand for labor far exceeds the available supply. The same applies to other factors of production: materials, equipment, and commodities in general are demanded in far greater volume than the current rates of production. The ability of the Soviet Government to maintain, through the planning system, a condition of permanent overfull employment is one of the greatest economic assets of the regime. We err when we interpret evidence of shortages in the Soviet economy as signs of economic weakness; they are rather indications that the economic engine is racing with the throttle wide open.

But just as an engine does not work at its maximum efficiency when it is working at its maximum capacity, so the Soviet economy pays a certain price for the advantages of overfull employment. It is the perpetual shortages of supplies that account in large measure for the losses due to overordering and hoarding. The hunger for goods by both firms and consumers encourages the deterioration of quality. The "sea of ink" associated with materials allocations, price fixing, priorities, and all the rigmarole of a controlled economy nurtures the spread of the tolkachi and the use of influence for personal gain.

The normally functioning American economy does not confront our managers with this kind of problem. Hoarding makes no sense when materials are in adequate supply. Competition and consumer resistance force the quality of production up to standard. The role of influence is narrowly circumscribed when the bureaucratic machinery of Government controls is removed. The biggest problem of American managers under normal conditions is marketing, not purchasing. The energy spent by the Soviet firm on obtaining materials is spent by the American firm on selling and advertising.

Thus, the major differences between the practice of American and Soviet management are to be ascribed to the differences in the economic environment. The interesting question is, How do American managers behave when placed in an environment that approximates that of the Soviet manager? The obvious test case is war. During World War II the national emergency forced us into a state of overfull employment. Along with this came the total immersion of Government into economic life, with a great burgeoning of materials allocation, price fixing, cost-plus contracting, and a prevailing shortage of supplies.

It is interesting to note that the rate of growth of production during the war rose to levels rivaling the current rates of Soviet economic growth. The implication of this fact is important; it means that there is no magic in the Soviet economic system. Our economy could grow as rapidly as the Soviet economy does if our people would consent to being pushed around as totally as the Soviet people are.

But like the Soviet economy, we paid for our high rate of production in various forms of waste. One of the first consequences of the introduction of materials controls was the rise of the black market. The only full-scale study of the black market, to my knowledge, confirmed what many people felt to be the case at the time.

During the war at least a million cases of black market violations were dealt with by the Government. Illegal profits ran into billions of dollars. Business interests and Government vied with one another in estimating the seriousness of the black market; business estimates, curiously, often being higher than those of the Government. Such extensive conniving in the black market in illegal prices and rationed commodities took place among so many businessmen, ordinary criminals, and even the average citizen that serious questions might be raised as to the moral fiber of the American people.[43]

To understand the position of the Soviet manager, we must realize that the American black market flourished at a time when the nation was fighting for its life and public indignation acted as a restraint. But if the economic controls that led to violations could not be justified by a national emergency, they would be thought of as just irritating obstacles, as so many hurdles that the resourceful manager must overcome as part of the risks of the game. There is good evidence that the Soviet manager takes just this amoral attitude toward economic controls, and it is therefore quite understandable that the evasion of controls would be more widespread.

The high quality of American production in normal times is a byword in international markets. But the effect of the economy of shortages was similar to that in the Soviet economy. One of the techniques used by Soviet managers is to represent lower quality merchandise as of higher quality, and to sell it at the higher price. In the United States during the war, "upgrading was one of the most difficult violations to detect, particularly where no professional investigator was available who could appraise the grade or where there were no State or Federal grades stamped on the commodity." [44] The reports of Government investigators read like some of the indignant letters of complaint we read in the Soviet press: men's shorts made of cheesecloth, water-resistant baby's pants which permit a third of a glass of water to leak through after one laundering. "If you pick up a board by both ends without breaking it in the middle, it's No. 1 Select," testified an American businessman.[45]

One of the features of Soviet managerial life which helps protect the manager is the feeling of "mutual support" among various officials whose fortunes depend on the success of the enterprise. The Communist Party secretary doesn't report the manipulations of a successful director because the party benefits from the success of the enterprise; the people in the "home office" (the Ministry or the Council of the National Economy) are reluctant to fire a director who violates the laws in order to get the materials his

[43] Marshall B. Clinard, *The Black Market* (New York: Holt, Rinehart and Winston, 1952), p. vii.
[44] *Ibid.*, p. 224.
[45] *Ibid.*, p. 45.

plant needs, for while the next director may be more law-abiding, he may not succeed in fulfilling his plan. This tendency to maintain a solid front against authority is a source of great irritation to the Government, which periodically inveighs against it but has not been able to eradicate it. A similar sense of common front prevailed among the groups of businessmen in America.

Nothing better illustrated the degree of organization and consensus among businessmen than their reluctance to testify against each other. . . . Some businessmen felt that the trade would disapprove of behavior that might undermine the solid front against the Government as well as interfere with supplies.[46]

One of the major differences in the position of management in the two countries is the nature of the penalty for failure. Under ordinary conditions the unsuccessful manager loses his job. But the Soviet manager faces many more situations in which the action necessary to get the job done carries with it the threat of criminal action. Indeed, whenever the Soviet Government has found some managerial practice too damaging to its interests and too intractable to the normal sanctions, it has turned to the criminal courts. Immediately after the death of Stalin the punishment for economic transgressions was relaxed, but the new regime has not been able to continue operating without the courts. One of the severest economic problems following the decentralization of industry was the tendency toward "localism": that is, each economic region tended to favor the plants in its "own" region, and would discriminate against plants in other regions. When all exhortation failed, the Government had to turn to the law. Today, a manager who fails to honor the orders of plants outside his own region is subject to "administrative action, fines, or even criminal punishment." [47]

Financial penalties, such as fines, have rarely proved successful as restraints on Soviet managerial behavior. American managers seem to have reacted the same way to the fines imposed for black-market violations. "They don't hurt anybody." "It just comes out of profits, like a tax." "They make so much money on the black market they can afford to pay steep fines." But imprisonment was another matter. "Jail is the only way; nobody wants to go to jail."

46 *Ibid.*, pp. 306-307.
47 *Planovoe khoziaistvo*, No. 7 (1958), p. 14.

132   JOSEPH BERLINER

"A jail sentence is dishonorable; it jeopardized the reputation." [48]
This would not be quite the same in the case of the Soviet manager.
At least during Stalin's lifetime some of the best people served their
time in jail, and it definitely did not destroy their reputation among
their neighbors; although the neighbors might be wary of as-
sociating with them. One has the impression that large numbers of
Soviet managers feel the chances are fair that some day they will do
their stretch, hopefully for a minor transgression.

The wartime economy of shortages injects the government into
business life not only as an agency of control but also as the largest
customer of many firms. In the Soviet case we have noted the importance of the tolkach, the expediter, the peddler of influence. We
might note in passing that the economic system of Nazi Germany
in which government had also assumed a dominant role, also gave
rise to this chap. The Germans called him the "contact man." As
described by an American student of the German economy:

To influence the powerful agencies of control, however, he (the German
businessman) has good use for what might suitably be called a private relations department. Under the Nazi system of control of business by an
absolute government, the contact man, or graft, or both, take the place
of the public relations executive. The contact man is primarily a political
figure. His job is to pull wires. He knows the influential members of the
all-pervading Nazi Party in a position to bring pressure successfully to
bear upon the men in charge of controlling agencies. . . . Two types of
contact man are known to be used: one is an independent agent whom
the businessman hires, or attempts to hire, whenever necessary; the other
is carried on the payroll of the business in a more or less permanent
capacity.[49]

The words might well have been written about the Soviet
economy. In that sector of the US economy in which Government
plays a dominant role as customer, the symbols of the mink coat or
Dixon-Yates, depending upon one's political persuasion, come to
mind. "Washington," wrote Senator Paul Douglas, "is indeed full
of lawyers and 'representatives' whose primary commodity is 'influence'." [50] The techniques of the American influence-peddler

[48] *Ibid.*, p. 244.
[49] L. Hamburger, *How Nazi Germany Has Controlled Business* (Washington,
D.C.: The Brookings Institution, 1943), pp. 94-95.
[50] Paul H. Douglas, *Ethics in Government* (Cambridge: Harvard University
Press, 1952), p. 56.

differ little from those of his colleagues in the Soviet or Nazi economy. Gifts and *quid pro quo* favors are standard among Soviet tolkachi. Another way in which Soviet enterprises manage to exert influence is to have one of "their" men placed in other organizations that can be of use, rather like the unusually high employability in industry of retired military personnel. During the war the problem was particularly acute because of our Government's desperate need for skilled managerial personnel, many of whom were on loan from corporations with which the Government placed contracts. But the use of influence is not confined to Government-business relations, as Senator Douglas pointed out in his critical defense of the ethics of Government personnel:

As a matter of fact, the abuses which have been exposed and properly denounced in the field of Government are quite widespread practices in private business. Thus the "padding" of expense accounts is so common that they are often referred to as "swindle sheets." Purchasing agents and buyers frequently exact toll from those who seek to sell to them, and their Christmas presents and other prerequisites appreciably increase their income. Business managers and directors think nothing of awarding contracts, insurance, and underwriting privileges on the basis of friendship and relationship rather than the quality and prices of the goods and services supplied. All this is taken as a matter of course in private business, although it obviously increases costs and intercepts gains which should go to stockholders and consumers.[51]

While gifts, payoffs, and bribery play their role in the Soviet scheme of things, the subtler and much more pervasive technique of influence is known as *"blat."* To have good blat with someone means that one has an "in"; one can always count on him for a favor because of friendship or family ties or some other relationship of confidence. Blat may be used to obtain everything from a new apartment to a carload of coal. The prominent British observer, Edward Crankshaw, has called blat the most significant word in contemporary Russia.[52] The way in which the American equivalent of blat is cultivated is described in one final quotation from Senator Douglas:

Today the corruption of public officials by private interests takes a more subtle form. The enticer does not generally pay money directly to the

51 *Ibid.*, p. 25.
52 *New York Times Magazine* (June 3, 1951), p. 35.

public representative. He tries instead by a series of favors to put the public official under such feeling of personal obligation that the latter gradually loses his sense of mission to the public and comes to feel that his first loyalties are to his private benefactors and patrons. What happens is a gradual shifting of a man's loyalties from the community to those who have been doing him favors. His final decisions are, therefore, made in response to private friendships and loyalties rather than to the public good.[53]

Summarizing, many of the differences between Soviet and United States managerial behavior spring from differences in the economic climate in which they operate. The stress on quality and appearance, the drive for innovation and technological development, and the interest in cost reduction reflect the force of competition and the buyer's market. Such similarities as have been observed in managerial behavior spring from features of the economic environment that are common to the two systems, such as large-scale organization and the intrusion of Government into the economy. Under wartime conditions our economy takes on more of the features of normal Soviet economic life, and the consequence is that our managers adopt more of the normal practices of Soviet management.

SUMMARY

The rewards in income and prestige in the United States and Soviet economies are such that a larger proportion of the best young people in the USSR turn to careers in heavy industry, science, and higher education, whereas in the United States a larger proportion of the best talent flows into such fields as heavy or light (consumer goods) industry, finance, commerce and trade, law, medicine, etc. Higher education, particularly technical, is more of a prerequisite for the attainment of a top business career in the Soviet Union than in the United States.

The principal managerial incentive in Soviet industry is the bonus paid for overfulfillment of plan targets. The incentive system is successful in the sense that it elicits a high level of managerial effort and performance. But it has the unintended consequence of causing managers to engage in a wide variety of practices that are contrary to the interests of the state. Managers systematically conceal their true production capacity from the planners, produce unplanned types of products, and falsify the volume and quality of production. In the procurement of materials and supplies they tend to order larger quantities than they need, hoard scarce materials, and employ unauthorized special agents who use influence and gifts to ease management's procurement problems. The incentive system causes managers to shy away from innovations that upset the smooth working of the firm.

Since American managers operate in a different economic environment, their problems and therefore their practices differ from those of Soviet managers. But in those aspects of economic life in which the US economy approximates the operating conditions of the Soviet economy, American managers develop forms of behavior similar to those of Soviet managers. The separation of management and ownership characteristic of the modern corporation leads to conflicts of interest between managers and stockholder-owners, and management's pursuit of its own interest leads to activities similar to those of the Soviet manager striving to defend his interests against those of the owner-state. The spread of legislation constricting the freedom of operation of the American firm leads to the evasion of laws and regulations characteristic of the Soviet economy, though on a larger scale there. Finally, under wartime conditions the burgeoning of Government controls and the dominant role of the Government as customer alters the operating conditions of the US economy in such ways that it closely approximates some of the normal operating conditions of the Soviet economy. The change is accompanied by black-market operations, hoarding, quality deterioration, and the use of influence, practices which are normal in the peacetime Soviet economy.

10

New Managerialism in Czechoslovakia and the Soviet Union

S. BENJAMIN PRASAD

Europe is witnessing a transformation that ranks in significance with the genesis of the European Common Market on the one hand, and the march of American firms—many via joint entrepreneurship—into Europe. The transformation exemplifies a blend of expansive private enterprise, extensive social welfare programs, and selective governmental intervention. As some Italian thinkers have recently labeled this phenomenon, it is *neocapitalism*—a system in which workers and management find common goals and interests. It is also typified by a change in the enterprise philosophy in Western Europe. Prewar devotion to lower wages, higher prices, restricted markets, and higher tariffs are discarded by private enterprises which are endeavoring to emulate American business organizations. Western Europe's neocapitalists have created a mass market and the technology that is necessary to cater to such a market; they have sought to minimize their differences with the labor sector; and they have softened their opposition to the governmental role in the private sector.

Since the early days of industrialization in the West, there has been a gap between the levels of living standards of East and West Europeans. Although some observers would ascribe this to Sovietization of Eastern European economics, Mares offers another plausible reason: "the conflict between the centrifugal forces of their national aspirations and the centripetal forces of modern production techniques." [1]

While neocapitalism is spreading in Western Europe, there has emerged a new managerialism in Eastern Europe which includes Bulgaria, Czechoslovakia, East Germany, Hungary, Yugoslavia, Poland, and Rumania as well as Russia. In this paper, the exploration of the new managerialism is restricted to only two countries of Eastern Europe,[2] namely, Czechoslovakia and Soviet Russia. For purposes of illustration of the new managerialism, these two countries may be regarded as unique. The Soviet Union and Czechoslovakia both own 100 percent of the industrial sector, which in both cases contribute more than 50 percent to their national income. The recent growth rates of industrial production in both countries have been approximately 10 to 11 percent per annum. But the Soviet Union, other than its military and political power, is large with a population of about 225 million people while Czechoslovakia is comparatively smaller with about 14 million people. Besides, Czechoslovakia has been regarded by many observers as being the most "conservative" among the Soviet bloc countries. Some of these similarities and dissimilarities reinforce the above rationale.

The following discussion is limited to 1. the old managerialism in the Soviet Union and Czechoslovakia, 2. salient features of the new managerialism in these countries at the *macromanagement* level and the *micromanagement* level, and 3. plausible implications of the new managerialism.

OLD MANAGERIALISM IN RUSSIA AND CZECHOSLOVAKIA

"Managerial Capitalism" is the name for the economic system of North America and Western Europe in the mid-twentieth century, a system in which production is concentrated in the hands of

---

[1] Vaclav Mares, "East Europe's Second Chance," *Current History* (November, 1964), p. 272.

[2] For some main aspects of Eastern Europe's breaking of its bond, see the special report in *Business Week* (November 20, 1965), pp. 177-198; and "What the Czechs Need" in *The Economist* (November 20, 1965), pp. 817-818.

large joint stock companies.[3] In contrast, there is the managerial socialism which typifies the organization for production in the Soviet Union and Soviet bloc countries, including Czechoslovakia.

The significant difference between managerial capitalism and managerial socialism lies rather in the character of the rules of the production game than in who sets them. In capitalism, these rules emerge indirectly from a body of law and custom, founded on the concepts of private property. These rules represent the formal structure. As Victor Thompson has observed, "the important difference is between the formal structure, and not in the informal behavior of the two people."[4] The United States, exemplifying managerial capitalism, may be described as formally *pluralistic* while the Soviet Union and Czechoslovakia may be characterized formally as *monocratic*. Thompson uses the terms—pluralistic and monocratic—in the sense of hierarchical relationship.[5] What have been some of the salient features of the *monocratic managerialism* in the Soviet Union and Czechoslovakia?

The Soviet economy is analogous to a gargantuan corporation rather than a pluralistic collection of distinguishable economic units.[6] There is an overlap of political and economic factors in the Soviet Union (and Czechoslovakia) and this introduces great complications in the study of top management.[7] Soviet top management is identified by Barry Richman as *macromanagement*.[8] This is the management of the entire economy. Although this term, by Richman's definition, approximates "administrative" actions by a central or federal government, in the case of the Soviet Union and Czechoslovakia it is the central feature. It is pervasive and detailed.

[3] Robbin Marris, *The Economic Theory of Managerial Capitalism* (New York: The Free Press of Glencoe, 1964), p. 1.

[4] Victor Thompson, *Modern Organization* (New York: Alfred A. Knopf, 1961), pp. 79-80.

[5] *Ibid.*, p. 38.

[6] Harry Schwartz, *Russia's Soviet Economy* (Englewood Cliffs, N.J.: Prentice-Hall, Inc., 1954), p. 183.

[7] Ralph James, "Management in the Soviet Union," in Frederick Harbison and Charles Myers, eds., *Management in the Industrial World* (New York: McGraw-Hill Book Company, 1959), p. 322.

[8] Barry Richman, *Soviet Management* (Englewood Cliffs, N.J.: Prentice-Hall, Inc., 1964), p. 8.

Macromanagement, or planning and management of the entire economy, is "the function of executive leadership involving planning, organizing, and controlling the basic directions of economic activity assumed to be those of the top echelons of the party state." [9]

In contrast to macromanagement, management of the individual productive enterprise is termed by Richman as *micromanagement*.[10] It is also referred to as enterprise management, plant management, and so on. "The basic organs of micromanagement are the economic councils to which the activities of the plant managers (directors) are subordinated." [11] As Ralph James has warned, "In analyzing Soviet management consideration must be given to the apparatus above the plant and not merely to the individual enterprise." [12] This is true of Czechoslovakia too.

Enterprise management appears to be largely "production management," with the decision-making and coordinating function lodged higher up in the apparatus. As Richman points out, "management of the Soviet enterprise is quite similar to management within an American company, particularly an American factory. . . . In many respects the Soviet enterprise resembles an American firm producing almost entirely for one customer such as the Government. . . . Although production is the major function of the Soviet enterprise, it also undertakes accounting, procurement, finance, and, in most cases, research and development." [13]

The role of the manager at the enterprise level is to meet and exceed the production targets with specified inputs. As Joseph Berliner [14] has emphasized, plant directors (or managers) attempt to manipulate their production targets and this indirectly affects the setting-up of output targets. As one plant manager revealed to a Western observer earlier this year: *"Nelzya zhit bez vala,"* meaning you cannot live without *val* or production quota.

9 Nicholas Spulber, *The Soviet Economy* (New York: W. W. Norton & Company, 1962), p. 10.

10 B. Richman, *op. cit.*, p. 8.

11 N. Spulber, *op. cit.*, pp. 10-15.

12 R. James, *op. cit.*, p. 323.

13 B. Richman, *op. cit.*, pp. 20, 25, 53.

14 Joseph Berliner, *Factory and Manager in the USSR* (Cambridge: Harvard University Press, 1957).

With a view to motivating the enterprise managers to meet and to exceed production quotas, macromanagement in the Soviet Union has developed a bonus system. "The bonuses are designed to motivate managers to make those decisions that the Government considers to be in its own interest." [15]

The bonus system [16] for managers in the Soviet Union has created a corps of managers dedicated to their work and responsive to production demands made upon them. Higher technical education is a prerequisite to the attainment of managerial positions. Because of the emphasis on heavy industry and the managerial prospects there, the young Soviet is likely to choose engineering as his path of entry to managerial cadres.

The line that separates the motives of a Soviet plant manager from those of a plant manager for a large American corporation is thin. Bonuses for both are, in essence, based on the profit motive. Self-interest or pursuit of personal goals is the driving force. In both cases, ownership is separated from management—in one case by the State, in the other by private stockholders.

Berliner and other Western observers of managerial socialism in the Soviet Union have held the prevailing bonus system responsible for motivating enterprise managers to make a variety of operational decisions contrary to the intent and interest of the state.[17] Barry Richman identifies these undesirable managerial practices.[18] They are undesirable in the sense that they are contrary to the goals set by the state. Some examples of these undesirable managerial practices are: 1. the constant search for the organizational slack—difference between the stated and actual enterprise capacity; 2. understating the capacity; and 3. multifarious distortions of information and communications.

Another factor as significant as the bonus system fostering "managerial misbehavior" in the Soviet Union is the supply barriers. The enterprise manager constantly faces shortages of materials. The theme that he spends time and financial resources to

[15] Joseph Berliner, "Management Incentives and Decision-Making: A Comparison of the United States and the Soviet Union," Ch. 9 in this volume.

[16] For an illustrative bonus scale see, Table 5.1 in Abram Bergson, *The Economics of Soviet Planning* (New Haven: Yale University Press, 1964), p. 76.

[17] J. Berliner, "Management Incentives and Decision-Making," *op. cit.*

[18] B. Richman, *op. cit.* See Ch. 8—Managerial Behavior—pp. 150-183.

break through these supply barriers has been dealt with by Berliner [19] and Granick.[20]

Soviet managerial behavior as typified above may be described, not explained, in terms of role interaction in the promotion of organizational goals and in the pursuit of personal goals. As Victor Thompson [21] hypothesized, behavior within the organization is oriented to personal goals. Although his frame of reference was the American business organization, one can visualize a close parallel in the Soviet enterprises.

The year 1957 was notable in the Soviet economy. A reorganization [22] of industry took place. Its main effect was to alter the lines of authority. As Michael Florinsky observed, "The reform aimed at decentralization of administration but not of control; its declared object was to establish a closer relationship between the supervising agencies and the producing enterprises." [23] The reform resulted in a replacement of the departmental attitude by a regional attitude, and also, in diverse ways, in the increase of the power of *Gosplan*. A further step toward decentralization was taken in 1963 as a result of the meeting of the Communist Party Central Committee in November 1962.[24] The *Gosplan* was abolished in its original form and replaced by the Union Council of National Economy which was assigned administrative powers to make decisions on resources allocation and other day-to-day problems of economic management.[25]

By a decree of July, 1959, industrial enterprises were required to institute a new system of payment of premiums to leading personnel.[26] Under this procedure, the cardinal criterion was performance regarding costs.

Soviet economists are now debating another reform. Evsei Liber-

[19] J. Berliner, *Factory and Manager in the U.S.S.R., op. cit.*

[20] David Granick, *The Red Executive* (New York: Doubleday & Company, 1960).

[21] V. Thompson, *op. cit.,* p. 81.

[22] On the industrial reorganization of 1957, see Oleg Hoeffding, "The Soviet Industrial Reorganization of 1957," *American Economic Review* (May 1959), pp. 65-67.

[23] Michael Florinsky, "Trends in the Soviet Economy," *Current History* (November 1964), p. 269.

[24] See Harry Schwartz, "Khrushchev is moving to spur the Soviet economy," *New York Times* (November 25, 1962, Section IV), p. 46.

[25] Lynn Turgeon, *The Contrasting Economies* (Boston: Allyn & Bacon, Inc., 1963), p. 215.

[26] Abram Bergson, *op. cit.,* p. 87.

man's proposal entails relating bonuses to a novel scale of "profit-ability." In other words, the contemplated revision is, in essence, one of managerial success criteria. This departure from the "old" managerial system in the USSR and other countries in the Soviet bloc, Czechoslovakia in particular, is arbitrarily labeled "new managerialism," a discussion of which follows.

NEW MANAGERIALISM IN CZECHOSLOVAKIA AND THE SOVIET UNION

Beset by economic problems such as mounting inventories of unpurchased consumer goods, poor quality output, and the sluggish introductions of innovation that stem largely from doctrinaire macromanagement, the nations of the Soviet bloc are turning to many capitalistic managerial techniques. The planners and leaders were quite aware of these techniques but had hitherto overtly condemned them as "bourgeois" methods. Now there is a change in the air. Advocacy of an idea of implementation of a technique seems to emanate from the academic economists,[27] and in a few instances, such as those in Rumania, from the younger enterprise managers. Prominent among the Soviet economists has been Evsei Liberman of Kharkov University. Ota Sik has been most articulate in Czechoslovakia.

Liberman has advocated the adoption of the "profit motive" as the incentive for micromanagerial action, and has called for the creation of a new bureaucratic agency to spread the idea throughout the Soviet economy. Recent reports suggest that Liberman's ideas have been partially and tentatively accepted. The ideas are experimentally being tested in Soviet industrial and other enterprises. What Liberman has suggested is a profit index as the sole measure of the performance of an enterprise and its managers.

Other than serving as an incentive to micromanagerial effi-

27 See for example, Evsei G. Liberman, "The Plans, Profits and Premiums," *Pravda* (Moscow) September 9, 1962; E. Loebl, "On Dogmatism in Economic Thinking," *Kulturny Sivot* (Bratislava, Czechoslovakia), September 28, 1963; Ota Sik, "The Survival of Dogmatism in Political Economy Must Be Overcome," *Nova Mysl* (Prague, Czechoslovakia), November 9, 1963, and "On the Levy to Be Paid by Enterprises on Fixed Working Capital," *Figyelo* (Budapest, Hungary), January 1, 1964.

ciency, the profit index may also rectify managerial malpractices. The role of the enterprise manager, which has so far been simple, in the sense of being devoid of significant innovation abilities and actions, may become a little more complex. Soviet planners and economic councils may insist that an enterprise manager enter a new field or adopt an innovation.[28]

Liberman is also advocating managerial type decision-making for the enterprise managers. He also wants to release the enterprise manager of a factory or retail outlet from the confusing and often conflicting array of performance goals now set down by the planners. In essence, it is a plea for decentralization of some phases of enterprise management.

Although Liberman advocates a profit index as the criterion for measuring the performance of the enterprise and its managers, he insists that the profit motive is not inconsistent with managerial socialism. "In the USSR profit belongs to society as a whole and is not the sole purpose of production. It is merely the means of raising living standards, for extending and improving production." [29]

28 See Barry Richman, "Innovation Problems in Soviet Industry," *Management International* (1963), pp. 67-69.

29 The following is the letter written by Professor Evsei Liberman to *Time*, March 5, 1965, reproduced with Professor Liberman's permission.

Sir: You consider as a sign of "failure" of one of Communism's cardinal creeds the fact that the USSR accepts the profit motive (*Time* cover, Feb. 12, 1965). In reality the notion of profit in the Soviet economy has existed for quite a long time. Actually, it is thanks to this profit that since 1923 the Soviet Union has been able to set up all its funds and industry, whose level is 60 times higher than that of Czarist Russia. However, those in the West often make believe that profit was formerly denied in the USSR. And now they allege that the Soviet Union has all of a sudden started zealously deriving profit.

Denial of profit by socialism and recognition of profit by capitalism has never served as the feature distinguishing socialism from capitalism. The difference is in the way profit is formed, appropriated, and used.

In the USSR, profit belongs to society as a whole and is not the sole purpose of production. It is merely the means for raising living standards, for extending and improving production. Under the conditions of a planned economy, profit can and must express actual efficiency of methods of production. Many Soviet economists think that profit can be used as an index for assessing and encouraging the work of our enterprises. However, this does not mean that the Soviet state intends to relinquish its centralized planning management, which will suffer no harm from the improvement of assessment and encouragement, but on the contrary will grow stronger. Your article ignores the role of centralized planning in the Soviet economy and emphasized profit.

Centralized planning in the USSR ensures rapid development of the Soviet

Czechoslovakia was rightly considered by Western students as among the most rigid and most conformist of Soviet Russia's European partners. But things began to change substantially during 1963-1964. The post-Stalin liberalization trends began to creep into Czechoslovakia surprisingly on a broad front. "More recently and most importantly the Marxist-Lenin economic doctrine itself has come under sharp scrutiny, and the entire system of communist economic planning and management is being drastically refashioned along lines that contradict some of the fundamental concepts hitherto held sacrosanct in the communist orbit." [30]

Several factors seem to have contributed to this rather sudden change of scope and direction in Czechoslovakia. They are deStalinization, Soviet rapprochement with Yugoslavia's Tito, the impact of the Polish and Hungarian revolutions of 1956, the ideological split between Russia and China, and more importantly, the declining economic situation. The growth of industrial production and national income slowed down substantially in 1961 and 1962. Quantitative indices showed decline while qualitative results remained less than satisfactory. As a result the Third Five-Year Plan had to be revised, downwardly, twice in 1963. A year later, with the slump growing even worse and Czech economists becoming more and more critical of the orthodox communist system of planning and management, in its session on January 21 and 22, 1964, the Party's Central Committee approved a number of measures to induce Czechoslovakia's economy to regain its lost momentum.

Various palliative measures such as closing down of nonprofitable enterprises, enhancing premium payments to foremen, and so on, were undertaken. Soon the inadequacy of these was realized. In September 1964, the Party adopted the new "Draft of Principles for the Perfection of the Planned Direction of the Na-

economy without crises. With the purpose of fulfilling general plan assignments, each large enterprise or production association should get orders from its customer establishments on the basis of direct contract relations. These contracts are not the product of sporadic market fluctuations but are rather the embodiment and realization of centralized planning. That is why the new system will never lead to unemployment. We intend to assess the work of enterprises, first of all, by the way in which they carry out orders placed with them, and only then shall we make appraisal of and encourage their efficiency.

[30] Edward Taborsky, "Change in Czechoslovakia," *Current History* (March 1965), pp. 168-174, 180-181.

tional Economy" embodying virtually all the main desiderata of the Czech economists—prominent among whom was Ota Sik, who is regarded as the architect of the new decentralization plan. This draft, in fact, amounted to a far-reaching change in the macro-managerialism.

The salient features of these changes may be summarized as follows:

1. Central planning will concern itself with setting overall economic goals and perspectives leaving elaboration of short term plans to enterprise managers.
2. Enterprises will have to do their own developmental financing except major investments.
3. Interest will have to be paid by the enterprises for all loans and capital advances from the state budget.
4. A realistic and flexible price system will gradually be introduced taking into account production costs, and the market forces of supply and demand.
5. The performance of individual enterprises will be measured by profits emanating from actual sales to customers.
6. Each enterprise must pay for its interest expense on borrowed capital, repayment of loans, taxes, and new investments.

These changes hardly appear radical to those accustomed to managerial capitalism; nevertheless, by the norms of Marxist-Lenin managerial socialism, they are drastic. As the draft concedes, it is a "reevaluation of the present conception of the character and substance of the Socialist System of economic management."

These changes are not without opposition and not without serious structural problems. However, the new managerial elite whose authority would be substantially augmented under the new decentralized system might assume increased political importance in the future.

Furthermore, implicit in the new managerialism is a greater emphasis on more economic contact with the West. This contact will certainly be in the area of trade as evidenced by the recent negotiations with foreign firms. It may be in the area of management education, too. Taborsky quotes a Czech economist saying, "I cannot imagine a Socialist expert in industrial management who did not become personally acquainted with methods by which significant enterprises are managed in Western Europe and the United States." [31]

CONCLUSION

The new managerialism—the new changes in the economic philosophy of the Soviet Union and Czechoslovakia—has also been emerging in other countries of the Soviet bloc. For example, in Poland thirty-six enterprises are involved in a pilot project to determine if the quantity and quality of goods can be improved by aligning production to some rate of profit. East Germany has relegated planning to a group of enterprises and is experimenting with the idea of profit incentives. Hungary has already introduced a form of profit sharing—a deviation from Soviet economics, and a unique feature in the Soviet bloc. It has also imposed a 5 percent interest on machinery and supplies to encourage enterprise managers to use capital more efficiently. In Rumania, the younger enterprise managers are believed to be one of the prime forces behind the creation of incentives for managers and workers.

The new managerialism, should its scope and direction continue, may bring managerial socialism close to the working style of managerial capitalism. That is to say, one may hear more of such capitalist managerial techniques as marketing research, performance appraisal, and decision-making at the micromanagerial level in the Soviet bloc.

The new managerialism may also put the Socialist factory manager on the factotum pole. Early in October 1965, Premier Aleksei Kosygin declared a new bill of rights for the enterprise manager in the Soviet Union. This, in essence, is meant to delegate more decision-making authority to the plant managers [32] than before. Under the rules of the old-style Soviet model of planning there was little room for initiative by individual managers of enterprise. They were told what to produce, how to produce it, at what price to sell and often to whom. Supplies of both working capital and investment funds were strictly controlled. The resulting red

---

[31] *Ibid.*, p. 172.

[32] For an interesting discussion of this point see *Time* (October 8, 1965), p. 48; see also *Business Week* (April 16, 1966), p. 76.

tape was staggering. As recently as 1962, some 18,000 products were centrally planned and allocated in the Soviet Union. The maze of authorities in other Comecon economies was hardly less tangled. In practice, managers in virtually all Comecon countries through the early 1950s concentrated on meeting quantitative targets—if need be at the expense of quality and marginal cost. Clearly under these circumstances there were advantages to be gained from some trimming back of the detailed supervision by the Central authorities. This has been done by reorganizing industry into gigantic trusts or cartels and these, in turn, have been given considerable powers of decision-making.

The new managerialism in the Soviet Union and other countries of the Soviet bloc might pave the path of a "theory of convergence" which suggests that while the USSR and other Socialist countries are taking small steps in the direction of private capitalism, many Western nations are borrowing bits and pieces from socialist state planning. This theory of convergence is more significant to the Western European countries and especially to the United States, although similar convergence has already taken place in many Asian and African countries which, in one fashion or other, purport to be following a "socialist pattern" of society. There is a need for research to systematically test this convergence hypothesis.

11

Managing Productivity in Developing Countries*

KEITH DAVIS

In South America recently, a consultant from the United States was called to study why West German machinery in a cellophane plant owned by South Americans was not operating properly. (This single preliminary sentence gives insight into the complications of international management because it shows that already three different cultures were involved in this problem.) When the consultant arrived, he studied the situation for several weeks. I happened to be in that area at the time he was making his report, and I talked with him about it.[1] His conclusion was that there was nothing at all wrong with the machinery. It was of excellent quality and in perfect adjustment. The raw materials and other supporting factors were entirely satisfactory.

The real problem was that the supervisors had a father image in the patriarchal mill manager, and were unable to make operating decisions without his approval. They referred to him as their elder and superior. When something in the mill went wrong, they

* Reprinted from *Management International*, No. 2 (1964), with permission from the International University Contact for Management Education, Rotterdam, The Netherlands.
[1] Some of the ideas herein are presented by the author in a chapter in *International Management Handbook* (New York: McGraw-Hill Book Company, in press). See also Keith Davis, *Human Relations at Work* (New York: McGraw-Hill Book Company, 1962).

waited indefinitely for his decisions before they would correct the problem. Since he had other business interests and was frequently out of the mill for part of the day, or even for two or three days, they permitted the continuous production to produce scrap cellophane for hours or even days because of some minor maladjustment which they could have corrected. The mill manager tried to delegate decision-making on these control matters to his supervisors, but neither he nor they were able to overcome the custom of deference to authority which existed in their culture. As the consultant finally summarized the problem to me, "the problem is the men, not the machines."

International management offers many new situations of this type which involve a blending of various cultures and require new adjustments by all persons involved. A manager who enters an underdeveloped country to install advanced technological equipment and get it operating will have to make adjustments in the leadership habits which he employed in the advanced country from which he came. Also, native employees in this new installation will find that they can no longer follow the way of their old, less-productive culture. In other words, each must change. There must be a fusion of cultures in which both parties adjust to the new situation of seeking greater productivity for the benefit of both the enterprise and the citizens of the country in which it operates.

Almost every civilized country of the free world has established as one of its national goals an increase in the productivity of its people.[2] To accomplish this goal, its own people will have to adjust to new ways of working as determined by modern technology and scientific management. These conditions require an international manager to have a greater understanding of human relations and social systems than he would need in his own country to an understanding of productivity.[3] In order to integrate the imported and native social systems, a foreign manager will need cultural empathy for local conditions. Having this empathy, he must then be adaptable in order to integrate the community of interest of the two (or more) cultures involved. A ten-year study by the International Gen-

2 For a general discussion of productivity see Robert A. Sutermeister, *People and Productivity* (New York: McGraw-Hill Book Company, 1962).

3 John H. Kilwain, "Working with Latin Americans," *Personnel Journal* (June, 1963), p. 297.

eral Electric Company of overseas personnel failures reported that 60 percent resulted from poor cultural adaptability (42 percent incompatible to a country, and 18 percent could not adjust— rigidity).[4]

In spite of the evident need for imported managers to have social empathy and to be flexible, often a manager arrives unprepared for his overseas position. Selection may have been based solely upon his performance in the home country, with little regard for the fact that he will be doing business with people whose traditional beliefs are different from his own. He may not know the native language and may have little interest in becoming a part of the local community. Rarely is he given predeparture-training, at least in the United States, because a survey of large United States corporations reported that only three of them gave their overseas personnel predeparture-training.[5]

In many cases, a native social system lacks a cultural heritage toward achievements.[6] Its people have had little experience with modern concepts of productivity and hence are either blind to the idea or antagonistic to it. For example, in some cultures of the world the idea exists that the more education one has, the less work he should do. An educated man may surround himself with aids whose primary job is to do errands for him rather than to work as a team toward productivity. In some instances, an educated man looks upon work as degrading which certainly does not endear it to his subordinates who should be becoming more productive. Sometimes social caste and rank interfere with teamwork and communication. In India, in some retail stores, when a cashier finds that a clerk has made an error in a sales check, he will not correct it himself or tell her what is wrong. He simply returns it to her while the customer waits for her to try to find the error.[7] On other oc-

---

[4] Richard B. Blomfield, "The Importance of Foreign Language to a Career in Business," *Journal of the American Society of Training Directors* (October, 1961), p. 35.

[5] Francis X. Hodgson, "The Selection of Overseas Management," *Business Topics* (Spring, 1963), p. 53.

[6] For a discussion of the achievement drive in different cultures see David C. McClelland, *The Achieving Society* (Princeton, N.J.: D. Van Nostrand Company, 1961).

[7] Ernest Dale, "Management Gives India A Lift," *Think* (June, 1961), p. 11.

casions, social customs interfere with understanding. In the United States, a supervisor feels that when he is talking to a man, that man should look him in the eye. In fact, if an employee evades his direct glance, a supervisor judges that the man is "shifty" and may be trying to hide something. In some other countries, however, it is a long-established custom for a person never to look an elder or supervisor in the eye. To do so is considered impertinent. Consequently, a supervisor from the United States who tries to deal directly with his men in this manner may find that he cannot establish good human relations with them.

Similarly, culture in the United States emphasizes face-to-face thrashing out of differences. Hence, companies in the United States have been able to develop bargaining systems which in most industries are built around local face-to-face negotiations by the persons directly involved. In Latin America, where status differences and authority are more significant, it is more difficult to deal directly with an employer. Hence, bargaining is more dependent upon an intermediate role by government. Workers have no difficulty telling an intermediary—government—how they feel about management; but they are not culturally prepared to tell management directly.[8]

It is unlikely that cultural deficiencies in achievement and productivity can be overcome in the two or three years allowed to make a new plant productive; hence, these cultural restrictions must be absorbed into the production system or by-passed temporarily. If, for example, a one-hour *siesta* must be accepted, perhaps siesta hours can be staggered so that equipment can be kept operating. If there is patrimonial management, which is the common first stage in a country's march toward economic development, then members of the patriarchy can be given intensive training in productivity so that they can use their influence to sell productivity throughout the organization.[9]

[8] William F. Whyte, *Man and Organization* (Homewood, Ill.: Richard D. Irwin, Inc., 1959), p. 9.

[9] Patrimonial management in underdeveloped countries is discussed in Frederick Harbison and Charles A. Myers, *Management in the Industrial World: An International Analysis* (New York: McGraw-Hill Book Company, 1959), especially pp. 69-73.

MAKING CHANGES

My second point concerns change, which is the effective device by which different cultures are integrated. The culture of a nation changes slowly; and in so doing, it gives stability and security to society. This is an advantage. However, there is the offsetting disadvantage that culture makes change more difficult for each of us. The international manager's job is to try to retain in his management practices the essential elements of both old and new cultures so that his group may work with the security of some old practices, but also with greater productivity than the old culture has normally accomplished.

As we have learned in both experience and research, change is a human relations problem as well as a technological one. The technological part of change is usually solvable by the logics of science, but the human relations part is dependent upon the art and skill of supervision. The following incident in the United States indicates how change may be made acceptable through a simple adjustment.

On the plains of Texas at the beginning of World War II, one of the first blackout aircraft factories was constructed. As was the pattern in those days, this factory had no windows or skylights, making possible its operation at night without showing lights to attract enemy aircraft. The building was air conditioned by the latest equipment to control temperature, humidity and air circulation. Since the ceiling was over fifty feet high, most of the air exits were high on the walls and ceilings.

As soon as the first group of employees started work, they began to complain about the inadequacy of the air conditioning—it was too humid, too hot, and too close feeling. Air conditioning engineers were called to check the equipment and the temperature, humidity, and circulation of air throughout the building. They reported that the air conditioning was excellent—providing exactly the air conditions that scientific studies showed the human body needed. Still, the complaints persisted. In fact, they grew worse until they were definitely undermining morale and productivity.

Finally, one alert manager recognized the problem. He reasoned that most of the workers were rural people who were new to both industry and air conditioning. They were used to an outdoor life and felt restricted in a windowless plant where they could neither feel a breeze nor see it blowing. Since the vents were too high for employees to feel the air, they needed to see that it was stirring. This manager simply had tissue streamers tied to the ventilators high on the walls. Anyone who felt uncomfortable could look up to see the paper fluttering in the breeze and be assured that he was getting plenty of air. The result was that employee complaints soon became negligible. That which was technically right was finally made humanly right.

The paper-streamer device was later used many times in areas where air conditioning was new. It is rarely seen today in the United States because people are adjusted to air conditioning, but it can be seen in other parts of the world. In 1960, I was teaching in a South American executive program, and mentioned the paper-streamer incident to participants. A few days later, we visited a new factory and observed the streamers in use. I asked why and was told that employees claimed that there was insufficient fresh air in the new building, and foreign consultants had advised management to use the streamers to demonstrate that there was fresh air. This action was a simple application of good international management —a recognition of the human factors in a technological change and an effort to apply human tools to achieve a workable result.

GAINING EMPLOYEE SUPPORT FOR CHANGES

Since management initiates most changes, it has primary responsibility for handling them in such a way that there will be satisfactory adjustment. Though management initiates change, the native employee controls the final decision to accept it or reject it, and he is the one who actually accomplishes it. Under these conditions, employee support becomes essential. Rather than trying to get employees to "accept" change, we really want them to join in producing it.

Management has developed a number of ways to encourage employee support of changes. One of these is to set up various pledges to protect employees from economic loss or from decreases in status and personal dignity. Each worker needs to feel that he personally will not suffer from the change, or better yet, that he will gain from it. In fact, if workers can be assured that they will share the benefits of a particular change, this will be their positive motivation toward acceptance. Sometimes, when supervisors introduce changes which may be resisted, they attempt also to introduce personal conveniences at that time, such as floor mats, chairs, ventilators, and better lighting, thereby showing that they are interested in the whole job process, including the worker.

Communication is also an essential element to reduce resistance to change. People tend to fear that which they do not understand; consequently, the full meaning of a change should be communicated even though some aspects of it may be bad. Naturally, positive aspects need to be emphasized as much as possible. Since people resist change for both logical and emotional reasons, communication should deal with both logical and emotional viewpoints of the employee. *Logic alone is not the best way to influence attitudes.*

A foreign manager also reduces resistance to change by preventing trivial and unnecessary changes which are not central to the productivity he is trying to achieve. Individuals can tolerate only so much change, and if they are bombarded with irritating small changes, they will be less apt to accept major changes that occur later. If a group can be encouraged to participate in recognition of need for a change, then change will be even more supported. Since changes require unlearning of old habits, some attention must be devoted to removing old habits instead of simply adding new ones on top of the old. Take the situation of a native supervisor who is taught by an overseas management new ways of leading employees. What sometimes happens is that he retains most of his old approach also, so that now he has a strange mixture of newer, positive practices which are substantially offset by holdover practices from his old habit patterns. As a consequence, there is little net benefit from his new practices. If he does not substantially believe in these new practices, he tends gradually to return to his old ways of doing things because these ways are more secure. Even when he does believe in his new practices, he may become frustrated because his old habits (and those of his manager) interfere.

Change should be made on the basis of the impersonal requirement of a work situation rather than on personal grounds. A manager who says, "I want this done," is less likely to gain acceptance than one who says, "Men, this is a need of ours which we can solve by doing it in this way."

Old habits can be changed only through long-run creation of new conditions rather than by short-run temporary adjustments in management effort. I can illustrate this with the smoking habit of a man who usually smokes two packs of cigarettes a day.[10] On the other hand, he sometimes smokes less, such as near the end of the month when he is running short of money to purchase cigarettes, or when he reads a news article or receives a warning from his doctor about the possibility that cigarettes may cause cancer. At other times he smokes more, such as when he is nervous or worried. However, observe that generally he returns to his old habit of two packs a day. These temporary pressures have not been effective in changing his long-run habit patterns. Neither will a temporary lecture or reprimand by a foreign manager be effective in changing the habit patterns long established by his men in their different social system. There must be a long-run effort based upon new long-run conditions.

Likewise, the manager himself must make some adjustment. In the United States, for example, it is the custom for people in face-to-face conversations to maintain some physical distance between them, perhaps a foot or two feet. In some cultures, however, it is the custom for people who talk face-to-face to do so quite closely, at perhaps six inches' distance. A manager from the United States may be uncomfortable in a conversation of this type. I observed one manager overseas who, by the end of a short conversation, had backed halfway across the room trying to increase the distance between himself and the employee who, of course, kept following him in order to keep the cultural distance of six to nine inches with which he was familiar. Under these conditions, it is

10 This illustration was first brought to my attention by Robert R. Blake at a management conference.

difficult to develop good human relations with subordinates because the manager appears uncomfortable in their presence.

COMMUNICATING THE IDEA OF PRODUCTIVITY

A third important idea in improving overseas management is to communicate the real meaning of "productivity" to the people involved. The modern industrial concept of productivity is not really understood in many cultures of the world. Simple social communication between people of different cultures is difficult enough; but when one steps up to the level of abstraction involved in the idea of "productivity," effective communication is almost impossible.[11] The image which the sender transmits is not likely to be what the receiver interprets, because he will see the image from his cultural point of view. In terms of the famous fable of the blind men and the elephant, the sender may perceive the elephant's trunk while the receiver perceives the elephant's tail. Communication is made even more difficult by the fact that a foreign manager's communication with workers is usually secondhand through a native supervisor who may attach his own values to what is being transmitted.[12]

Even when the image received is accurate, it is difficult to get action on the basis of that image. I have observed that even when natives are able to talk about productivity in an intelligent way, they still may not be able actually to apply the concept in their day-to-day work, because they refuse to give productivity priority over other cultural values which are inconsistent with it.

In one country, I observed a crew of seven men unloading one-half-inch steel rods from a flat-bed truck. In normal circumstances, this job should have been accomplished in an hour or more, but in this case it took more than one day. On the truck bed, there were four men. Three men lifted the rods one-by-one and threw them to the ground. A fourth man on the bed counted rods. On the

11 Edward T. Hall and William F. Whyte give an excellent discussion of the difficulties of intercultural communication in "Intercultural Communication: A Guide to Men of Action," *Human Organization* (Spring, 1960), pp. 5-12.
12 Claude McMillan, Jr., "The American Businessman in Brazil," *Business Topics* (Spring, 1963), p. 74.

ground, two men picked up the rods and moved them about five feet to a stack. A third man in a coat supervised the entire operation.

Of particular interest to me was the fact that one man on the truck bed always picked up a rod on its wrong side. Two men were on one side of the rod and he was on the other, so that when they stepped to the edge of the truck bed to throw off the rod, his head always was in the way! At that point, he had to turn loose of the rod, stoop under it, and grasp it on the other side before it could be thrown off the truck. The foreman watched this operation all day without offering any suggestion for improvement in productivity. Furthermore, the truck could have been driven adjacent to the stack so that the rods could be thrown on to the stack or skidded on to it. However, this was not done. It would appear in this case that the supervisor as well as his men did not have an abiding interest in productivity; consequently, they were unable to discover means to improve their productivity as they worked.

It is possible to make large increases in productivity while still keeping enough of the old culture to maintain security for the persons involved. In other words, the old culture is blended with the new. Oil companies in the Middle East have effectively blended cultures and thereby accomplished considerable productivity. Similarly, in its rise to advanced industrialization Japanese industry was able to retain much of its old culture and still be competitively productive. Japanese workers are hired virtually for life, and managerial promotions are mostly by seniority. However, within this cultural context, most of the technological improvements of modern industry have been introduced. What the Japanese factory loses in rationality and efficiency, it seems to gain back in stability and employee loyalty. Culture is used to reinforce production needs rather than to interfere with them.

MOTIVATING PEOPLE

A fourth point in improving international management is to apply motivation in terms of an advanced industrial economy. Most companies desire to hire native supervisors, but there is usually a meager supply of properly motivated and trained supervisory aspirants.[13] First priority must be given to developing a competent local supervisory group. There is little use trying to motivate workers if their supervisors are not motivated according to modern industrial standards. What is effective motivation in one environment may not be so in another.

In a South American factory, for example, accidents were high. The six native superintendents were not following management's instructions for accident prevention. They seemed agreeable, but somehow failed to sell accident prevention throughout the organization. The overseas top management of the company then tried a high-powered safety publicity program of the type used in its own home plants. This was of no avail. Finally, a wise staff man offered an effective solution. Papier-mâché heads of the six superintendents were molded and colored, with the idea that each week these heads would be arranged on a "totem pole" at the front gate in the order of the weekly safety rank of each department. No superintendent wanted to see himself as low man on the safety totem pole, so the accident problem was quickly corrected. In this case, management used existing cultural values of this country in order to accomplish the desired result of better safety.

Modern psychology reports that new human needs take priority whenever former needs are reasonably satisfied. In other words, man is motivated more by what he is seeking than by what he already has. Human needs are generally recognized to be in some order, with physiological and security needs preceding social and ego needs.[14] In underdeveloped countries, most employees are still seeking basic physiological and security needs. Hence, some of the more sophisticated and elaborate motivational devices of modern industrial management may not be appropriate in these countries. The needs of their workers may be more simply reached by direct motivation. In some instances, they have worked in economic systems which had little direct connection between how effectively they worked and how well their needs were satisfied. Therefore, they require management to show them simple, direct evidence that if they work more effectively, they will receive more. In other words,

[13] Peter F. M. McLoughlin, "Business and Its Managers in Africa," *California Management Review* (Summer, 1963), p. 45.

[14] A. H. Maslow, "A Theory of Human Motivation," *Psychological Review*, L (1943), pp. 370-396.

work must be interpreted in terms of their immediate needs, rather than waiting for indirect results through a complex economic system. Accordingly, action which would be inappropriate in an advanced country may sometimes be workable in the underdeveloped country, as illustrated by the following example.

In South America, an international petroleum company employed about twenty natives in an oil well perforation team managed by a non-native executive. In spite of management efforts, each perforation job averaged nine days. Since a similar job with similar equipment was done in the United States in one and one-half days, management reasoned that, even considering the more primitive operating conditions in South America, the job could surely be done in six days or less. Since the job did require genuine teamwork and they worked in isolated locations less subject to direct supervision, management decided on a drastic step to break the cultural pattern. It offered nine days' pay for each job regardless of actual work days. This dramatic economic incentive proved sufficient to alter long-standing cultural habits.

The employees' attitude changed gradually. Within four years they had reduced perforation time to one and one-half days, the same as in other efficient countries. Team members readily offered suggestions to improve teamwork and adapt technology to the special conditions of that area. On two occasions, the team encouraged transfer of men who would not change their habits and were thus holding back the team.

CONCLUSION

Management in underdeveloped nations is filled with many inconsistencies and difficulties if one approaches it from the culture of an advanced industrial economy. But if the situation is approached with the view of integrating the best of modern technology and scientific management with the best culture of the underdeveloped nation, then better productivity is sure to follow. In the accomplishment of this better productivity the wise international manager will pay particular attention to the integrating social systems, making changes carefully, communicating the idea of productivity and motivating people in terms of their needs.

12

Some Managerial Aspects
of the African
Economic Problem

S. BENJAMIN PRASAD

A recent study of the external factors primarily contributory to economic development in Africa, by Guy Benveniste
and William Moran,[1] concluded that the major problem in Africa
was to recognize all sectors of economic life so that an accelerated
growth can be achieved. The investigators further suggested that
there are so many tasks to be undertaken in Africa that no single
approach will be sufficient. A more recent study done for the National Planning Association [2] suggested that in tropical Africa today, there are inadequate numbers of indigenous entrepreneurs
eager and able to avail themselves of the opportunities for productive private investment made possible by the growth of infrastruc-
ture, the expansion of commercial agriculture, and the increasing
number of skilled workers and technically trained persons. The
authors of this monograph recommended that US missions in
African countries and appropriate US Government agencies in

[1] Guy Benveniste and William Moran, *Handbook of African Economic Development* (New York: Frederick Praeger, Inc., 1962), pp. 131-137.
[2] Theodore Geiger and Winifred Armstrong, *The Development of African
Private Enterprise* (Washington, D.C.: National Planning Association, 1964), p.
121.

Washington should establish continuing facilities for assisting African entrepreneurs to obtain the services of US management, production, marketing, and other technical-business specialists. This NPA recommendation may be construed as one of the many tasks to generate a contributory factor to economic development.

Walter Krause observed that "concern is exhibited in major countries as to whether the newly emerging countries of Africa can prove viable as distinct economic entities." [3] The distinct African economies becoming entities is a long road which many of the African countries are traversing rather slowly and with many difficulties. This may be designated as the long road of the "agro-industrial revolution." Although there are linguistic, cultural, and social differences among the African nations, the frame of reference for this analysis is Africa as a whole excluding Egypt and the Union of South Africa. It is assumed that for Africa industrialization is a nationalistic goal, and for purposes of analysis "organization of production" is taken up here as part of the core structure of industrialization. This paper attempts to 1. briefly point to the duality of the African economies, 2. classify business enterprises or "organization of production," 3. reflect some African managers' behavior, and 4. formulate research questions concerning the managerial aspects of the African economic development strategy.

At the outset, several special conditions which envelop the "organization of production" in the African continent should be noted. The economic and political circumstances surrounding private business enterprise produce a strikingly different business environment from those of North America or Western Europe. As Peter McLoughlin has warned, "because African industrial firms assume discrepant complexions and forms, direct comparisons of any specific aspect of private business firms in developed Western economies with that aspect of firms in Africa is perforce suspect." [4] A feature which distinguishes business enterprises in Africa from those in Western countries is the strong cultural group identification with one or another type of business. There prevails a sort of "caste-system" among indigenous entrepeneurs.

3 Walter Krause, "The Regional Approach to Economic Development," *Iowa Business Digest* (Spring, 1961), p. 30.
4 Peter McLoughlin, "Business and Its Managers in Africa," *California Management Review* (Summer, 1963), p. 43.

Many of the African countries fall under level I in the typology developed by Frederick Harbison and Charles Myers.[5] These are the countries whose economic and social progress is dependent upon the continued employment of foreign high-level manpower in a wide variety of key positions in major public and private enterprises. As Harbison and Myers have inferred: "most of the under-developed (level I) countries would have had little or no modern development without expatriate high-level manpower." [6]

Scarce resources, and in some cases nonexistent resources, in African countries, make it imperative for active governmental participation, in one form or the other, in the process of economic progress. "Government is the only cohesive, viable, economy-wide agency competent and large enough to contemplate and affect desired economic changes." [7]

External factors are and will long continue to be important to economic growth in Africa, even though primary responsibility for this growth will, of necessity, rest with Africans. As Benveniste and Moran observed, "the principal factors are governmental assistance in men and money, foreign investment, and trade." [8]

Most large-scale industries in Africa are concentrated in a few cities such as Salisbury and Bulawayo in Southern Rhodesia, Elisabethville and Léopoldville in the Congo, Dakar in Senegal, Algiers in Algeria, Casablanca in Morocco.

THE DUALITY OF AFRICAN ECONOMIES

For many areas of the world, the first major transformation involves what may be called the incorporating of the subsistence sector into the commercialized market system of the national economy.[9] The subsistence sectors in many African countries exist apart from the balance of the society, and they neither produce a surplus nor provide a market for the products of industrial enterprises.

The subsistence sectors of the traditional African economies are

[5] Frederick Harbison and Charles Myers, *Education, Manpower, and Economic Growth* (New York: McGraw-Hill Book Company, 1964), p. 31.
[6] *Ibid.*, p. 185.
[7] Peter McLoughlin, *op. cit.*, p. 46.
[8] Benveniste and Moran, *op. cit.*, p. v.
[9] Wilbert Moore, *Social Change* (Englewood Cliffs, N.J.: Prentice-Hall, Inc., 1963), p. 96.

quite distinct from the modern market sector of the economy. The latter is oriented toward exports and is usually monopolized by the European community. Africans do benefit from this sector of the economy primarily through employment but rarely in positions above clerical levels.

Until very recently the whole continent, except South Africa, Southern Rhodesia, Egypt, Ethiopia, and Liberia remained in a state of political preparation. The essence of colonial status was that economic power as well as political sovereignty was in alien hands. Major economic activities such as banking, commerce, currency, shipping, taxation, and a host of others were all in the hands of the foreigners. Raw materials were produced for export, and sometimes processed by entrepreneurs from whichever European country wielded political power over a particular territory. As Benveniste and Moran put it: "Colonies were operated as a part of a foreign economy, that of a colonial empire. They were treated as units within this larger economy and were not developed in terms of African or regional possibilities or requirements but in terms of their place in the colonial scheme." [10]

TYPES OF BUSINESS ENTERPRISES IN AFRICA

Private business enterprises in Africa may be classified according to three distinct types: 1. The expatriate European; 2. The resident but non-African; and 3. The African.

The expatriate European business organizations are large and dominant in such activities as trading, shipping, insurance, oil, machinery, and banking. They are either branches or subsidiaries of multinational firms. The top managers as well as middle managers are almost always nationals of European countries. It is in this type of business organization that the problem of "Africanization of personnel" persists.[11]

The resident but non-African business enterprises are smaller than the expatriate European firms and are concentrated in retail-

10 Benveniste and Moran, op. cit., p. 5.

11 See Raymond Vuering's paper, "Problems of Industrial Management in Developing Countries," Ch. 13 in this volume, for details of the problems of Africanization of managerial personnel. In addition, it should be noted that foreign personnel will be needed for a number of years in the newly independent countries but their employment also presents problems. No matter how

ing, wholesaling, construction, and light manufacturing. These enterprises are owned and managed by non-African groups such as Arabs, Armenians, Greeks, Indians, Japanese, Lebanese, and many others. These firms are geared primarily to local markets. They supply their own managerial and supervisory personnel from among their own groups. "Though historically traders and real estate and inventory dealers, and *not* manufacturers, they increasingly employ expatriate technicians and managers when necessary to expand into construction or manufacturing industries." [12]

The African enterprises are only small-scale trading, jobbing, and shipping (internal) firms. Historically, lack of skill or lack of opportunities to acquire skills, experience, and capital have precluded Africans from entering the twentieth century economic patterns.

The concept of *corporate management* is applicable in some respects to the expatriate European firms. The concept of *small business management,* as understood in the US, is comparable to the small-scale resident but non-African business enterprises while native African firms are hard to describe.

The vital role of economic leadership has been performed in African countries by foreign personnel. In recent years the state has been participating in such leadership. Africa has not had what economists call *entrepreneurs.*[13] In some respects this role is now assumed by the state. The economist who emphasized the role of entrepreneur was Joseph Schumpeter whose books—*Theory of Economic Development* and *Capitalism, Socialism and Democracy,* are studded with major insights into the role of the entrepreneur in economic development.

---

badly such personnel are needed, they cannot be used unless their old attitudes change. Hundreds of Europeans have found it necessary to leave the newly independent states because they could not accommodate to independence. As Sierra Leone and Tanganyika found that out of 1,700 top British civil service administrators who had served under the Protectorate, 308 retired; 1,250 retained the right to retire at any time; and, only 150 volunteered to remain through the important first two years of independence. For interesting details, see Benveniste and Moran, *op. cit.,* pp. 20-22 and 65-70.

[12] Peter McLoughlin, *op. cit.,* p. 46.

[13] Some exceptions to this may be the emerging African businessmen, particularly in Nigeria. For an interesting note about the Nigerian millionaires, see *Time* (September 17, 1965), p. 122.

Non-Schumpeterianism

In African countries, the innovating entrepreneur assumed in the Schumpeterian system simply does not exist. The innovating entrepreneurs are, in part, the result of a different society from that which exists in most African countries, and, in part, they are themselves the product and result of economic development. Here is a truly vicious circle for the African countries whose problem is to start development, rather than continue it. Therefore, the building up of a private sector, and thereby a set of private entrepreneurs (managers) is a recognized goal of many governmental programs. As Singer [14] points out, "from this point of view the Schumpeter system is not really a theory of economic development in the sense it is a theory of how such a development starts. Rather, it is a theory of how economic development continues and proceeds, once it has reached a certain state characterized by creation of innovating entrepreneurs, and the creation of the kind of society in which they can operate." Singer, in view of the non-Schumpeterianism which has prevailed in Africa, advocates developing innovating entrepreneurs in small-scale business enterprises.

Singer's Thesis

African countries are, in Rostow's terminology, "traditional societies" or societies in the early phases of precondition stage. Following the particularistic approach, and taking into account the special circumstances that have prevailed in African countries, Singer [15] advocates the development of small-scale industries as the desirable path and type of industrialization in Africa. His arguments can be summarized as follows:

1. There is a greater chance in Africa than elsewhere to develop autonomous technology, i.e., technology adjusted to the resource endowments of the African countries. Autonomous technology would result in typically smaller-scale units of production than in Europe and North America.

---

14 H. W. Singer, *International Development: Growth and Change* (New York: McGraw-Hill Book Company, 1964), pp. 56-58.
15 *Ibid.*, pp. 109-204.

2. The efficient management of large-scale industries is not yet accessible to a large enough number of Africans. However, Africans have already shown and had the opportunity to develop business or managerial skills in running the small-scale enterprises and personal forms of organization rather than big complexes and corporate organizations. Therefore, the choice is not entirely an economic choice between small-scale industries and large-scale industries. Rather, the choice is between *African* small-scale industry and *foreign* large-scale industry.

3. The development of small-scale enterprises of many kinds can be a stepping-stone to large-scale enterprises—a part of the learning process. There is an organic link between small-scale, medium-scale and large-scale forms of business organizations.

4. Given the African desire for independence, personal identification, and the present weakness of business talent, the real alternative to the development of small-scale industry would *not* be the development of large-scale industries but rather the development of trade and speculative activities.

5. In small-scale industries, there is an element of self-employment. Parenthetically it should be noted that this may be a vital factor as McLoughlin points out that "the modern-minded African tends to prefer two main routes to higher socioeconomic status, one of which is through small-scale business independence." [16]

6. The development of small-scale industries in African countries has the advantage of building on something that already exists.

Singer's arguments lead to the hypothesis that *small business* management, which he believes is organically linked to large-scale enterprise management, has a very vital role to play in African economic development.

AFRICAN BUSINESS MANAGERS' BEHAVIOR: SOME ASPECTS

The most fundamental decision which a manager, be he an African, an American, or a Russian, makes is to prepare himself to

[16] Peter McLoughlin, *op. cit.*, p. 47.

be a manager. We know that properly trained managerial personnel are meager in African countries, and this paucity may be attributed to lack of training facilities, both educational and in-plant. But why do many Africans who are college educated shy away from entering the managerial hierarchy? This is a more complex question, and plausible explanations for such a behavior of potential managerial workers are:

1. University-trained Africans with college degrees in commerce or economics rarely choose private firm employment. As discussed earlier the major business organizations are *not* owned and managed by Africans, so, there appears to be a reluctance on the part of the college graduates to identify themselves with foreign enterprise.
2. Public employment—civil service—appears to be more attractive to these people than private foreign employment, in terms of higher salaries, greater security—even retirement programs.
3. Another attraction of civil service for the educated is that government employment offers more occupational variety and mobility.
4. Many Africans cherish small-scale business independence.

According to Singer,[17] the businessmen of North East Africa suffer from three main weaknesses in their managerialism:

1. There is a mania for "keeping the business in the family." The family nature of enterprise is a great weakness. Not only is there a total dependence upon one or two individuals in the family set up, but there is also a high degree of reluctance to drawing outside sources of finance, to seek outside advice or assistance.
2. There is a tendency to do everything within the factory. For example, engineering factories produce their own spare parts, and even whole pieces of new machinery. Many factory workshops have their own foundries. Not only are these trends detrimental to specialization, but they also result in unutilized industrial capacity.
3. While owners and managers of plants take great pride in their workshops and machinery, there is among them a surprising indifference to social conditions of workers. "I was continually struck by the contrast between the pride of businessmen in their

17 H. W. Singer, *op. cit.*, pp. 269-271.

workshops, their side lines, or some mechanical improvement, on the one hand, and their lack of interest in the social conditions of their workers, on the other. I even had the feeling that the provision of special factory services was more a result of legal requirement or a showpiece than evidence of social concern." [18]

Aid From Other Developing Countries

Many African countries are interested in comparable experiences of Israel, India, Mexico, Japan, and others. Israel, for example, has been providing assistance in cooperative effort, community development, and agricultural extension, notably in Ghana.

Recently the Government of India proposed to invest $42 million in joint industrial ventures in Ghana and certain East African railways and harbors. Already such ventures exist in Sudan and Uganda mainly in the form of suppliers, credit loans for purchase of capital goods and establishment of industrial projects, participation in equity capital in Government sponsored projects, and encouragement to private Indian industrialists to collaborate with African governments or industrialists to start joint industrial ventures.

So far six projects for industrial collaboration in ten African countries have been negotiated. Included in these are cotton textile factories, woolen and jute mills, light engineering manufacturing, and a host of other consumer products.

A start has also been made in the matter of extending technical cooperation to developing countries in Africa. Indian industrialists, it has been reported,[19] have come forward extending full cooperation to the Government. The India-Africa Development Association provides facilities for "in-plant training" for African technical personnel in Indian factories and business establishments.

CONCLUSION

The duality of the African managerial problem can be restated as two vital questions:

18 *Ibid.*
19 Embassy of India, *India News* (March 15, 1965), p. 3.

1. How to minimize the continued dependence upon foreign high-level manpower? One approach to this problem is the increased Africanization of personnel. Of course, in order for this to eventually succeed, other corollary problems need to be solved.

2. How to augment managerialism among the indigenous Africans, or in economic terminology, how to develop entrepreneurs? Assuming there exist organic links between small-scale industrial enterprises and large-scale enterprises, one feasible approach to develop entrepreneurs appears to be that of small-scale industrial development. Thus "small business management" may have a vital role to play in African managerialism and industrial development.

13

Problems of Industrial Management in Developing Countries*

RAYMOND VUERINGS

Decolonization, which in the course of twelve years has spread across the African continent, confronts private firms established, or wishing to establish themselves in the new African states, with novel problems. To ensure their survival, these firms must revise or adapt their traditional policy and structure.

In the colonies of old, the large, European-owned, capitalist firms formed a pressure group carrying sufficient weight with the central government at home to ensure private enterprises a commanding position. Authority, both private and public, centered mostly in the metropolitan hierarchy. Thus metropolitan enterprises were favored with a position accentuated by a system of preferential tariffs which operated to the disadvantage of other nations. Many firms owned by powerful financial groups, exercised and still exercise *de facto* monopolies in colonial territories. Investors are sometimes reluctant to finance sectors of the colonial economy that may be thought to stand in competition with interests

* Reprinted from *Management International*, No. 4 (1964), with permission from the International University Contact for Management Education, Rotterdam, The Netherlands.

owned by the colonizing country. Often, investments are decided by their compatibility with the interests of the metropolitan economy rather than the needs of the colonial economy and its *multiplier effects*.

The indigenous population of the major part of the states in Black Africa thus remain to this day strangers to the great Western industries established in their midst. For a variety of reasons they participate neither in owning capital nor in the management of these industries which thus have created a truly "closed economy." The capitalist sector characteristically comprises resources controlled by merchants and their salaried personnel. This concentration of wealth includes only a tiny minority of the native born inhabitants. Side-by-side, the traditional subsistence economy, based on communal tribal society life, continues to survive to the present day on a substantial scale.

Considerable numbers of this rural population have since the last world war migrated to the towns where the inelastic modern economy cannot absorb them. As a result, these people form a "lower echelon" proletariat, always in the grip of chronic unemployment.

It is certain that these conditions account for much of the frustration encountered by the governments of the newly independent African states. Having, little by little, become aware of the realities of their situation, they consider the gradual removal of what economic subjection to the old colonial powers remains as one of their primary tasks. They also seem to realize that the mechanism of capitalist economy is incapable of achieving the full development of their country which makes it incumbent upon them to strive for planned, if not forced, economic growth.

Is it to be inferred, therefore, that the governments of the new African states will adopt a policy of socializing their economy fully? At present, that does not seem to constitute their immediate objective. They are aware that private capital cannot be dispensed with if their economy is to be developed fully. However, taking the weakness of their economy into account, they are not disposed to leave development to the control of private enterprise. They want the firms concerned to subscribe to a plan for growth determined by the government.

How will firms and private foreign investors react when confronted by that attitude? Before dealing with that point I should like to examine the factors which dominate the new environment and how these factors will, in all probability, develop.

THE NEW GENERAL CONTEXT OF INDUSTRY

It is important to say, first of all, that accession to full sovereignty by the new African states has in no way changed the essential characteristics of their economy, i.e., underdevelopment.[1] On the contrary, independence has often engendered a series of changes which are likely to compromise economic development of the young states to a serious extent.

It is obvious that many governments find it difficult to establish their authority firmly enough to get their decisions respected throughout the national territory. Effective administration is generally less than perfect. Cliques and political jobbery, corruption, incompetence, apathy, and lack of professional ethics among office holders often paralyze constructive action, just as much for the public authorities as for private firms. In certain countries, such as Guinea, Mali and Ghana, reputedly ruled by a strong regime, governments successfully imposed their will by creating a single political party and thus managed to mobilize and control the masses in accordance with the central plan, with a fair measure of success by using partisan regional and district machinery.

Practically all the new states have frequently had to face strong inflationary pressure. Broadly, the root cause is public finance deficits.[2] This deficit springs from adopting a way of life out of keeping in relation to the real resources of those states: salaries and increased social security for civil servants, politicians and diplomats, status expense (air lines, merchant marine, armed forces). In addition, a shrinking flow of tropical produce to the world markets leads in turn to smaller fiscal receipts, and customs duties play an important role in their national economy. It must also be admitted that those paid do not always reach the Treasury: fraud, embezzlement, and corruption taking their toll. Nevertheless, some govern-

[1] See, for example, L. J. Lebret, *Dynamique concrète du développement* (Paris, 1961), pp. 50-62.
[2] At Léopoldville, the overall deficit assumed enormous dimensions rising to around 1,116 Congolese francs a month in 1962.

ments, e.g., Senegal, the Ivory Coast, Madagascar, Ghana, and Mali are beginning to understand the dangers of inflating the state budget and have made their first attempts to practice austerity.

Another factor in the economic milieu concerns the shortage of foreign currency, mainly due to deteriorating rates of exchange,[3] fraud,[4] and reduced volume of exports.

The attitude of governments in the newly independent African states to foreign private enterprise shows two specific tendencies: the first which one might call "National Revolutionary Socialism" (*socialisme révolutionnaire nationaliste*) is adopted by such countries as Ghana, Guinea, and Mali. The second is less extremist and applying to most of the other countries has been dubbed "individualized communal socialism" (*socialisme communautaire personnaliste*).

Initially, the national governments tried to secure rapid development of their economy by imposing a central, authoritarian plan. Its implementation envisaged virtually immediate state control of various sectors of the economy, coupled with strict control of foreign investment. Foreign trade is usually the section nationalized first, because the operation is comparatively easy and profitable. Next in line are the large public utilities and mining enterprises, the banking system, agriculture, domestic trade, etc., a method which follows closely the procedure adopted by communist countries. The African countries which have shown themselves so far most anxious to establish economic relations with the Eastern countries and to benefit from their financial and technical assistance are Ghana, Guinea, and Mali.

Nevertheless, African revolutionary socialism does not altogether preclude foreign investment. Dr. Kwame Nkrumah, [former] President of Ghana, unceasingly repeats that his socialism is well able to team up with private capital. However, such alliances come under tight control. The governments do not conceal their preference for mixed-economy firms where the state claims part, often half, of the capital, which allows it to control management of the

[3] For example, in Nigeria, exchange rates have deteriorated by 21 percent since 1954. In Ghana they worsened by 85 percent since 1954. *Afrique Express* (January 25, 1963), p. 24.

[4] The Mali minister, for example, gave himself the following percentage losses by fraud in the total export traffic from Mali to neighboring countries, particularly in the case of cattle: With Mauritania and Ghana, 46 to 65 percent; with the Ivory Coast, 35 percent; and, with Guinea, 40 percent.

firm directly. Otherwise, private investment is encouraged only when it is linked to one or more phases of the government's economic and social development plans.

Moreover, inducements offered are often hedged by reservations which go far enough to make the inducements ineffective. The Mali law of 13 January 1962, designed to encourage foreign investment, strikingly demonstrates this policy.[5] According to that law certain private firms were accorded privileged positions in the development plans and have succeeded in making agreements with the Mali state recognizing them as such. These approved firms secured certain privileges, such as full guarantees allowing them to transfer their investment in case of liquidation, unhampered transfer of profits and a fifteen-year guarantee against increase in monetary imposts. However, there was no freedom from or reduction of taxes on profits transferred out of Mali; the fiscal advantages were abrogated by treating the profits accrued as an increase in investment; the management of the firm must submit to the government's plans for investment, production, export and employment; once approved, execution of the plans is enforced down to the last detail; any significant deviation causes the risk of unilateral total abrogation of all or part of the benefits agreed upon in the original arrangement.

Sometimes the states require that part of the profits be officially assigned to them or reinvested in the country, that the ownership of the buildings and installations of the firm be transferred to them after a set period, that the Africanization of the staff of the firm be completed by a certain time, etc. Such conditions obviously are likely to discourage private foreign investors considerably.

It seems, nevertheless, that the tide is beginning to turn and that the states which adopted revolutionary socialism are reverting to a more liberal policy; Mali always excepted. Various reasons are at the root of this change: misconceptions which engendered dalliance with the East; realization that planning in the USSR had suffered setbacks when it solicited Western help to overcome a cereal shortage; their own experience with the state industries which proved inefficient, and disquiet at seeing private investment disappear, thus endangering fulfillment of the development plans.

In Ghana, Dr. Nkrumah announced, in October 1963, a num-

[5] *Industries et travaux d'outre-mer* (June 1962), p. 472.

ber of measures designed to avert the dangers of an economic crisis,[6] more particularly:

1. Abolition of the forced savings plan, through which all salaried persons must put 5 percent of their incomes, and all employees 10 percent of theirs, into National Bonds, theoretically repayable after ten years by the Ghana National Development Board.
2. A fiscal amnesty for the capital of Ghanaians placed abroad which could be repatriated to Ghana without risking penalties.
3. The suppression of obligatory reinvestment: Foreign companies established in Ghana would no longer be forced to reinvest on the spot 60 percent of the global amount of their profit.

In Guinea, as a result of the difficulties encountered by the nationalization of industry, Sekou Touré and the Political Bureau decreed (after the national conference on business held at Conakry from 7th to 10th October 1963), the closure of state stores from the 1st of November 1963, except in districts where there were no private merchants.[7]

Henceforward import licenses will be granted to private business on the same conditions as to state firms and the marketing of all local produce will be in the hands of free enterprise. By virtue of the same decree, diamond mines, nationalized two and a half years ago, will be worked again by private firms.

It remains to be seen whether the progressive governments feel that they have proceeded too quickly on their road towards socialism, or whether they feel they have come too far. In the first case, the new policy represents perhaps only a necessary pause (particularly for the formation of a sound national structure and the accumulation of fixed capital) before deciding once again to return to the objectives of socialism. In the second case, such a partial return to liberalism has chances of consolidation and even extension.

In any case, the adherents of individualistic communal socialism, most strongly represented in Senegal and the Ivory Coast, praise the rallying of the "revolutionaries" to the prudent ideas which they have always defended. They, in fact, exert themselves to

6 *Moniteur africain du commerce et de l'industrie,* Dakar: Abidjan (October 26, 1963).
7 *Ibid.* (October 19, 1963).

attract private capital by respecting the property of firms, desisting from discrimination and vexatious interference in their management. Their development plans are above all plans to give direction to the economy. Private investments are channelled toward the activities foreseen by the plan by offering special concessions to firms in line with a special statute concerning privileged enterprises or benefit agreements which carry serious guarantees and are free from restrictive clauses.

Until now those states which subscribe to that policy have intervened directly only in the agricultural sector, which they wished to reform fundamentally, by founding a vast network of cooperatives destined to stimulate and rationalize the production and marketing of agricultural products and thereby to put an end to old trading methods. By creating cooperatives and communal development centers, they tried to mobilize the productive forces in the rural centers because they considered this an essential foundation for the development of the country. It is precisely that procedure which has given rise to the description "communal socialism." This "socialism" wishes nevertheless to be "individualistic," that is to say, to take care of and preserve the integrity of the individual.

THE ATTITUDE OF FREE ENTERPRISE

In Regard to Investment

Generally speaking, private investment declined from the end of 1956, the date on which decolonization in Africa got under way. Between 1951 and 1955 it amounted to 147 million American dollars per year; between 1956 and 1959 this had fallen to 83 million.[8] Indeed, the nationalist movement was not the only cause of the decline, but it most certainly constituted an important factor.

Private capital looks firstly for security. A large number of Western industries, having settled in Africa, often took fifteen to twenty years to make their first profits. They agreed to run this risk, without doubt, because from the date when their long term fore-

---

[8] Source: United Nations, "Courant international de capiteaux à long terme et donations publiques, 1951-1959."

casts permitted the conclusion that once the firm became solvent, ultimately profitable operation would always follow. For example, the United Africa Company has had for thirty-three years out of the thirty-four of its existence, smaller profits than that of the Unilever parent company which works in industrialized countries.[9]

It is precisely that prospect of long term stability, that view of lasting business life, that is really lacking in Africa. Private firms show reluctance and hesitate when faced with both political and economic risks: expropriation, confiscation or sequestration, political instability, discriminatory measures against private firms, withdrawal of concessions, and the whole grisly gamut of expropriations such as restriction of imports, unjustified tax impost, prohibition to repatriate capital and revenues, restrictions imposed on the powers of the shareholders, exchange control, and the creation of state monopolies.

It is certain that the policy of progressive nationalization of sectors of the economy in Guinea—overseas trade, home trade, the banking system, underwriting, and public services—have greatly diminished the flow of private investment and have led to the sanctions imposed by the government of Guinea on the Bauxite Company of the Midi.[10] Likewise, the socialist revolutionary policy of Mali, after relations with Senegal had been broken off, has seen all private foreign investment dry up. At Léopoldville, in the Congo, most Belgian firms facing a situation aggravated by physical insecurity, an unproductive, weak, and corrupt administration, control of exchange and overseas trade (which did not prevent fraud on a grand scale), refused to produce fresh capital at such high risk.[11]

On the Ivory Coast, nevertheless, the moderate liberalism of the government has ensured that French capital is still being invested in several branches of the economy. The same thing is true, moreover, for Nigeria, the largest nation of independent Black

9 Declaration of N. J. K. Clark (Economic Adviser, United Africa Company, Ltd.), in the *"Journée africaine"* of the International Fair.

10 *Industries et travaux d'outre-mer* (December 1961), p. 83.

11 Such were the conclusions arrived at by a group of twenty-seven top managers of firms operating in the Congo, during a seminar on "The Future of Private Enterprise in the Congo and in Africa," held in Louvain, Belgium (October 2-5, 1963).

Africa, with 40 million inhabitants, which has become the preferred field of action for American investors.[12] That state, profiting already from having an important home market, by a common language, by a stable government and by willing cooperation, encourages Americans "to demonstrate to the new nations of Africa that the best way to realize their political and economic aspirations lay in democratic institutions cooperating with the free world."[13]

Without doubt, the African countries have realized the need for safeguarding private foreign investors. Nearly all the states in the French sphere of influence have issued investment codes or *ad hoc* enfranchisements offering advantages (principally fiscal mandates or stated guarantees) for the transfer of the capital, profits and revenues of exiles. In spite of evident interest in these measures, it seems that they do not represent a decisive factor in attracting capital. The attitude African governments take in relation to private foreign firms is what matters. When the National Assembly of Guinea adopted an Investment Code, it thought it prudent to recall "that expropriation and other acts of nationalization undertaken so far concerned issues of sovereignty and the abandoned or exploited sectors of the economy."[14] It is significant that those countries which did not promulgate—or did so only on a very limited scale—special legislation affecting foreign investments, attracted most private capital.[15]

Restrictive measures laid down by the developing countries needing to import capital suffer from the basic weakness of being internal laws which do not form part of a network of international obligations. These measures may thus be repealed or withdrawn unilaterally and with impunity by the countries which promulgated them.

Systems of guarantees and assurances for foreign investors, instituted in capital exporting countries, prove indispensable. Such

[12] When the European Economic Community approved $730 million in five years to member countries, the Agency for International Development by itself supplied to Nigeria in six years $225 million for the carrying out of its plan. (*Industries et travaux d'outre-mer* [January 1963], p. 3.) For a discussion of the Ivory Coast's search for US capital, see *Time* (June 11, 1966), p. 133. [Editor]

[13] *Industries et travaux d'outre-mer, Ibid.*, p. 3.

[14] *Industries et travaux d'outre-mer* (May, 1962), p. 405.

[15] M. Brandom, "The Encouragement and Protection of Investment in Developing Countries" (London, 1962), p. 3.

a system now flourishes in the US, in Germany, and Japan. They are being studied in Switzerland, Great Britain, the Netherlands, and France.

The African Public Authorities

One of the first consequences of independence is the transfer of political power from the once powerful colonizers to the government of the new state. In dealing with that body, firms are obliged to take certain susceptibilities into account which in effect considerably reduce their chances for exerting pressure. Constructive relations between the private individual firm and the independent State can only be established if the former scrupulously respects the sovereignty of the latter over its wealth in natural resources.

First of all, firms must recognize that the relations between private enterprise and public authorities are no longer centered on their capital city. Decentralization must be carried out to allow management on the spot to treat directly with the new administration. Nothing is more annoying for managers than to negotiate with directors of firms who have to ask every time for permission of their governing board in Paris, Brussels, or London before making the smallest decision. It is noteworthy that in certain firms this change has not been accomplished easily: top management often tenaciously resists any delegation of its powers.

It follows also that free enterprise has every inducement to seek active collaboration with the independent State, particularly in the inception and realization of its national development plan. This collaboration reduces the danger of nationalization, because the firm has adjusted its own objective to those of the sovereign state. Quite simply, the approved firms are those which fulfill certain conditions imposed either by the legislature in an Investment Code or by an "Investment Commission." The recognized firms conclude definitive contracts with the government which gives the firm specific guarantees in return for specific obligations. Here the possibilities are practically limitless, seeing that the content of each contract or agreement depends on negotiations between two sides. As has already been said, the principal danger to be avoided is too much meddling by the state in the management of industry. For the sake of efficiency, industry must preserve its autonomy in respect of its internal

management. In other respects, it is not always easy to set a limit
to absolute autonomy.

The Africanization of Staff

It is only too evident that one of the most serious obstacles to
economic and social development of young African nations is a
lack of competent native-born staff. Independence has speeded up
the Africanization of these staffs, not only in the public sector where
the transmission of power has been absolute, but also in the private
sector where the ex-colonists still keep most of the authority. The
state, however, often demands, in setting up agreements with new
industries, that Africanization be progressively carried through
within a specified time.

It is in the owner-managed or very small firm that foreign
managers have shown a hostile attitude to the promotion of Africans. To these managers, who for a long time were the owners,
Africanization is almost synonymous to handing the enterprise
over. Some have nevertheless maneuvered skillfully enough to let
the Africans manage their business while they themselves remain
owners or at least co-owners.

Some large firms have been sufficiently farsighted to anticipate
the Africanization movement long before independence, which enabled them to build up effective African staffs quickly. It is generally
firms of worldwide scope which have been able to profit by their
experience in other developing countries which achieved independence. They accomplished the recruitment and training of African
personnel within the framework of an overall plan of improvement
and promotion, based on on-the-job studies about the level of education and professional qualifications required by different categories of workers, consideration of their chance of improving themselves, and on the specific needs of the firm for qualified staff.

Finally, there remains a nucleus of European managers, who,
while not hostile to Africanization, are nevertheless somewhat scep-
tical that it can be organized in a systematic and rational way. This
scepticism involves, in its turn, doubts as to the possibility of turning out competent African managers. In these circumstances, one
often hears of "political promotions" of Africans, that is to say,
promotions to higher grades (usually involving increased authority

for making decisions or granting privileges) made for appearance' sake or quite simply to create a spokesman for public occasions.

The two principal obstacles which hamper rapid Africanization of the staff of private firms at present are: 1. the poor level of general education of the African staff employed, and 2. resistance of the ex-colonists to Africanization. It is not reasonable to expect that the first obstacle will be rapidly overcome. It is extremely difficult to raise those with only elementary or secondary education, to manager level, by means of a training which will be in any case sketchy. Elsewhere, external recruitment for the middle manager level is limited by the fact that most of those who finish their secondary schooling go on to higher education. Finally, there is the attraction of Public Administration which, in the eyes of many Africans, university graduates and others, offers most security and immediate jobs. It remains to be seen if, in the future, a grave shortage of native-born middle managers will make itself felt in the young countries of Central Africa.

As for the second factor, the success of Africanization will depend on active participation of higher and top management in training the African. Insofar as the ex-colonial managerial staff can function effectively as instructors, they must be trained for this role to enable them to assume it and execute it with the enthusiasm required. It is absolutely vital to consider the normal duties of European staffs in the light of the urgent necessity to train Africans for managerial posts. Preparation for these creative roles means that Europeans should be taught the essential techniques of teaching. In order to give them a chance to play this role, it will be necessary to free them from part of their ordinary duties, which will often mean the engagement of more staff. Finally, so that they should be interested in this new occupation, their own promotion should be linked with their success in training their African successors. In other words, the ex-colonists must be given guarantees regarding their own future when the time comes for their African colleagues to take over.

CONCLUSION

Consideration of the recent changes which have taken place in the environment which surrounds private Western firms since Central Africa achieved full sovereign status, leads to the conclusion that they will be forced to introduce reforms if they wish to continue to participate in the development of these countries. The reforms required must be aimed at aligning the objectives of the private firms to those of the new African states. In fine, these comprise:

1. Active cooperation with the state in the inception and carrying out of its development plan while undertaking to negotiate mutual agreements for setting up the plan and exploiting resources.
2. Much more decentralization, giving to managers on the spot more freedom of action and the necessary authority for negotiating directly with the local government.
3. The "naturalization" of capital by the adoption of mixed economy arrangements or attraction of private native-born stockholders.
4. The internationalization of capital, in order to divide the risks by joining with private investors of different nationalities.
5. The training and progressive Africanization of staffs.

Finally, it would appear to be highly desirable to reinforce the cohesion of all private firms so as to secure both concerted mutual action and improved coordination with the aid policies and technical assistance programs of Western governments.

14

Some Aspects of
Israeli Management *

MILTON DERBER

Typically, American managers make their own decisions on what and how much to produce, where to produce, and
what prices to charge; they make most decisions on how to produce,
although they often share decision-making with worker representatives on certain aspects, such as the speed of operations and the
workload; and they codetermine wages, hours, and employment
conditions with worker representatives. In general, American unions
have been content to confine their responsibility to the job territory [1] and have rarely challenged the managers' exclusive role in
the financial and engineering areas, let alone the selection of management personnel.[2]

European unions, espousing socialist and welfare state ideolo-
gies, have often sought a wider voice in the management process.
In Britain, syndicalist notions of workers' control got nowhere, but
joint consultation has been adopted, with limited success, in both

---

* Reprinted with permission from *Industrial Relations*, Vol. 3, No. 1 (October, 1963). Copyright, The Institute of Industrial Relations, University of California, Berkeley. The original title was "Worker Participation in Israeli Management." This is an abridgment.

1 Well-known exceptions to this generalization are the activities of the
clothing unions in making loans to distressed employers, furnishing engineering
advice, and cosponsoring sales campaigns.

2 Except for the foremen in certain industries like printing and construction.

nationalized and privately operated enterprises.[3] In Germany, a more far-reaching program of "codetermination" was introduced by law first in the steel and coal mining industries and then in other industries.[4] In Yugoslavia [5] and, for a brief time, in Poland [6] workers' councils schemes carried worker participation in management to its furthest point.

The experience in Israel adds another interesting, although still incomplete, chapter to the history of worker participation in management. Despite its small population (2.3 million) and the recency of its industrialization, Israel provides an extremely varied scene for study.[7] Sizable numbers of enterprises are run both by private entrepreneurs and government corporations, and by the labor movement itself. In each sector, organized labor (predominantly the Histadrut, the general federation of labor) is a powerful factor and is in a position to exercise considerable influence in behalf of the workers.

The experience in Israel may therefore shed some important light on the nature of worker participation, its possibilities, and the difficulties that arise in dealing with the concept. On the other hand, any conclusions must be qualified by recognition of Israel's unusual circumstances—its Zionist origins, the vast number of new immigrants from widely different cultures, the problem of defense against hostile Arab neighbors, and a serious balance-of-payment condition. Furthermore, like many newly industrializing nations, Israel has numerous workers who lack understanding of industrial practice and discipline and it suffers from a shortage of experienced managers.

[3] See H. A. Clegg, *A New Approach to Industrial Democracy* (Oxford: Basil Blackwell, 1960), Ch. 4; and A. Flanders and H. A. Clegg, eds., *The System of Industrial Relations in Great Britain* (Oxford: Basil Blackwell, 1954), Ch. 6.

[4] Clegg, *op. cit.*, Ch. 6. See also, W. H. McPherson, "Codetermination in Practice," *Industrial and Labor Relations Review*, VIII (July, 1955), pp. 499-519; and W. Michael Blumenthal, *Codetermination in the German Steel Industry* (Princeton, N.J.: Princeton University Press, 1956).

[5] Clegg, *op. cit.*, Ch. 7, and John Dunlop, *Industrial Relations Systems* (New York: Holt, Rinehart and Winston, 1958), Ch. 7.

[6] See Adolf Sturmthal, "The Workers' Councils in Poland," *Industrial and Labor Relations Review*, XIV (April, 1961).

[7] The following analysis is based mainly on interviews and observations in eighteen of Israel's larger enterprises during November, 1961-March, 1962.

WORKER PARTICIPATION IN PRIVATE ENTERPRISE

In the private sector of industry, worker participation in management differs only in degree from American practice, although Israel has a system of joint production committees which are rarely found in the United States and which potentially could extend worker participation considerably. The main areas of participation are indicated by the collective bargaining agreements: wages, hours, and conditions of employment. In respect to hiring and dismissal, the influence of the workers is more extensive than in the typical American manufacturing establishment. The voice of the workers extends to technological changes which affect wages or jobs. Transfers of employees in general, as well as upgrading, promotion, and downgrading, require prior consent of the workers' committee in most of the establishments studied. In some, however, management can transfer without consulting the workers' committee, as long as neither wages nor conditions of the employee are adversely affected. The employee can always raise a grievance if he is discontent with the change. . . . The most significant extension of worker participation in the management process, compared with American practice, is in the area of productivity.[8] Largely as a result of the Histadrut initiative and pressure, the Manufacturers' Association, on May 26, 1952, signed an agreement to establish Joint Productivity Councils in all plants affiliated with the Association and employing 50 people or more. . . .

In theory JPC is a mechanism through which the workers may be involved in virtually every aspect of plant life on a consultative basis. The Histadrut leaders view it as an essential means of making Israel's industry competitive in world markets, raising worker living standards, and developing industrial democracy. . . . Practice, however, has fallen far short of Histadrut theory because few workers and even fewer managers share its broad viewpoint. . . . More serious, however, to the Histadrut theory is the reluctance of many worker representatives on the JPC's to interest themselves in

8 For an account of the early experience of Israel's productivity movement, with particular reference to the work of the Productivity Institute, see Hy Fish, "Raising Productivity in Israel," *International Labour Review,* LXVIII (October-November, 1953), pp. 375-392.

the broader aspects of productivity such as waste reduction, over-head costs, and quality control. The norms have a direct and immediate tie to effort and earnings. The other elements do not. The Histadrut thus has a major task to convert the workers' limited interest into a broad-gauged participation in productivity analysis. It seeks to do so by classes and conferences, by widely publicized financial awards to workers and managers significantly contributing to production in their enterprises and by direct participation of their specialists in JPC meetings. Management resistance is another obstacle to the use of JPC as a source of worker participation. The Manufacturers' Association accepted the JPC with considerable dubiety and reservation. . . . Many employers genuinely feel that the workers have too little experience or knowledge to make a useful contribution, and it is true that the mass of immigrant workers require long education before they can fill the role which the Histadrut envisages. In general, however, managers do not conceive that they have any responsibility to educate workers to this role.

WORKER PARTICIPATION IN GOVERNMENT ENTERPRISES

In addition to the traditional functions of government, the Israeli government carries on a limited number of industrial activities either through a regular ministry, such as defense, or through special public corporations. Two of the four enterprises visited are regarded as among the nation's leaders in labor relations. . . . Another factor in the labor relations approach of these governmental enterprises is the dominant role of the Mapai Party (the major labor party) in both the Government and the Histadrut. As a result, the top managers are either members of Mapai or acceptable to its national executives. . . . In view of labor's controlling position, we might expect a much higher degree of worker participation in management in these establishments than in the private sector. This is not the case. Perhaps the most important reason is the intensity of the top managers' determination to further the enterprise's output and efficiency and their belief that this can be best accomplished by a clear-cut definition of the manager's functions and "prerogatives" and a reduction in the barriers to them, whether on the part of government bureaucracy or union rules and procedures. . . .

Significantly, only one of the four establishments has utilized a joint production committee. Although managers in the other three see some utility in safety and social committees, they do not believe that the workers can contribute much to matters affecting productivity. Nor has there been any pressure from the workers for involvement in a joint production committee.

WORKER PARTICIPATION IN HISTADRUT ENTERPRISES

One of the most unusual features of economic life in Israel is the ownership and operation of a substantial sector of industry (over 20 percent in terms of value product) by the Histadrut. Most of the "heavy" and "medium" goods manufacturing establishments in the Histadrut sector are subsidiaries or associates of its industrial company called *Koor*.[9] Koor's thirty-odd establishments include the nation's only iron and steel mill, the largest foundry, the major cement factory, the leading glass and ceramics factories, and a diversity of other producers.

Koor offers a remarkable opportunity for the testing of ideas about worker participation in management, since the enterprises belong to the labor movement and "industrial democracy" is one of its most important expressed values. The ideology of democratic socialism which has characterized Histadrut from its inception lends added force to the conception that workers should take an active interest and play a major part in the running of their enterprises. . . .

It was generally agreed by participants who were interviewed that workers viewed Histadrut enterprises as different from private establishments, but only rarely in the sense of making special efforts in behalf of the enterprise; instead they expected better employment conditions and economic returns, and were more likely to be critical of the managers for securing preferential benefits for themselves. They frequently saw the Histadrut trade union department

[9] Some manufacturing (mainly of consumer goods) is also done by other Histadrut organizations.

representatives as taking a "management" position rather than supporting the workers.

The difference in perspective and interest was equally pronounced on the management side of Koor. Although not shared by every manager and personnel director interviewed, the prevailing view was that management was a "function" in Koor no less than in private or governmental plants, that the managers' job was to produce as efficiently as possible and to expand output, and that workers were neither competent nor interested to pursue this line.[10] The failure of Koor establishments to achieve the climate of mutuality essential to the maximum worker participation in management is demonstrated in the experience with joint production committees and councils. . . .

CAN GENERAL WORKER PARTICIPATION BE SUCCESSFUL?

Through a combination of political and economic power, the Israeli labor movement has been able to take the initiative in the formulation of national economic and industrial policy in a society where national planning and regulation are necessarily far-reaching. Despite what would appear to be a highly favorable climate for its success, however, worker participation in management at the factory level does not appreciably differ from that in the United States or Britain, except in the limited sectors of Kibbutz industry and producers' cooperatives. Nor is the workers' role markedly different in Histadrut and government establishments than it is in private establishments.[11] Worker representatives do exercise great influence on wages, fringe benefits, hours, and a wide array of employment conditions, but outside of the job territory their influence is negligible. The joint production committees have strongly affected norms and premiums, but have not had an important impact on

10 Confirmation of this finding that Koor managers saw industrial relations in basically the same terms as private and government managers was provided in an attitudinal study by Y. Rim of Technion, Israel's Institute of Technology, *Attitudes of Israeli Executives and Trade Union Leaders to Industrial Relations.*

11 A distinction, of course, must be made between the managerial activities of national Histadrut leaders in running Histadrut enterprises and the role of workers in the plants.

other aspects of productivity. The workers do not have a voice in choosing the managers of their enterprises, except for the first-line foremen in some Histadrut and government plants. Neither do they help determine the products to be manufactured, the materials to be used, the methods of work (except where a job loss or change of duties is involved), the prices to be charged, plant investment, plant expansion, customer relations, accounting practices, and a host of other basic aspects of management. In brief, worker participation is limited rather than general.

Part of the explanation for this seeming paradox inheres in a number of internal developments in Israel. For one, the growing industrialization of the country depends in considerable measure on the ability to attract private capital. Investors of such capital are not inclined to favor more worker participation and the national leaders are sensitive to this fact. Secondly, socialist ideology, which dominated the thinking of many of the early pioneers, has waned appreciably in influence. This applies not merely to the bulk of new immigrants and to the increasingly important professional class but also to many of the "old-timers" occupying major administrative and policy-making positions. In the third place, the leaders of the Histadrut face exceedingly complex organizational problems in accommodating a highly centralized policy-making system to the powerful pressures for greater national union and local plant autonomy. The leaders are therefore disinclined to press controversial new programs which may further complicate their roles. Finally, managerial leadership is progressing in knowledge, skill, and self-confidence. Only if managers can be persuaded to view more worker participation as a desirable goal are such programs likely to succeed; there is no sign that they are being so persuaded.

The Israeli experience, however, also raises some intriguing questions about management and organizational behavior in general:

1. Is there something inherent in the process of management which imposes effective limitations on worker participation in management, especially in large-scale enterprise?
2. Can workers serve as co-managers and at the same time maintain the support of the people who chose them as their representatives?

3. Does the concept of industrial democracy necessitate participation of workers in all phases of the plant government or society of which they are "citizens"?

DOES THE MANAGEMENT PROCESS LIMIT PARTICIPATION?

Management is the process of determining the objectives of an enterprise and guiding its human and other resources in a way which will best serve to satisfy those objectives.[12] The objectives may be the production of goods or services of a particular quality and quantity, achievement of high economic returns for the owners, provision of employment for a community, earning foreign currency in world markets, or a combination of these and other ends. The test of management is how successfully the objectives are achieved, always subject to one condition—the survival of the enterprise.

Objectives that are unwisely or unrealistically selected from the standpoint of the enterprise's economic or political environment may lead to the destruction of the enterprise, even though the objectives themselves are successfully attained: for example, the objective of high output or high employment which fails adequately to take into account competitive cost conditions. Under certain limited emergency circumstances (e.g., a war), economic cost may be a secondary or even unimportant consideration in the management process. However, where product competition prevails, the level of per-unit costs becomes an essential element in management.

As here defined, management is a process. People must guide the process. The managers are the people formally selected or approved by the owners or controllers of an enterprise to do the managing. Successful managers are those capable of formulating realistic objectives for the enterprise and seeing to it that they are achieved. They have an interest, too, in satisfying their own personal needs and wants (e.g., status and material reward), as well as the objectives of the enterprise. To the extent that these are compatible or

---

[12] Management is also often defined more narrowly as the people who manage, but for the purpose of this discussion a distinction is warranted.

that personal needs are subordinated to institutional objectives, the management process is facilitated.

Groups other than the formally designated managers may, of course, also share in the process of formulating objectives for the enterprise and of making decisions for their attainment. In a unionized establishment, the union officials or representatives of the workers play such a role. Like the managers, they have distinctive needs and goals as organizations and individuals. If these needs and goals are compatible with those formulated for the enterprise, the management process is again facilitated.

To be successful, management necessitates: 1. a strong interest in the economic welfare of the enterprise, 2. ability to formulate goals and plan for their attainment, 3. expertise in handling men and materials, and 4. ability to make and execute decisions in a timely and flexible way. This list is, of course, not all-inclusive, but it may serve adequately for the present analysis. The question is to what extent the qualities possessed by worker representatives are likely to be consistent with these qualities.

Interest in the Economic Welfare of the Enterprise

Both managers and workers have a strong stake in the economic position of the enterprise. Jobs and income for both depend on it. Management, however, also requires cost consciousness. Managers, confronted directly with budgetary restraints or market competition, are likely to share this consciousness and make efficiency a major consideration, even though it often creates problems and conflicts for them which they would like to avoid. When they can pass costs on to their customers in a period of excess demand or because of cost-plus arrangements, they may take advantage of the opportunity. But workers do not (cannot) see the relationship between costs and the enterprise's economic welfare so easily, because their daily jobs are much more removed from budgets and markets. The larger the enterprise, the more difficult it is to perceive the relationship. Moreover, short-run and immediate relations are better understood by workers than long-run and indirect consequences. Hence, worker representatives are in an ambiguous position if they attempt to share in management decisions which require cost reduction. The worker leader who moves too far from his electorate is very likely to be repudiated. Workers can be sensitized to the cost problem, but it is a long, slow process.

Planning Ability

Effective planning calls for imagination, experience, and knowledge. It also calls for extensive information on costs, markets, etc. Planning is not a one-time task; it is a continuing process. In such a process, worker representatives can contribute more to the formulation of objectives than to designing methods for achieving them. Worker representatives can perhaps serve most usefully as critics of planners, forcing them to justify their positions, to clarify their thinking, and to see various aspects and consequences which they might otherwise have ignored.

Coordinating Men and Materials

This is another phase of management in which worker representatives can better serve as constructive critics than initiators of action. Determination of such matters as layout of equipment, allocation of skills, and speed of machines, are, in the first instance at least, technical decisions to be made within a total plan. To assure maximum efficiency the decision must be made by production specialists. Workers, from their experience and knowledge, can best contribute ideas for fill-ins or revisions of the main plan. Technically sound decisions, however, are not always the best decisions from a human standpoint. Traditional work habits, fear of losing skills, and ideas of fair treatment may necessitate a different series of steps or a slower timetable. Worker representatives are usually better judges of probable worker reactions than managers and are thus in a position to suggest wiser management decisions.

Timeliness and Flexibility

Successful management requires not only the formulation and execution of sound policies and decisions, but doing so at the right time and place. An enterprise is not a debating society; it needs *timely* decisions and actions. One man can always act more swiftly than several men of similar ability. A committee of similarly minded men can invariably reach decisions faster than a committee of men with varied interests. Hence worker participation in management has an implicit tendency to slow down the process of decision-making and execution. If, however, joint discussions produce wiser decisions, they may be worth the extra expenditure of time.

It follows from this limited discussion that worker participation in management introduces a number of elements which have a tendency to complicate and obstruct the management process, although participation also adds or has the potential of adding some qualities that are beneficial to the process. To some degree, adverse elements can be corrected by education in the plant and through outside programs. The beneficial aspect of worker participation is that it adds a new dimension to management. The workers' viewpoint is obtained prior to the making of decisions, thereby reducing conflicts. While workers are capable of making some useful technical contributions out of their work experience, this is most likely to occur at the departmental or shop level and least likely at the overall plant level. In other words, worker participation in management is not a useful means of tapping the same kind of talents and ideas which are supplied by managers, but rather is a way to utilize different values and experiences. Worker representatives are most valuable playing a criticizing, modifying role rather than an initiating one.

WILL WORKERS SUPPORT THEIR REPRESENTATIVES?

Even if managers welcome the idea of worker participation in management, can it succeed on the workers' side? This question has been discussed in the literature with conflicting conclusions. Studies of codetermination in Germany and of workers' councils in Yugoslavia suggest an affirmative answer. Other students, on the basis of experience in Britain and the United States, tend to give a negative answer.

The obstacles are twofold. First, it takes a long time and considerable training before a worker representative is capable of contributing usefully to the management process. The longer the worker representative serves in this capacity and the closer he gets to management, however, the greater is the danger that he will lose his sensitivity to rank-and-file opinion. Frequent turnover is disturbing to management, but congenial to union democracy. The other obstacle is that when worker representatives share in decision-making with managers, they often have to defend decisions which are unpalatable to the rank-and-file. Opposition leaders play the role of critic, and the incumbent leadership may be defeated in a subsequent election. Neither of these obstacles is impossible to hurdle. However, the co-manager role takes unusual qualities of sympathetic insight into the problems of both the enterprise and the work force, firmness in resisting pressures which are politically threatening but factually unjustified, and capacity to persuade men to accept one's judgment. Not many worker leaders have such qualities or the desire to fill the role.

DOES INDUSTRIAL DEMOCRACY CALL FOR PARTICIPATION?

Worker participation in management as an aspect of industrial democracy has been a subject of analysis and debate going back at least to the Webbs in the 1890's. It carries over into industry the political assumptions of the virtues of self-government, that workers should have the same rights and responsibilities, as citizens within industry, that they have as citizens of a city or state. Unions are justified as instruments of representative government. It is possible to translate the political analogy into an industrial model in which workers share with other industrial citizens (shareholders, managers, creditors, and perhaps even the customers) responsibility for electing executives and legislators and, through them, for enacting laws or rules.

Many managers would reject outright the application of the concept of democracy to management. Representative of this view is a statement reportedly made by A. W. Robertson, former chairman of the board of Westinghouse Electric and Manufacturing Company: "Good management is the rule of the best minds. It is anti-democratic, although private organizations flourish best in democratic countries. However, the democratic rule of the majority will frustrate and defeat any management. The crew cannot run the ship." [13]

H. A. Clegg, in contrast, uses the concept of industrial democracy to argue against extending worker participation in management.[14] Clegg holds that central to any democratic system are recognition of a diversity of interests, fear of unrestrained concentration of power, and encouragement of independent opposition to a ruling body. He sees trade unions as representatives of the workers' interest and whose principal task is to oppose any abuse of authority by the managers of industry. "If trade unions were too closely connected with industrial management they would not be able to do that job." [15] Hence, efforts to achieve more worker participation in management are a mistake. It is inherently sounder for unions to function as critic and watchdog (the "loyal opposition") and to rely upon collective bargaining to safeguard and enhance the workers' interests. Clegg sees only one possibility for extending worker participation in management and that is in those limited sectors of industry where present managerial functions can be transfered entirely to small, self-governing groups of workers.

The writings on the Works Council Plan of the Glacier Metal Company in Britain suggest, on the other hand, that it is possible to reconcile and integrate worker participation in management with independent interest-group representation, leaving intact both the managers and trade unions as separate entities.[16] Peter F. Drucker, who is acutely aware, like Clegg, of democracy's need for a strong independent opposition to any ruling power, adopts a middle position.[17] He would leave with the managers the responsibility for the economic government of the enterprise, with "economic performance its governing rationale," and with the union the responsibility for functioning as the "loyal opposition." But he would

---

[13] Quoted, with strong approval, by Jackson Martindell in *The Scientific Appraisal of Management* (New York: Harper & Row, 1950), p. vii.

[14] Clegg, *op. cit.* Ch. 3, Ch. 17.

[15] *Ibid.*, p. 28.

[16] Elliot Jaques, *The Changing Culture of a Factory* (New York: Holt, Rinehart and Winston, 1952); Wilfred Brown, *Exploration in Management* (London: Heinemann, 1960).

[17] *The New Society: The Anatomy of the Industrial Order* (New York: Harper & Row, 1949), part 8.

turn over to an autonomous plant community of workers and supervisors the responsibility for social affairs.

CONCLUSION

Worker participation in management has been advocated for
various reasons: to improve the efficiency of management by making use of the workers' viewpoint and experience; to give workers
a more creative and satisfying role in their work place; and to
achieve a fuller measure of industrial democracy. These are appeal-
ing reasons and justify strong efforts to implement them. The preceding discussion, however, casts some doubts on the extent to which
the premises underlying them may be generalized.

With the increasing professionalization of management, it becomes clear that even well-trained and properly oriented worker
representatives can contribute, in a positive way, only supplemental
ideas—apart from the personnel area, where they have a higher degree of expertness. The workers' potential for contributing positively
to management efficiency increases the closer one comes to the shop
level, where the workers' experience is most applicable. Through
the role of critic, workers can make a substantial contribution, but
this role is perhaps better played from the outside rather than
within the managerial domain.

A major assumption underlying most proposals for increased
worker participation in management is that workers desire it. A few
sociological and psychological studies lend support to the thesis
that workers enjoy and fulfill their work lives more if they have a
voice in the decisions affecting them.[18] The evidence, however, is
scanty and further research is needed. . . .

The role of worker representative in co-management at higher
levels creates a special sociopsychological situation. Here, the worker
is placed in the dual role of representative of the interests of his
fellow workers and of formulator of enterprise policy which may
not be acceptable to these interests. This psychological situation
may be disturbing rather than satisfying. . . .

I conclude from the Israeli experience, as well as from observations and literature on other countries, that worker participation

[18] See, for example, the writings of Erich Fromm and Georges Friedmann.

in factory management confronts many obstacles when extended beyond issues of a job-related nature, although there are enough exceptions (e.g., Kibbutz industry, German codetermination, the New York garment industry) to discourage any effort to draw a fixed line. To extend worker participation into aspects of management which do not directly or obviously affect job security, income, safety, or work effort, certain conditions seem essential:

1. The warm approval of the managers, so that they will not only support but actively cooperate and even lead.
2. Sufficient understanding and interest on the part of rank-and-file workers as well as their elected leaders.[19]
3. Involvement of workers at the shop level as well as representatives at the enterprise level.
4. Monetary and other incentives to encourage sustained worker interest and effort.

Industrial management has undergone many changes during its century-long history and there is no reason to believe that it will not continue to change. The diversity of forms currently existing in the world and the experimentation which goes on afford ample supporting evidence.

[19] I have not attempted in this paper to analyze the problem of communications, which is an important aspect of worker participation in management. For some detailed observations on the Israeli communication problem, see my article "Plant Labor Relations in Israel," *Industrial and Labor Relations Review* (October, 1963).

III

Managerial Models
in World Perspective

15

The Comparative Approach
to the Study of
Business Administration *

J. BODDEWYN

Q. "How's your wife?"

A. "Compared to what?"

This uncommon answer illustrates the necessity of comparison in human affairs, and represents the essence of a method which is gaining greater acceptance in the study of business administration: the comparative approach.

In other disciplines, the comparative method has been explicitly incorporated in publications, curricula, and research in comparative economics, sociology, psychology, law, education, religion, literature, and so forth. In business administration, however, formal interest in the comparative method is more recent, although books, articles, courses and research projects are fast multiplying—particularly international comparisons of marketing and management systems.[1] This cultural lag may be in part explained by: 1. feelings of

---

* Reprinted with permission from the *Academy of Management Journal* (December, 1965).

1 See, for example, F. H. Harbison and C. A. Myers, *Management in the Industrial World* (New York: McGraw-Hill Book Company, 1959) and other publications of the Inter-University Study of the Labor Problems in Economic Development. In marketing, post-1959 textbooks have included chapters or data on international marketing, and R. Bartels has edited *Comparative Marketing* (Homewood, Ill.: Richard D. Irwin, Inc., 1963).

US superiority in the field of business administration; 2. a fairly widespread disinterest in business history; and 3. the insularity of American business, at least until the postwar period.

Conversely, greater involvement in international affairs has created the need and provided some of the data for comparative studies. Another factor has been the growing interest in developing general or universal theories in the field of business administration —an interest likely to benefit from the use of the comparative approach.

While "Compared *to what?*" is of the essence of the method, it has to be supplemented by the questions of "Compared *as to what* [elements]?," and "Compared *for what* [purposes]?" This paper addresses itself to these questions as well as to the methodology and prospects of the comparative method for research and teaching in business administration—especially in the fields of management and marketing.

COMPARED TO WHAT?

In its scientific form, the comparative approach consists of the systematic detection, identification, classification, measurement, and interpretation of similarities and differences among phenomena.

The locus of the comparison is either in time, space, or among sectors: [2]

1. Temporal (historical) comparisons deal with differences and/or similarities among phenomena removed in time but otherwise

[2] The social anthropologist S. F. Nadel has suggested a somewhat different organization of these elements in the comparative study of societies: "1. We could consider a single society at a given time and analyze the broad variations in particular modes of action or relationships occurring in that society. 2. We could consider several societies of generally similar nature which differ in certain modes of action or relationships; more precisely, we could here compare either different and perhaps contemporaneous societies, or the same society at different periods, if these exhibit some limited cultural changes. 3. We could compare several, perhaps numerous societies of widely different nature yet sharing some identical feature; or different periods, showing radical change, in the life of the same culture." S. F. Nadel, *The Foundations of Social Anthropology* (London: (Cohen & West, Ltd., 1951), p. 226. Ch. 9 of his book contains an excellent section on "The Comparative Method."

identical or similar as far as space and sector are concerned.[3]

2. Spatial (geographical) comparisons focus on differences and/or similarities among phenomena located in spatially removed units (e.g., continents, cultures, nations, regions, cities, and sites) but otherwise identical or similar as far as time or sector are concerned.[4]

3. Sectoral (sub-cultural) comparisons concentrate on differences and/or similarities among segments of a single spatial unit (e.g., a nation) at a single time (or period).[5]

The comparative approach goes beyond uncovering similarities and differences, or establishing what is "universal, related, and unique." [6] It provides interpretations that lead to the establishment of logical relationships between instances and principles, as in all true sciences. It aims at demonstrating the invariable agreement or disagreement between the presence, the absence or the change of a phenomenon and the circumstances where it appears, disappears, or changes.[7]

COMPARED AS TO WHAT?

When comparing, for example, the names of US corporations of various periods of US business history, or British management to

[3] For example, W. Lloyd Warner and J. O. Low have used historical data to compare the Yankee City Shoe Industry at different periods of its history as far as technology, form of division of labor, form of ownership and control, producer-consumer relations, worker relations, and structure of economic relations are concerned. *The Social System of the Factory* (New Haven: Yale University Press, 1947), pp. 54-65.

[4] See, for example, Harbison and Myers' *Management in the Industrial World* where the role of management as an economic resource, a system of authority, and a class is compared in twelve nations.

[5] All sorts of "sectors" can be used for comparative studies: profit versus non-profit enterprises; small versus large business; department stores versus discount houses; staff versus line; superordinate versus subordinates; negro versus white executives; sales versus production, and so on. For example, Norman H. Martin has made a comparative study of the levels of mangement and their mental demands: "Differential Decisions in the Management of an Industrial Plant," *Journal of Business*, XXIX, No. 4 (October, 1956), pp. 249-60. (This article by Martin and an excerpt from the book by Warner and Low are reprinted in W. L. Warner and N. H. Martin (eds.), *Industrial Man* (New York: Harper & Row, 1959), pp. 422ff, pp. 276ff.

[6] C. Kerr *et al.*, *Industrialism and Industrial Man* (New York: Oxford University Press, 1964), p. 10.

[7] Nadel, *op. cit.*, p. 323.

US management, or the financing of small firms to that of large firms, the comparison must focus on some features of the entities compared: What in corporate names, in British and American management, in small and big business financing—or, for that matter, between your wife and someone else's wife—will be compared?

Quite a few things can be compared, depending on one's and other people's interests or needs, the availability of data and other resources, and the state of the art and science in the field. Yet, after allowing for the freedom of the curious, the genius, and the iconoclast, it appears advisable to conduct comparative studies within a theoretical framework in the context of which hypotheses can be tested.[8]

COMPARED FOR WHAT?

Comparisons are for knowledge's sake or for action—whatever may be the relationship between the two in the short or the long run.

For Knowledge

There is afield a significant amount of interest in general and universal theories of management and marketing, although there is also disagreement regarding the remoteness or even the possibility of such theories.[9] In any case, the development of such theories will require many comparisons.

More modest yet closer to the purpose of the comparative method is the desire to sift what is the universal from what is related or unique in various business, management, and marketing systems. Here again numerous comparisons will be required.

---

[8] This author has proposed that comparative analysis focus on actors, processes, structures and functions—their features, interrelationships, changes and/or strains. See J. Boddewyn, "A Construct for Comparative Marketing Research," *Journal of Marketing Research* (May, 1966). Alternative schemes for comparative analysis can be found in the writings of R. Bartels, R. N. Farmer, B. M. Richman, and J. D. Thompson. See also: R. C. Macridis, *The Study of Comparative Government* (New York: Random House, Inc., 1955), pp. 24ff.

[9] R. W. Millman, "Some Unsettled Questions in Organization Theory," *Academy of Management Journal*, VII, No. 3 (September, 1964), pp. 189-95.

Even more basic but certainly essential to the advancement of scientific business administration, is the realization that comparison is inherent in science.[10]

Science aims at uncovering regularities: such patterns can be discovered only by studying as many systems of phenomena as possible in the light of common analytical categories. Although one may well be interested in a unique event—e.g., the business philosophy of Henry Ford—it remains that such a study can only gain perspective by being contrasted explicitly or implicitly to other business philosophies. All analytical sciences thus require the use of the comparative method.

In the social sciences, however, it represents the equivalent of the experimental method in the natural sciences—the experiment being nothing but the comparative method where the cases to be compared are produced to order and under controlled conditions.[11]

For Action

In the planning stage, knowing what has worked when and where, and under what conditions, is eminently useful in identifying and selecting alternative courses of action, although indeed such knowledge does not preclude the innovation of policies and programs.

In the controlling stage, comparison is of the essence—with the past, with others, with plans or norms.

METHODOLOGICAL PROBLEMS

Among many apparent methodological problems, these seem especially worth noting. Obviously, comparison can only be made among comparable phenomena: "The study of co-variations is

[10] The sociologist S. A. Stouffer stresses that: 1. all research is implicitly or explicitly comparative; and 2. research ought to fit into some overall theoretical scheme. "Some Observations on Study Design," *American Journal of Sociology*, LV, No. 4 (January, 1950), pp. 355-61. This article is reprinted in F. A. Shull, Jr. and A. L. Delbecq, eds., *Selected Readings in Management*, Second Series (Homewood, Ill.: Richard D. Irwin, Inc., 1962), pp. 69-77.

[11] T. Parsons, *The Structure of Social Action* (New York: McGraw-Hill Book Company, 1937), p. 743.

bound up . . . with judgments on similarity and partial identity, the very concept of variations implying a sameness of facts which yet permits of some measure of difference." [12] Involved here are problems of 1. the quantity and the quality of the data compared—an important technical problem which promises, however, to subside in the future; and 2. the intrinsic identity or similarity of the phenomena compared—a crucial philosophical problem unlikely ever to wither away. This problem of identity must be handled in one of three ways:

1. By assuming that identity in name is a relevant one, i.e., that the boundaries of phenomena are prescribed by the concepts used in classifying these phenomena, and by the names given to them.[13] In this view, for example, it is quite legitimate to label as "marketing" certain types of behavior in primitive societies and compare them with what is similarly named "marketing" in the US. Naturally, it is important here to guard against the twin pitfalls of assuming too much under a single name such as "marketing," [14] and using ready-made classifications such as "capitalistic" and "socialistic" which straitjacket comparisons.[15]

2. By clarifying the contents and the context of the entities compared. Comparative analysis—like any other type of analysis—requires that the phenomena compared be abstracted from what in practically all cases is a complex reality. Ultimately, everything hangs together; yet, for research or teaching purposes, it is usually necessary to concentrate on some aspect of the universe studied.

[12] Nadel, *op. cit.*, p. 225. He equates the comparative method with the study of "concomitant variations" (or co-variations, for short), i.e., the study of the related presence, absence or change of two or more phenomena (p. 229). Nadel defines it also as "the analysis of social situations which are at first sight already comparable, that is, which appear to share certain features (modes of actions, relationships) while differing in others, or to share their common features with some degree of difference" (pp. 222, 225).

[13] *Ibid.*, p. 225.

[14] Karl Polanyi has challenged the application of terms such as "marketing" or "economic behavior" to older and non-Western societies. *The Great Transformation* (Boston: Beacon Press, 1957).

[15] Comparative economics has particularly suffered from such straitjacketing. One is reminded here of the cautious distinction allegedly made by a Polish intellectual: "Capitalism consists of the exploitation of man by man, while communism is *vice-versa.*"

Such loss of concreteness is largely unavoidable in scientific inquiry. It can be partially compensated by the careful delineation of the scope of the comparative study, and by judicious use of definitions and assumptions.

3. By subsuming what may appear at first as "apples and pears" under some higher classificatory category such as "trade" or "exchange" (in the case of marketing), or "decision-making" (in the case of management). Yet, in so doing, one must guard against the pitfall of tautology, whereby the universality of a phenomenon is implicit in its broad definition.

In the search for similarities and differences, one must assume that phenomena are not random although recognizing that there is usually some variability of behavior which falls within the normal curve of distribution:

> The method of co-variations implies the general postulate that social situations are not made up of random items, but of facts which hang together by some meaningful nexus or intrinsic fitness.[16]

The comparative approach is also opposed to viewing events as unique.[17] Instead, it views the "unique" as a residue left over after similarities and differences have been established and explained. Thus, the comparative method differs from the historical approach which—while often covering some span of time—focuses on the development of some unique event rather than on its explicit comparison with other events.

Comparison goes beyond the juxtaposition or the parallel description of phenomena which are potentially comparable.[18] While

[16] Nadel, *op. cit.*, pp. 224, 226.

[17] "Uniqueness and understanding simply do not go together; nor do infinite variety and explanation. The rejection of 'types,' 'laws,' or uniformities in general, is tantamount to rejecting all that science stands for. Such an approach leads, at best, to a preliminary survey, and at worst, to some 'general picture' based on nothing firmer than the impressions of the observer." Nadel, *Ibid.*, p. 393. "Science (as distinguished from history or biography) is not concerned with the particular, the unique, but only with the general, with kinds, with events which recur. . . .": A. R. Radcliffe-Brown, *Structure and Function in Primitive Society* (London: Cohen & West, 1952), pp. 190ff.

[18] Although the design of its editor was different, the contents of R. Bartels' *Comparative Marketing* (Homewood, Ill.: Richard D. Irwin, Inc., 1963) is better represented by its subtitle *Wholesaling in Fifteen Countries*.

more descriptive studies of the anatomy, morphology, taxonomy, and ecology of various business, marketing, and management systems are needed, it is well to recognize that such studies are not comparative studies. The latter require some explicit contrast and explanation, whether done throughout the body of the study or in its concluding section.

The range of the comparisons made, i.e., the types, number, or length of the times, spaces, or sectors compared, is a function of the level at which comparison is meaningful and possible. Phenomena may be comparable yet yield only minor comparisons not offering an adequate range of variations; or data may be available at one level (world, culture, nation, economy, industry, firm, department, individual) but not at another. The range also depends on the level and the comprehensiveness of the theories available.

The comparative approach must be distinguished from the normative approach where the comparison is made to some norm, ideal, or expectation. Thus, studies where the business system of a particular country at some particular time—typically, the modern US business system—is used explicitly or implicitly as an ideal reference point, are really more normative than comparative.

Comparing phenomena in different spatial and temporal environments requires more holistic and interdisciplinary studies as many more things have to be considered and interpreted in such "foreign" environments. This is in contrast to typical studies of business administration in our contemporary environment which—because it is familiar—is usually assumed away as given.

PROSPECTS FOR RESEARCH AND TEACHING

The comparative approach is not completely foreign to the study and teaching of business administration. There are already quite a few courses, books (or chapters thereof), articles, monographs, and dissertations that incorporate its use. However, although a bibliography of publications on the comparative study of business administration is not yet available,[19] it appears safe to say that:

[19] This author is presently preparing an annotated bibliography on comparative business, management, and marketing systems.

1. these studies are still too few; and 2. they seldom fit into a comprehensive framework of analysis.[20] As such, there is obviously room for more research in the field.

On the one hand, it appears desirable at this point to have some suitable body of scholars organize committees, conferences, or workshops to map out the field by 1. establishing some priorities (What countries? What periods? What sectors? What problems? How, and with what resources?); and 2. suggesting suitable conceptual schemes of analysis.[21]

Meanwhile, there is need for more systematic descriptions of "foreign" (time, place, sector) units according to some classificatory schemes, as a prelude to more and better comparative studies in business administration.

Yet, the lack of data should not prevent research at the conceptual, technique development, hypothesis-making stages since such research suggests the type of data needed—new, better, sustained.[22] Also, more research should be designed to include hypotheses to be tested through "foreign" units.

In teaching, it should be made apparent that the comparative study of business administration does not have to be considered as a separate branch of knowledge but as a point of view, a way of approaching any significant problem. As such, it can be incorporated into any course which can at least implicitly be made com-

[20] As mentioned earlier, a notable exception is represented by some of the books prepared under the auspices of the Inter-University Study of the Labor Problems in Economic Development—notably Harbison and Myers' *Management in the Industrial World*. More recently, one may note R. N. Farmer and B. M. Richman, *Comparative Management and Economic Progress* (Homewood, Ill.: Richard D. Irwin, Inc., 1965). See also J. D. Thompson *et al., Comparative Studies in Administration* (Pittsburgh, Pa.: University of Pittsburgh Press, 1959).

[21] Special conferences and committees dealing with problems presented by the comparative method in the field of political science were organized by the Social Research Council in 1953-1954, and by the International Political Science Association in 1954 (Macridis, *op. cit.,* p. ix). Two conferences to exchange views on the direction and organization of research in comparative economic growth and structure were held by the National Bureau of Economic Research in 1958 (NBER, *The Comparative Study of Economic Growth and Structure,* 1959). A standing committee on comparative marketing was appointed by the American Marketing Association in 1959 (Bartels, *op. cit.,* p. v).

[22] NBER, p. 178.

parative through the inclusion of foreign data.[23] Some schools may want special comparative courses; others may prefer to integrate comparative findings into existing advanced theory courses; all can include comparisons in the contents of basic introductory courses once suitable publications have become more readily available.

[23] The NBER study suggested the massive infusion of foreign data in standard economics courses (NBER, p. 178).

16

International Management *

NARENDRA SETHI

As the horizontal expansion of the managerial system begins to transcend the subsystems of nationalism, cultural groupism, and industrial community, the resultant focus will begin to mark an *internationalization* of the managerial structure, both in terms of organizational constants as well as in terms of human values. The trend is quite noticeable at the present time both in the conceptual field of management literature and in the operational field of management practice. The *global concept* of management which some marketing generalists seem to propound, and the *universalist* view of business system which is being developed by management scholars seem to converge in the synthesis which international management offers. As a matter of fact, one might be tempted to consider this internationalization as the intrapersonal and intra-organizational growth carried to a nongeographical apex.

Our frame of reference in this study is primarily an interdisciplinary one whereby one may hypothesize about the present constituents and the future indications of this international managerial system. It appears logical to interpret this model of emergent extranational system of administrative theory as one of both industrial and sociological import. An effort has been made in this paper to
1. analyze the values comprising the totality of this internationalization in terms applicable both to the individual of a single cultural

* Reprinted with permission from the *Seton Hall Journal of Business* (May, 1964).

affinity and to the organization cutting across these self-imposed cultural boundaries; 2. describe the actual operational criterion for the effectiveness of this system, in terms of ecological, socioeconomic, institutional, and technological components; 3. interpret the broad essential themes of international management relative to industrial development concept, and 4. conceptualize the significant patterns of futurity in the development and fulfillment of this energy-based system of managerial growth. A few hypotheses in each of these areas of enquiry have been suggested.

THE VALUE-STRUCTURE

Writers like Harlan Cleveland and G. J. Mangone, Fayerweather, Harbison and Myers, Niles and Sethi have on occasions described the basic constituents of international business. They have also at times ventured to understand the desirable values and characteristics of the business executives engaged in foreign business activities. It appears, however, that the connotation of international business or foreign business as understood by a majority of writers is somewhat different than the one held by this writer. It is also felt that relatively little scholarly attention has yet been paid towards measuring the value-analysis of international management. For example, Cleveland and Mangone are more interested in *overseamanship* rather than in a nongeographical concept of international management. Fayerweather appears to place a heavy emphasis upon the marketing strategies in international business. And, finally, Harbison and Myers seem to prefer a focus upon the geographical and national components of global business. In this way, it appears that, so far, international management has not been treated in a way different from geographical or national trade-centered classifications.

Judged in a value-centered perception, international management refers more to a set of extensive concepts of administration which cut across frontiers of self-imposed social and political units. For our purposes, geographical subdivisions are not necessarily essential in this interpretation. In other words, in the present frame of reference, one can well visualize a system of international management without actually crossing national boundaries or regions.

The fact that we do see different geographical units mentioned in an analysis of international management is incidental but not essential.

Value 1. International management is a concept of universal power-reflex.

Value 2. It addresses itself to the task of energy-release in a broad scope.

Value 3. Since its nucleus is a cultural subsystem of administration, it moves along the horizontal path of anthropological-structure and the vertical path of liberal enterprise-structure.

Value 4. Basically, international management transcends the physical subsystems of authority which one finds in almost all cultural systems, and begins to create its own authority-process.

Value 5. Considering the dichotomy of formality and informality of the organizational behavior, international management moves nearer to being more informal in substance and formal in character.

Value 6. Integration between communal acceptance and societal acceptance is easier to achieve in international management than otherwise.

Value 7. Barriers to communication and information flow often play a more subdued role in this perspective than they otherwise might do.

These seven-odd values which have been stressed here point towards two significant issues. These are:

1. An individual in an international organization identifies himself not with any one subsystem of power and energy, but with all the subsystems therein. This in turn leads to a greater mobilization of its resources.

2. Correspondingly, the organization too experiences a multidimensional sequence of growth: along different loci and different patterns. This in turn leads to a greater energization of its resources.

Judged in this way, the value-structure of international management becomes one of a concrete movement: that is, both the dy-

namics of time-distance, and the dynamics of personality-distance.
The constants to be enumerated in this pattern are the following:

1. The cultural delimitations and their release.
2. The universalization of conceptual administration.
3. The pattern of mutuality and conformity—though in a sur-
   charged environment.

The variables are to be enumerated as follows:

1. The element of time dimension: the genesis of international
   management may have been in the present, while its extension
   may either have been in the past or will be in the future.
2. The element of cross-cultural dimension: the constituents of
   international management will vary in proportion to their basic
   allegiances and original attitudes.
3. The element of institutional power dimension: the functional
   power of institutions comprising international management will
   vary greatly.

THE OPERATIONAL SYSTEM

Writers like Agarwala and Singh, Barlow, Galbraith, Islam,
and Ward have on occasions discussed the active operational criterion for international business practices. But it seems that there
has been relatively little attention paid to the mechanism of international management from its direct functional and growth-centered
role. To most of these writers, international management appears
to be synonymous with industrial development. This identification
of these two significant terms does not appear to be realistic. For
example, Agarwala and Singh overly emphasize the role of industrialization in the context of underdevelopment. Bryce seems to
identify economic growth with industrial development and actually
suggests some guidelines for better internationalization of this concept. Barlow tends to prefer a financial and tax-based perspective
in this context—thereby overly "money-mending" the concept of
international management. Galbraith, in his recent book on economic development, does offer to weigh down the dichotomy of developed and underdeveloped countries, but fails to suggest an ac-

tive operational philosophy for the emergent growth. Islam, a Pakistani author, establishes an overly enthusiastic and optimistic correlation between capital accumulation and the international management movement. Last, but not least, Barbara Ward, an eminent writer on political economy, prefers to use the often-repeated cliché of "the rich nations and the poor nations," and, in doing so, she carries this geographical-cum-financial myth of international management further. In this way one finds very few reassuring classificational models in the available literature.

Perhaps one growth-centered approach toward developing a functional model of operational international management might be one of the following components:

1. The ecological system
2. The socioeconomic system
3. The institutional system
4. The technological system

The Ecological System

International management, inasmuch as it conceptualizes the broad extensions of individuals along varying patterns, remains in entirely an ecological complex. This means the integration of various communities, groups, and behavioral patterns in the identity of international management. One might think that this ecological system is identical with a geographical totality (which we have rejected throughout). As a matter of fact, when one refers to the ecological groupism in international management, one is not referring to the patterns set up by national boundaries but to the community of various interest-groups. In this analysis, the concept of ecological subsystems in international management refers to the different levels of industrial enterprises and communities therein.

Further, an executive performing in this environment will become a member of several communities at the same time. How will this modify his complex judgment and behavior? And, how then will he qualify as a decision-maker in such a cross-communal setting? These questions cannot be answered before elaborating the issue of the origin, the growth, and the sustainment of the ecological systems.

Value 1. It appears a logical phenomenon that the groupism of international management is related to the degree of communal mobility.

Value 2. Movements within these environmental units will be related to the degree of ecological acceptance within an individual rather than within his original political unit.

Value 3. In the final analysis, finite ecological units will disappear giving place to a sharply dynamic system of intra-ecological development in international management.

The Socioeconomic System

Because of its eclectic and integrated nature, international management lends itself rather well to socioeconomic analysis. In the present reference, this socioeconomic system refers more to the blending of societal and economic manifestations of the business enterprise in an international setting than to a naive interpretation of the social or economic needs of the people involved. It appears that in the need-centered function, the cultural needs occupy a greater position that the limited rationale of socioeconomic needs. However, this socioeconomic system can be looked at from the following perceptive approaches:

1. As an entrepreneurial complex
2. As a developmental complex
3. As an organizational complex

The first approach refers to the creative and pioneering urge of the individuals motivated to cut across cultural lines to establish a new subsystem of societal and economic gains; the second primarily addresses itself to the theory of a centralized planning procedure which in turn seeks to accomplish the industrial development of the society through economic resources; and finally, the third refers to the processes of coordination which may integrate the other two functions for the greater release of energy in the society.

Value 1. International management addresses itself to the welfare of the society: both in terms of societal gain and individual gain. This it does without regard to the primary source of its growth.

Value 2. In this inference, it is the secondary movement from the original society to an adopted society that may distintinguish the salient features of this socioeconomic subsystem in international management.

The Institutional System

In a historical perspective, it can be argued that international management is constantly moving in the direction of rigid and formal institutionalization. As referred to above, various international and intercultural agencies and associations are taking participative measures to achieve such an institutionalization. Perhaps an institution of this kind and magnitude might be treated in a way different than a normal type of institution. As a matter of fact, the foundations of the international management institution are being laid on negative, indirect, and often wrong premises. Some of these can be enumerated here as follows:

1. The degree of class consciousness evident in belonging to more cultural, societal, and economic subsystems than one.
2. The relative attraction for ego involvement, self-adventure, and personality exploration evident in the overly emphasized geographical divisions therein.
3. The identification of governmental approval with international business undertakings and consequent status-extension.
4. The nonregulatory conditions prevalent in the existing ventures of some kinds and their general universalization and subsequent disruption of the administrative flow.

Fundamentally, this writer does not seek to play down the institutionalization of international management, but he does very convincingly and positively wish to point out the follies of the above-mentioned premises and notions on which such institution is being built. With the passage of time and the relative ease of international process, perhaps the earlier hypotheses of this institution might break, but the negativistic view that they might have introduced and integrated in the organism by then would be a very difficult barrier to its future development. Therefore, such an institutionalization should be preceded by the following subsystems and approaches. The list enumerated here is by no means an exhaustive one; it is only a suggestive one. It is as follows:

Value 1. The institutionalization of the international concept of management should not be considered as a distinct entity from any other institutions of professional management.

Value 2. The "symptoms" of institutionalization in international management should include at least an awareness of the broad integrative power of cultural frontiers and an equal degree of the legitimacy of informal interrelationships evident in the functioning of this managerial operation.

Value 3. The present emphasis upon the institutionalization must not be identified with any obvious class symbols and status pointers because these in turn have a tendency to thwart the operational development of international management.

The Technological System

Used in the present structure of our analysis, the technological subsystem of international management refers to the developing features of industrial consciousness, bureaucratic awareness, and the resultant focus upon the automatization (as distinct from automated) of the production-cum-distribution mechanism. In many developing regions around the world, the need for such technological transfer is quite obvious, perhaps sometimes it is a bit too immature as well. However, international management, because of the extensive changes and modifications that it introduces both in the 1. structural and the 2. organizational behavior of the business enterprise, unconsciously begins to identify itself with a technological compendium of values.

The interrelation between the "human" and the "technical" components of international management are evident in these technological features. We can enumerate the more salient of these features as follows:

1. The momentum of optimum work-energy.
2. The strengthening of productive-use complex.

3. The relative ease of movement from one value-mix to another.
4. The incorporation of "futurity" in basic operations and decisions.
5. The emphasis upon the changing "norms" of factory culture, in relation to the indigenous and the imported norms.

It appears that the technological subsystem of international management has a tendency to shine out from the other subsystems mentioned above and to occupy a relatively more distinguished place. The reason for such misdirected emphasis is within the human orientation and attraction towards the more tangible, and outer visible symptoms of managerial extension. Therefore, while admitting the necessity and the functional role of the technological variables, an attempt is made to modify its content-analysis more in terms of nontechnical and dynamics-oriented judgment.

Value 1. International management does not refer to the movement or the unilateral transfer of one technology to another, nor does it refer to the application of one in a different environment.

Value 2. A more stimulating approach will be to see the technological movement within the international managerial perspective as one referring to the ease and harmony of movement from one cultural system to another. The ease of transfer between the two is emphatically the more significant point of them.

Patterns of Futurity

We have outlined the broad essential themes of the actual operational criterion of international management in terms of the ecological, the socioeconomic, the institutional, and the technological subsystems present therein. We had also indicated earlier about the incorporation of the new discplines and new dimensions in the identity of international management. Writers like Van Wagenen, Rostow, Rottenburg, Lerche, Lassalle, and Hickman have tried to visualize the future trends in the international business scene. But with few exceptions, their primary frame of reference is governed by an overly enthusiastic motivation towards *technological* future. For example, Hickman seems to postulate the expansion of "technology and culture of the Western world . . . upon all the lands and peoples of the earth." Lerche opines that the impact of unifying technology will result in making the world "a truly technological unit." Rottenburg builds his entire thesis on the fact that the "United States business firms promote technological progress." Rostow shifts the major emphasis but still seeks to suggest a geographical expansion of the futurity in international management. Lassalle is content with only a generalized survey of the concept of public relations in this scene without dwelling on any other future trends. And, finally, Van Wagenen discusses the recent research findings and hypotheses in the area but seems to confine his analysis to a political and agency-oriented approach.

Therefore, existing literature does not seem to provide us with any comprehensive treatment of the future indications of international management in a nontechnological context. Since simulated research cannot yield effective results in this reference, we can only hypothesize about the general future trends that we visualize, in overall harmony and confluence with our earlier assumptions. Some of these are as follows:

1. International management, in the future years ahead, will move away from a geographical-distance equation and will move towards a cultural-distance sequence.
2. The future years may also witness the development of a "global" view of the managerial process which in turn may lead us to revise the present thinking about individual and organizational relations.
3. It seems that the international management movement will emphasize more and more the indigenous character of the community-centered management operation rather than the imported and borrowed version thereof.
4. Greater focus will be put on the concept of "factory culture" in the growing international management field.
5. The process of conceptual administration will experience a universalization of its components thereby rendering it more powerful and effective.
6. Perhaps, international management, moving as it will do in a nongeographical context, may well be instrumental in establishing the oft cherished but seldom achieved "unity" of a single world.

7. Finally, international management will afford a better setting for the integration of liberal enterprise characterization and manpower energization than any other system of administrative management.

CONCLUSION

International management is fast becoming a positive tool of international relations and adjustment. But that is not its only objective. It must strive for the establishment and development of an integrated system of international community which in turn will result in an inspired synthesis of universal power, functional control, and sociological values. Judged in this way, international management can add newer dimensions of visionary truth and liberal process to the known frontiers of administrative theory.

17

A Model for Research in Comparative Management *

RICHARD FARMER
BARRY RICHMAN

Comparative management deals with problems of management and managerial efficiency in various countries. In exploring management theory to determine what tools and techniques can be utilized in this comparative area, it becomes clear that the existing management theory has some serious drawbacks in terms of its orientation and applicability to different types of cultures and economies. Traditional management theory usually deals with productive enterprises operating in a single environment. Management has been defined in one major work as "the accomplishment of desired objectives by establishing an environment favorable to performance by people operating in organized groups." [1] In this approach, the managerial functions of planning, staffing, direction, organizing, and control within the firm are analyzed. The firm attempts to operate as efficiently as possible in its environment, in the sense of trying to achieve its goals with the minimum use of resources.

---

* Reprinted from the *California Management Review*, Vol. VII, No. 2 (Winter, 1964). Copyright 1964 by The Regents of the University of California.
[1] Harold Koontz and Cyril O'Donnell, *Principles of Management*, 3rd ed. (New York: McGraw-Hill Book Company, 1964), p. 1.

Explorations of the management theory jungle [2] reveal that virtually all theories approach the problem of management as an internal problem within a productive enterprise. External factors, if considered at all, are assumed to be constant in most formulations. Hence, the universalists focus attention on functions and principles of internal management in a given firm in a given environment, seeking to determine how a firm might gain more effective and efficient operations. The various human relations and behavioralist theories of management focus on the persons in a given firm in a stated environment, again trying to determine how the firm might operate better. In a similar manner, the decision theorists, the students of bureaucracy, and social systems theorists, with few exceptions, view the firm as fixed in space and time.

This type of analysis certainly helps an individual firm achieve higher levels of efficiency. No organization is perfect, and close study of its major functions and personnel will usually yield insights into its operations which will increase efficiency. However, this analysis does not attempt to consider the problem of relative efficiencies between firms in different environments. If, for example, an efficient manager of a ball-bearing plant in Pennsylvania were placed in charge of a similar operation in Mexico City, he would initially be less efficient than he was in his American job. The man has not changed, but the environment has. The question of relative managerial efficiency and differences in managerial activity between cultures is the problem to be considered here.

It may also be true that managerial efficiencies may vary between industrial sectors in the same country. Thus railroads may be managed less efficiently than steel companies in a single country. Present management theories can perhaps point to ways of improving in both sectors, but they fail to explain why the two industries have different levels of efficiency.

PRESENT THEORY INADEQUATE

In effect, most studies of management have taken place within a "black box" labeled *management,* without much concern for the

2 The various modern management schools are examined in Harold Koontz, ed., *Toward A Unified Theory of Management* (New York: McGraw-Hill Book Company, 1964).

external environment in which the firm may operate. As long as this external environment is about the same for all firms, the approach is valid; however, in cases where the environment differs significantly, present theory is inadequate to explain comparative differentials in efficiency. Where environments do vary, as is the case between nations, it is necessary to examine the external pressures, or constraints, upon internal management.

The hypothesis presented here is that in cases where comparative situations are considered, existing management theory in effect assumes the absence of many of the crucial variables. As a result, it is rather inadequate to use as a research tool in the area of comparative management. Our purpose is to develop a new conceptual framework for such studies which hopefully will prove more useful in the analysis of critical comparative management problems.

EFFICIENCY AND OBJECTIVE

General Economic Goals

As a beginning for comparative analysis, it is useful to consider the question of what general economic goals most societies have. Management of productive enterprise does not take place in a vacuum: it may be defined as the coordination of human effort and material resources toward the achievement of organizational objectives. The organizational objectives ultimately reflect the desires of people for useful goods and services.

The basic assumption here is that virtually all countries want more goods and services and prefer higher level of per capita income to less. Or they may prefer the same per capita income they now have, produced with less inputs, in order to enjoy more leisure. In either case, the manager's problem is to become steadily more efficient over time.

Increasing productive efficiency has generally been considered a desirable goal for enterprise managers in most societies. In capitalist countries, improved efficiency means higher profits and greater rewards for firm owners and managers; in Marxist countries the planners stress firm efficiency so that the country can produce more goods and services with the same inputs. Since a country's total production will be the sum of production of component productive enterprises, the more efficient [3] each firm is, the more efficient the country will be.

National efficiency here can be considered conceptually as an engineering notion, namely:

$$E = Q/I$$

where E is efficiency, Q is output, and I is input. In economic terms, inputs consist of land, labor, capital, and management. Outputs are useful and desirable goods and services.

Measuring outputs and inputs with the elastic yardstick of money will not indicate real efficiency in any economy. Just as the inputs necessarily must consist of actual labor hours, real capital in the form of machines, plant, and so on, outputs must consist of real goods and services. The physical efficiency of a country will be measured by comparing real inputs and real outputs. Identifying and quantifying outputs and inputs is difficult, since different kinds of things must be added to determine what efficiency is.

However, there is a measure which can be used as a rough guide to managerial effectiveness in a given economy as compared to other economies. Comparisons of gross national product per capita between countries can be used.[4] It would be useful also to include a weighted value of the rate of growth in GNP per year over the past decade in making comparisons, since it is possible that a country will be interested in less income now in order to achieve more later. In part, the portion of GNP invested determines how big it will be in the future, but preparations for the future may not

[3] The problems of defining enterprise efficiency are great, given the difficulty of measuring varigated inputs and outputs. See Herbert A. Simon, *Administrative Behavior*, 2nd ed. (New York: The Macmillan Company, 1961), pp. 172-197, for a detailed discussion of this crucial point. It is important to point out that the concept of productive efficiency warrants an entire chapter in our book. In this chapter models of both firm and economic system efficiency having universal application will be presented.

[4] For a discussion of the concept of gross national product see Paul A. Samuelson, *Economics*, 5th ed. (New York: McGraw-Hill Book Company, 1961), pp. 212-237. As with many other aggregate concepts dealt with here, measurement of this item is much more difficult than the basic concept.

appear in national income accounts. Note, however, that a country could have a high rate of investment and still not get much growth if the investment were badly directed—which in effect would be saying that management effectiveness is low.

EXPENDED OUTPUT

This type of comparison of GNP, growth, and managerial effectiveness begs the question of whether or not a country or culture in fact wants to become more efficient. The implicit value judgment here is that such efficiency gains are desired badly enough so that a culture, given probable trade-offs to get more efficiency, will opt for more efficiency. But if a culture decides not to obtain growth, the entire analysis collapses. In such a case a country could be perfectly managed in the direction of no growth, orienting its energies to other, possibly more esthetic values.

Our argument here is based on evidence from dozens of countries which suggests the contrary.[5] Poorer countries are striving mightily to expand outputs, and development economics, almost unknown twenty years ago, is a thriving branch of general economic analysis. Governments uninterested in development have been overthrown, to be replaced by those who are. International commissions, agencies and bureaucracies have been organized to deal mainly with rapid economic progress. Wealthy countries worry about their rates of growth, while poorer ones steadily push for improvements in this sector. There are few countries in the world that fail to at least give lip service to the idea of development, and many countries, rich and poor, set national plans of achievement for the next five, seven, or ten years, always with some large per capita income growth indicated. There is overwhelming evidence to indicate that economic efficiency and improvement are desired; this is at least a good working beginning for analysis.[6]

[5] The authors have worked, lived, and studied in Canada, the United States, Mexico, the USSR, Poland, Czechoslovakia, Lebanon, Kuwait, Saudi Arabia, Egypt, and the United Kingdom. Experiences in these and other countries studied have served as a basis for much of the analysis presented.

[6] See Robert L. Heilbroner, *The Great Ascent* (New York: Harper & Row, 1963), pp. 75-88, for a further discussion of this point.

MANAGERIAL FUNCTIONS

The Concept of Managerial Effectiveness

All productive enterprise managers perform the same general managerial functions: planning and decision-making, control, organizing, staffing, and direction. This is as true for a large steel company in the United States as it is for a small candy factory in Moscow. The act of managing cannot be performed without engaging in these functions. Hopefully, managers are motivated to perform these functions as efficiently as possible, but as noted above, the measurement of efficiency in a complex economic situation is quite difficult. Thus it is useful to consider the problem as one of determining managerial effectiveness. This may be defined as the degree of efficiency with which managers of productive enterprises achieve their stated (or given) goals. Subjectively, at least, one can evaluate given enterprises in terms of how well they seem to perform. In the aggregate, for all productive enterprises in the economy, the rough measure of this managerial effectiveness is GNP per capita plus growth over fairly long periods. A specific act of a manager may not be quantifiable, but results for the whole economic system are.

To get at the question of why management is effective or not, it is useful to consider the relative importance of management in any economic system. Management is the active factor in such a system. A country can have endless resources of all sorts but, unless management is applied to these factors, the production of the system will be close to zero. Moreover, the better the management, the greater output will be. Managerial effectiveness is the critical factor in the economic system.

The basic hypothesis here is that managerial effectiveness determines productive efficiency, or:

$$E = f(X)$$

where E is productive efficiency, and X is managerial effectiveness. If managerial effectiveness can be determined, we should be able to say something about the efficiency with which a country converts its inputs into outputs. If efficiency can be measured by a GNP rate-of-growth index, managerial effectiveness should also correlate closely with this index.

External Constraints on Management

In making comparisons of management efficiency between countries with widely different social and cultural environment, difficulties can soon arise when traditional types of analysis are applied. We observe two managements in the same sector, and we note that in country A, managers seem far superior to their counterparts in country B. However, we cannot then state categorically that managers in A do their internal managing job better that those in B, since the nature of the external environment facing the two managements may be completely different. A may be a country with ample supplies of highly skilled labor, while B may have serious shortages of this important factor. A may also have a good low-cost transportation system, while B is faced with transport shortages, high-cost freight movements, and the need to build far larger inventories than in A. A may have an excellent credit system, which allows a competent firm to obtain adequate funds, while B may have no organized capital markets. The result could well be that the presumably inept managers in B are actually doing better than their counterparts in A, given their external constraints.

In such a case it is fruitless to argue that the firm in country B should improve its internal management. This is clearly possible in most cases, but the gains from urging changes in external constraints might prove much larger. The point here is that comparisons between internal managements in different cultures may prove useless unless the external environment is also studied carefully.

This external environment may be termed the *macromanagerial structure*. It consists of the crucial external factors which directly influence the activities and effectiveness of firm management. The external constraints act on managers to inhibit or aid their effectiveness. These external constraints may generally be grouped into the following sectors: economic, legal-political, sociological, and educational. Since managerial effectiveness depends on, or is influenced by, external constraints, we have:

$$X = f(C_1, C_2, \ldots . C_n)$$

where the C's are the various relevant external constraints.

A second critical point is that many of the external constraints are interrelated. Hence, a culture's view toward managers may well be closely connected with educational achievements, or the efficiency of the commercial banking system may depend at least in part on formulations of business law. The result is an extremely complex set of interrelationships which determine in large part how efficiently a country performs economically.

RANKING CONSTRAINTS

In an attempt to measure the importance of external constraints on internal managerial effectiveness, the approach here will be to give each major external constraint a numerical value suggesting its relative importance. For any given country, it is then possible to give values to these constraints on managerial effectiveness. The scores given will be based on a subjective evaluation of how the constraint affects management—the higher the score, the more helpful the constraint is in making internal management more effective. Hence, if the American central banking system is given a score of 100, a German might have a value of 90, and the Saudi Arabian a value of 10.

Clearly, such numerical evaluations are incapable of being refined values of the impact on such constraints. In effect, what is being done is to rank the effectiveness of each constraint between nations. Any observer making the rankings could, with some logic, give somewhat different evaluations of the impact on management of key constraints. The purpose of giving a numerical ranking, however, is to focus on the best available subjective evaluation of a given constraint. Most persons who are familiar with central banking problems would probably rank the three countries above in the same order, although they would give different numerical values to the constraints. But mere ranking fails to indicate that, if a country is really deficient in some respects, it is not just below a second country, but far below it.

If the constraints are really relevant in determining managerial effectiveness, the scores of the various countries rated would indicate the relative managerial effectiveness in the economy. The score would indicate the relative efficiency of the given economy as well —although this could also be obtained by comparing per capita GNP plus its rate of growth. The evaluation of the external constraints has the additional value, however, of focusing on the reasons *why* a country has poor management. The lower scores on selected constraints point to where the corrections needed in improvements in efficiency are to be made. Countries may have similarly low per capita GNP figures for quite different reasons, while, conversely, countries may be relatively wealthy for different reasons. This technique also allows for the evaluation of different economies in terms of specific factors which tend to influence managerial effectiveness. If a given country is strong in central banking and monetary policy, it will prove less important to devote time and skilled manpower to corrections here than in areas where more serious problems exist.

RELATIVE EFFICIENCY

The External Restraints

The list below shows the relevant external constraints affecting managerial effectiveness and their assigned weights. If a given country were perfectly organized from the standpoint of efficient management, it would be rated 500 on the suggested constraint scale. No country could presently receive a perfect score, because no country is perfectly efficient in its management. Note also that as long as there is any technical progress in the natural or social sciences, some improvements in managerial effectiveness over time could be expected. Deterioration could also occur if negative changes occurred in the constraints.

IDENTIFYING CONSTRAINTS

The method of constraint identification was to consider the various pressures in a country which could be seen to have some effect on internal management. There is a danger that this technique will lead to discussions of everything in the world. The variables mentioned are obviously very complex, and detailed study of even a few could take a lifetime. However, if only the portion of the constraint directly influencing management is considered, the task becomes somewhat simpler. Hence, we are not interested in all of law and legal theory but only the portions of law which bear directly on management. Similarly, our concern with education does not include all of pedagogy but only the portion which concerns managerial effectiveness. By focusing our attention in this way, it may be possible to gain some insight into how such constraints actually do affect internal managerial effectiveness.

External Managerial Constraints and Suggested Weights

I. *Educational Characteristics* (100)

C1.1: *Literacy level.* The percentage of the total population who can read and write, and the average years of schooling of adults. (50)

C1.2: *Higher education.* The percentage of the total population with post high school education, plus the quality of such education. Numbers and quality of colleges and universities in the country. The types of persons obtaining higher education. (20)

C1.3: *Specialized technical training.* Types and quality of technical trainings, including apprenticeship programs, engineering training, technical institutes, company training programs, and vocational high school training. The type, quantity, and quality of persons taking such training. (10)

C1.4: *Attitude toward education.* The general cultural attitude toward extensive education, in terms of its presumed desirability. (10)

C1.5: *Educational match with requirements.* Whether or not the type of training available in a culture fits the needs of productive enterprise on all levels of skill and achievement. (10)

II. *Sociological Characteristics* (100)

C2.1: *View of managers as an elite group.* The general social attitude toward managers of all sorts. (10)

C2.2: *View of scientific method.* The general social attitude toward the use of rational, predictive techniques in solving various types of social, business, technical, and economic problems. (40)

C2.3: *View of wealth.* Whether or not the acquisition of wealth is considered socially desirable. (10)

C2.4: *View of rational risk-taking.* Whether or not taking of various types of personal, corporation, or national risks is considered acceptable, as well as the general view toward specific types of economic and productive risks. (10)

C2.5: *View of achievement.* The general attitude toward personal achievement in the culture. (20)

C2.6: *Class flexibility.* The possibilities of social class mobility, both upward and downward, in the culture, and the means by which it can be achieved. (10)

III. *Political and Legal Characteristics* (100)

C3.1: *Relevant legal rules of the game.* Quality, efficiency, and effectiveness of the legal structure in terms of general business law, labor law, and general law relevant to business. Degree of enforcement, reliability, etc. (30)

C3.2: *Defense policy.* Impact of defense policy on productive enterprise in terms of trading with potential enemies, purchasing policies, strategic industry development, labor competition, and similar factors. (10)

C3.3: *Foreign policy.* Impact of policy on productive enterprise in terms of trading restrictions, quotas, tariffs, customs unions, etc. (20)

C3.4: *Political stability.* Influence on productive enterprises of revolutions, changes in regime, stability or instability over protracted periods, etc. (20)

C3.5: *Political organization.* Type of organization in constitutional terms, degree of centralization or decentralization, pressure groups and their effectiveness, political parties, and their philosophies, etc. (20)

C3.6: *Flexibility of law and legal changes.* Degrees to which relevant barriers to efficient management can be changed, certainty of legal actions, etc. (10)

IV. *Economic Characteristics* (200)

C4.1: *General economic framework.* Including such factors as the overall economic organization of the society (i.e., capitalistic, Marxist, mixed), property rights, and similar factors. (50)

C4.2: *Central banking system.* The organization and operations of the central banking system, including the controls over commercial banks, the ability and willingness to control the money supply, the effectiveness of legal policies regarding price stability, commercial bank reserves, discounting, credit controls, and similar factors. (20)

C4.3: *Economic stability.* The vulnerability of the economy to economic fluctuations of depression and boom, price stability, and overall economic growth stability. (10)

C4.4: *Fiscal policy.* General policies concerning government expenditures, their timing, and their impact; the general level of deficit, surplus, or balance; total share of government expenditures in gross national product. (10)

C4.5: *Organization of capital markets.* The existence of such markets as stock and bond exchanges, their honesty, effectiveness, and total impact; the size and role of commercial banking, including loan policies and availability of credit to businessmen, the existence of other capital sources such as savings and loan associations, government-sponsored credit agencies, insurance company loan activities, etc. (20)

C4.6: *Factor equipment.* Relative supply of capital and land, agricultural and raw materials per capita; skills and ability of work force. (20)

C4.7: *Market size.* Total effective purchasing power within the country, plus relevant export markets. (20)

C4.8: *Social overhead capital.* Availability and quality of power supplies, water, communications systems, transportation, public warehousing, physical transfer facilities. (40)

C4.9: *Interorganizational cooperation.* Degree to which various firms, government agencies, unions, and other relevant organizations cooperate with each other to achieve desired mutual goals. (10)

Perfect Score: 500

EFFECT ON MANAGEMENT

Constraint Evaluation

For a given country, the constraints can be evaluated by a person familiar with the general cultural, economic, business, and political environment in the country. Quantification of the external constraints is obviously subjective and difficult, but at least an effective ranking can be accomplished. The kind of evaluation desired is one which tries to weigh the effect of the constraint on internal managerial effectiveness in a country. The lower the assigned score, the greater the impediment to efficient internal management. High scores for given constraints suggest a favorable impact.

This ranking is posed basically only in managerial terms—it is not particularly relevant if a given external constraint aids the development of folk art or literature, for example. While such cultural activities may have a great deal to do with the quality of life in a country, as long as they have nothing directly to do with effective internal management they are irrelevant for our purposes.

The scores achieved by various countries in effect rank the country with other countries of the world. Total scores may be similar, but internal ratings may suggest weakness worthy of further study. Hence, country A and country B may have identical total scores of 275. However, A rates highly on sociological factors while B rates highly on economic characteristics. In this case, the strategies to be followed by the countries might be completely different. Both can improve managerial effectiveness, but in different directions. The usefulness of the rating scale is to focus on the kinds of serious problems which require analysis, change, and reform.

The variables noted are constantly changing over time, and it is impossible to pose this type of question in static terms. A country may have a poor but improving legal system, for example. Rapid change may occur when a country makes a major shift in foreign policy. The joining of a customs union such as the Common Market could have this sort of effect—as might the winning or losing of a war.

As a result, it is necessary to consider the external constraints over a fairly long period of time, and to rate trends as well as actualities. A decade should be long enough to consider the major shifts in constraints in this sense. Since change is continuous, rechecks of given countries would become necessary to determine what impact macromanagerial shifts had on managerial effectiveness.

CHANGE IN EXTERNAL FACTORS

The Impact of External Constraints

Examples of how the external constraints affect internal management may serve to illustrate the precise choice of constraints noted in the foregoing list. The basic idea here is that a given firm, with given internal managerial effectiveness, could actually have a given efficiency if external constraints shifted favorably. The discussion and examples which follow are intended to be suggestive rather than conclusive, since space does not permit an exhaustive evaluation of every constraint and its implications for managerial effectiveness.

Educational Constraints

The quality and efficiency of any organization depends largely upon the overall quality of the persons in the organization. Hence the nature and quality of the educational process within a country are critical factors in determining the level of managerial competence. If a manager has to staff only from illiterate, superstition-ridden peasants, he will have a much different organization than the man who has a choice among skilled workers and university graduates. In part, this educational factor consists of formal schooling and scholastic organization, but informal schooling is equally important. The English, with their sparse university population, appear weak in regard to formal education—but also to be considered is the high development of apprentice training available in that country. To produce large numbers of college or technical institute graduates may be worthwhile, but the quality of educational experience, as well as the quantity, is quite relevant.

BASIC LITERACY

The most important factor of all is basic literacy. Many a genius has been able to educate himself in quite astounding ways once he was literate—but the competent but illiterate person rarely has a chance to improve himself.

The types of highly educated persons in the culture also affect management. If managers are largely trained as lawyers, their work will likely reflect this education, and the enterprise they run will be quite different from one staffed largely by engineers. If the managers are trained as managers, which outside the United States has been rare, the firm will also be different. And if managerial training is largely informal, consisting of on-the-job training of intelligent, noncollege men, results will be still different. In any case, the types of persons available to the firm will in large part determine how well the firm does its job.

The educational complex of a country may also determine technical, as compared to managerial, efficiency. If a country is willing to finance extensive technical education for its citizens, it will benefit accordingly in this complex world. Failure to do so will result in poor performance for many productive enterprises.

Far too many countries have attitudes toward education which result in their educational systems being badly out of step with educational requirements for productive enterprise. Too many lawyers are produced, and far too few engineers and doctors. The familiar result in many countries is to find managers trained as agronomists, engineers serving as accountants, and lawyers working as technicians. The effect on efficiency is clear.

As with the sociological constraints, the problem of evaluating the impact here is difficult. Other things being equal, the firm with the best trained management and work force will be more efficient, and if "best trained" can be evaluated, some insight into the impact of these external constraints on internal management can be achieved.

ATTITUDINAL VALUES

Sociological Constraints

This set of constraints can also be discussed as a group, although in a detailed analysis the major constraints would be broken down and analyzed independently. It is clear that many of these constraints are extremely complex sets of variables in the environment which tend to affect managerial effectiveness considerably.

The general attitudes toward managers and management will influence the type of management and leadership effectiveness of managers. Managers may be seen as dynamic, entrepreneurial heroes, capable of performing great feats which enrich the culture and economy—or they may be seen as cynical exploiters of humanity concerned only with a narrow view of profits and crass commercial activities. If managers are regarded as heroes, the profession will not lack capable recruits, and managerial competence will tend to improve over time. Education systems, as well as popular folklore, will reflect this attitude. But if managers are considered only slightly better than mad dogs or vicious exploiters, it is quite probable that the profession will suffer accordingly. So, for that matter, will leadership and productivity.

Closely connected to this point is the way in which alternative elite groups are viewed in the culture. If the traditional elite occupations of the clergy, the central government bureaucracy, the military, and the law are regarded so highly and rewarded so well as to drain off talented young men from management, business organizations will suffer. The impact of such status rankings will not only be reflected in the quality of recruiting of competent young men, but also in the way managers see themselves, and in their influence on the society. In some cases, strong admiration for traditional elite groups, plus tight entry controls into these elite professions, may actually help business management, since highly qualified young people may be drawn to management or entrepreneurship as the only high-income occupation open to them in a tightly stratified society. Many European countries have large landed estates once owned by the traditional elite groups, but now serving as country estates for the previously despised managerial elite.

Social attitudes of this sort may also interact with the type of constraints business operations face in other sectors. A country which has small regard for management and business activity is not likely to have a government sympathetic to business problems, and constraints such as tax law, business codes and similar factors will reflect prevailing attitudes as to the importance of key groups in the society.

USE OF SCIENTIFIC METHODS

The general feeling toward scientific methodology will also strongly influence managerial efficiency and behavior. If a country has a strong traditional religious and cultural bias toward non-scientific behavior, it will prove difficult to introduce modern managerial methods, which are based on the same type of predictive, rational view of the world as are the more purely technical devices. A modern manager who operates efficiently spends much of his time trying to predict what might happen and altering his decisions accordingly, much as an engineer or scientist tries to predict behavior in mechanical or scientific phenomena and infers from what will happen how the situation might be altered to advantage. If the culture's view of the world is mystical or fatalistic, such future orientation will prove difficult. Many problems of presently under-developed countries stem from this constraint. Being unable to understand scientific methodology, citizens are unable to understand the reasons for the success of the Western economies which have utilized scientific techniques in a wide variety of activities including management. In a nonscientific culture, managerial and technical recruitment will prove difficult. Even if a few capable men exist, the problem of developing effective work forces will also be hard, since virtually all skilled personnel will require some training in scientific methodology and thinking.

The manner in which society regards wealth also will be relevant in determining the type of management it gets. Wealth can be seen as a passive, asset situation, where money is held mainly by a social class which deserves it for nonproductive reasons. Or it may be viewed as a dynamic income item, growing steadily as the forces generating wealth are steadily improved and expanded. If the prevailing view is the former, management is likely to be held in low esteem. If the rich are highly regarded in the culture, seekers after wealth will not be hard to find, and if management offers a path to riches, the profession will benefit. But if wealth is regarded with suspicion, or if certain kinds of wealth are considered better than others, productive enterprise may suffer. In many cultures, land-created wealth is considered better than industry-created riches, and industrial management suffers.

RATIONAL RISK TAKING

The uses of wealth also are relevant. Calvinist-oriented countries typically regard riches as something to be used to create further wealth, while other societies have a much more static notion of the uses of wealth. Conspicuous consumption instead of productive investment can have considerable impact on the manner in which enterprise develops and on the practice of management itself.

The social view toward rational risk-taking may also influence the type of management obtained. A society which sees large risks as desirable and acts accordingly will have considerably different managerial attitudes than one where reasonable risks are considered unsound. This attitude, as with others mentioned above, tends to shift over time at varying rates. Often a culture has a subgroup which may directly influence the types of managers and entrepreneurs in the society. The Chinese in Southeast Asia, the Lebanese in Africa, and the Armenians in the Middle East are examples of such subgroups who seem willing to take bigger business risks than the general population. The impact of such groups on management and entrepreneurship in these areas has been large.

Management will also be influenced by the general social view toward personal achievement. In cultures where personal drive and ambition are regarded as negative values, management will be hampered. If Horatio Alger traditions abound, the reverse will occur. The drive toward achievement may be collective as well. Some countries are known for their almost overwhelming desire to succeed, to achieve *grandeur* in the community of nations. If such achievements require better management of productive enterprises, it will probably be forthcoming.

If the culture deliberately or unconsciously prevents a significant number of citizens from entering the ranks of management, there will be some impact on efficiency. An obvious example is the tendency in most countries to exclude automatically all women from top-level management, thus throwing away half the intellectual potential of the country. Such restrictions as may be connected with race, religion, or social class would also be examples of this type of exclusion. The smaller the pool of acceptable managerial candidates as a percentage of the total population, the less likely it will be that a country will have effective management.

DIFFERENT LEGAL CODES

Political and Legal Constraints

The nature of legal constraints on business, such as contract law, patent and antitrust law, labor legislation, and tax law is relatively clearcut. Firms operating under Anglo-Saxon legal codes have different rules of the game than firms operating under Napoleonic codes or various forms of religious law. Hence, a firm in some Middle Eastern countries must do business under *Shariya* law, which is derived from the Koran. Business cases involving breach of contract and similar matters are evaluated by religious judges whose major precedent is koranic injunction. Since each case may be decided on its individual merits, precedents seldom are available to indicate what the next decision may be, resulting in considerable uncertainty in business decision-making. This legal code also bans interest payments entirely, and the effect of this prohibition on internal business operations can easily be seen.

Defense policy and foreign policy may also have considerable business impact. Americans are familiar with the kinds of differences in organization found in firms dealing mainly with the Defense Department; while one major reason for the remarkable success of West German firms since 1948 is that the very low defense budgets of the Republic have prevented a drain of valuable human and material resources into defense activities. Such foreign policy decisions as trade agreements, tariff rates, and import quotas can literally mean the survival or collapse of many business enterprises. This type of policy also has considerable effect on the price of both inputs and products sold. One major effect of the American fuel import policy, which sharply restricts the flow of low-cost crude oil into the United States, is to raise energy costs for productive firms and lower their efficiencies. No matter how capable a manager may be, he still has higher costs in this sector than many of his foreign colleagues.

Political stability also directly affects firm effectiveness. An enterprise trying to operate in a country which endures frequent revolutions, and which has complete turnabouts in major political policies from time to time, faces completely different uncertainty problems than a country which is politically stable. Where firms can be reasonably confident that present major government policies will endure, their internal effectiveness will be higher.

Countries whose political and legal institutions are strait-jacketed by tradition and inertia may have considerable inefficiency caused by their inability to change gracefully over time as economic and managerial requirements change. Firms may find that they are hampered by archaic customs, laws, and traditions, and that they are unable to operate efficiently as a result. All countries are afflicted with this type of problem to some degree, but some systems are much less flexible than others.

DETAILED STUDIES

Economic Constraints

The economic constraints affecting business efficiency have been covered in great detail in studies both by economists interested in determining levels of income in an economy and by development economists.[7] Since management is one key factor of production, the analysis of why it functions as it does, given other external economic conditions, has not been lacking. Hence, the economic constraints

---

[7] See Ralph K. Davidson, Vernon L. Smith, and J. W. Wiley, *Economics: An Analytic Approach* (Homewood, Ill.: Richard D. Irwin, Inc., 1958), pp. 115-226, for one of many studies of macroeconomics. See Paul Alpert, *Economic Development* (New York: The Macmillan Company, 1963), for one of many examples of modern economic work in the study of income growth.

developed in the foregoing list are taken from various sources in the economic literature, which has noted the significance of these factors in keeping a total economy in the position of having a relatively stable price level, with real income per capita rising as rapidly as possible. In developed countries, the avoidance of recessions and depressions has also been covered exhaustively.

Traditionally, economists have tended to place more weight on the factors of production than management, assuming managerial effectiveness. Thus in an analysis of the American economy, managers of productive enterprises are assumed to behave in a rational manner calculated to improve their profit position and internal efficiency. In the recent tax cut debate, as one example, the assumption was made (correctly) that if $11 billion of additional purchasing power were put into the economy, American businessmen would make the necessary additional sales efforts, invest intelligently in needed capital equipment required for sales expansions, and so on. Precisely how such activities would take place within the firm was not considered in detail by most economists.

THE DEPENDENT VARIABLE

Our analysis follows the usual economic analysis in that it is argued that a stable price level, with growing per capita incomes, freedom from recessions, and adequate supplies of capital directed properly to firms needing it are desirable for effective internal firm management. However, here we are proposing that the traditional economic approach be reversed: that is, if the economic constraints are of assistance to business enterprises, the internal efficiency of the firms will be greater, leading in turn to higher levels of per capita income. Management has become the dependent variable around which the economy revolves. There is an interrelationship here between the other factors of production and management which creates an endless interaction between the economic constraints and the efficiency of internal business management.

Examples of how the economic constraints affect internal managerial effectiveness are easy to develop. Consider a situation characterized by extreme price inflation, such as presently is occurring in Brazil. Enterprise planning in this case must necessarily revolve around the prospect of higher prices for both inputs and outputs tomorrow; the firm must steadily try to get out of money (the depreciating asset) and into goods (the appreciating asset). The effect of such external circumstances on the firm will result in management policy which is completely different from efficient management policy in a stable situation. Such behaviors may both be quite efficient, but they are not the same. An inventory policy considered completely unsound and inefficient in the United States could make quite good sense in Brazil at the moment. Similar impacts could be traced for such external factors as extreme economic boom or deep depression. Firms cannot escape such situations—they must adjust to them, but to argue that these economic factors are unimportant in their effect on internal management would be unsound.

Another example of the effect of economic constraints on managerial effectiveness would be when production is efficient only when the market reaches a given minimum size. Such economies of scale in production influence the organizing, staffing, and planning of a firm operating in an economy where it is unable to achieve minimal efficient size. The firm will be inefficient relative to similar firms operating in countries where such size in easily achievable. Hence, a Chilean steel mill may be unable to operate efficiently no matter how good its managers are, while a relatively inept group of American steel mill managers can easily achieve lower costs due to the size of the market.

ANALYSIS OF MATRIX

A Comparative Management Matrix

It is possible to construct a comparative management matrix using the external constraints developed above. Such a sample evaluation is shown in the table below. Here the constraints are arranged vertically, with various countries being evaluated listed horizontally. The ratings for each constraint are made for the country, and the totals are added. At this stage, such evaluations are definitely subjective—the purpose here is to demonstrate how a more complete study might be accomplished. However, for our book we intend to use a variety of techniques to assure that our rankings and weights are meaningful. For example, some use will be made of the "Delphi" technique developed at Rand Corporation.[8] In this connection, we plan to get specialists who are experts in a number of countries to rank those countries and assign weights to those constraints within their sphere of competence. Through a series of interviews and questionnaires, in addition to our own research, we are confident that meaningful rankings, weights, and values for the countries under analysis will emerge.

Total constraint scores are added for each country and compared to the index of GNP per capita and GNP growth in the past decade. The weight given here is 80 percent for GNP per capita and 10 percent for the growth rate. If the hypothesis that productive efficiency depends on managerial effectiveness is correct, there should be a close correlation between the GNP-growth index and the managerial effectiveness index.

SUBJECTIVE RATINGS

Again it should be noted that the scorings for the various external constraints are completely subjective at this stage. The statistical meaning of the number is nil, although this technique does have the virtue of forcing the investigator to ponder in his own mind the relative significance of various constraints affecting management.[9]

The matrix developed in the table below shows that the countries with higher rankings in their managerial effectiveness indices also have higher per capita income, when adjusted for income growth. Note, however, that the United Kingdom actually ranks higher (subjectively) than the United States on political-legal constraints. The relatively less developed countries show weakness in all areas, although the degree of weakness differs between them.

[8] Norman Dalkey and Olaf Helmer, "An Experimental Application of the Delphi Method to the Use of Experts," *Management Science*, IX, No. 3 (April 1963), pp. 458-467.

[9] The use of rank order correlation techniques would be more meaningful statistically. See A. C. Rosander, *Elementary Principles of Statistics* (Princeton, N.J.: D. Van Nostrand Co., Inc., 1951), pp. 618-629.

SUGGESTED COMPARATIVE MANAGEMENT MATRIX

EXTERNAL CONSTRAINTS	USA	USSR	UK	MEXICO	SAUDI ARABIA
Educational (100)					
C1.1	48	45	45	25	6
C1.2	15	11	10	5	1
C1.3	6	8	9	3	1
C1.4	6	9	5	5	5
C1.5	8	5	7	5	1
Total	83	78	76	43	14
Sociological (100)					
C2.1	5	8	4	5	6
C2.2	35	25	35	25	5
C2.3	6	8	5	6	8
C2.4	6	3	4	5	5
C2.5	12	15	10	10	8
C2.6	8	9	5	4	4
Total	72	68	63	55	36
Political-Legal (100)					
C3.1	25	20	28	20	10
C3.2	6	3	8	6	5
C3.3	10	5	15	12	5
C3.4	18	15	20	10	10
C3.5	6	5	8	5	4
C3.6	6	2	5	5	1
Total	71	50	84	58	35
Economic (200)					
C4.1	30	20	32	28	25
C4.2	18	10	19	12	3
C4.3	5	6	8	5	5
C4.4	5	5	6	5	2
C4.5	18	10	19	8	2
C4.6	16	12	10	6	6
C4.7	19	15	15	8	4
C4.8	35	25	30	12	6
C4.9	8	4	7	6	6
Total	154	107	146	90	59
Total (Constraint Index)	380	303	369	246	144
1960 GNP */capita	$2,300	$760	$990	$280	$110
1951-60 growth rate	1.5	4.0	2.0	1.5	2.0
Efficiency Index	405.0	272.6	178.2	37.8	19.8

* GNP data derived from United Nations, *Statistical Yearbook, 1961* (New York: United Nations, 1961), pp. 21-38; 486-489. The UN noted that inter-country GNP comparisons should be used with caution because of the statistical discrepancies between countries.

LABOR PROBLEMS

A company doing business in the United Kingdom, as compared to one in the United States, could expect to have considerable staffing difficulties, given the relatively low ranking on educational constraints. Highly skilled manpower for managerial and technical positions is likely to be in short supply. Firms in Saudi Arabia would have serious training problems with labor, given the very low literacy and other educational ratings. They might also be advised to consider their legal position quite carefully, given the low rating on this constraint.

Those concerned with increasing efficiency in the United States might well ponder the implications of the relatively lower sociological and political-legal rankings which suggest a mildly antibusiness climate. Russians, on the other hand, would be best advised to consider economic reforms which could improve the effectiveness of productive enterprises. The point here is that the matrix is designed to provide a focus on difficulties which a given country faces. If the reader disagrees with the authors, he is welcome to defend his choice and propose other ratings which could show other difficulties.

Intercorrelation of the various constraints also shows up in the rankings. If a country like Saudi Arabia has a very low literacy rating, it is likely that the country will also rank low on many other ratings, since basic literacy is a necessity for many facets of productive efficiency. It is difficult to imagine a situation where illiteracy would be coupled with a highly skilled labor force.

Hopefully, this type of focus on weaknesses will lead to debate and discussion as to ways and means of correcting deficiencies. If the alleged deficiency is in fact unreal, the problem then becomes one of finding which other factors cause lower per capita GNP figures. Readers are invited to rate countries in which they are interested, to determine if this approach casts any light on managerial problems within the given economy.

OVERSEAS PROBLEMS ANTICIPATED

This matrix might also be useful for American firms planning to establish branches overseas. Where weak points emerge in the host country, the firm could anticipate difficulties and plan accordingly. If the educational factors are rated low, the firm can anticipate training and staffing problems of a different type than would be found at home. If the legal structure is poor, careful advance planning with American and local lawyers to avoid difficulties would prove useful, and so on.

A final note is that on the table, our efficiency index for the Soviet Union places this country in rank order two, whereas the constraint index places it in rank order three. The reason for this is apparent—GNP growth rate has been so high in the past decade. Also relevant may be the way in which GNP is measured here—errors in intercountry comparisons can be large. Rather than "adjust" the efficiency index to account for this discrepancy, we have let it stand—to suggest that further work in refinement of the concepts discussed here is very much in order.

CONCLUSION: PURPOSE OF ANALYSIS

Our purpose in this paper was to consider the kinds of problems which arise when different countries are compared in terms of their relative managerial efficiency. Such discrepancies cannot be explained in terms of existing management theory; thus it is necessary to evaluate the nature of external constraints bearing on management. By examining such constraints considerable insight is gained into the reasons why various countries have more or less efficient internal management in productive enterprises. This type of analysis has already proved useful to the authors in their examination of various management problems in quite diverse countries, and it is hoped that it will provide some insight into other types of comparative management problems as well.

18

An Appraisal of the Farmer-Richman Model in Comparative Management *

S. BENJAMIN PRASAD

The purpose of a model is to describe, explain, and predict the performance of a system. To be most useful, the model should explain and predict the behavior of the individual components of a system. In Forrester's terminology [1] the Farmer-Richman model [2] approximates the "abstract-dynamic" model. However, for purposes of understanding, it can be construed as a theoretical approach in the field of "comparative study" of management systems.

The rationale for an appraisal of "A Model for Research in Comparative Management" is 1. the exposition of the approach is more verbose than lucid, 2. the authors' ideas, some of which are lost in the maze of their verbalism, could be more easily comprehended if presented in a slightly modified form, and 3. since this was a suggested research approach, an appraisal was in order.

This is an appraisal of their methodology and its logical implications for research. An examination of the merits and demerits

---

* Reprinted from the *California Management Review*, Vol. VIII, No. 3 (Spring, 1966), pp. 93-96. Copyright 1966 by the Regents of the University of California.

[1] J. W. Forrester, *Industrial Dynamics* (New York: John Wiley & Sons, and M.I.T. Press, 1961), p. 49.

[2] *California Management Review*, VII, No. 2 (Winter, 1964), pp. 55-68; Ch. 17 in this volume.

of the model follows a restatement of it in a more orderly fashion than presented by the exponents.

PURPOSE OF THEIR APPROACH AND CONCEPTS EMPLOYED

The purpose of Richard Farmer and Barry Richman is "to develop a new conceptual framework for comparative studies which will prove more useful in the analysis of critical comparative management problems." It should be noted that the authors, at the outset, recognize that "existing management theory has some serious drawbacks in terms of its orientation and applicability to different types of cultures and economies . . . where environments vary, it is necessary to examine the external constraints upon internal management."

There are four key concepts employed in this model.

1. *Comparative management*—which deals with problems and managerial efficiency in various countries. The question of relative managerial efficiency and differences in managerial activity among cultures is the problem of comparative management.
2. *Internal management*—defined as "the coordination of human effort and material resources toward the achievement of organizational objectives."
3. *External constraints*—external factors. The external factors constitute the external environment termed as macromanagerial structure. This influences the activities and effectiveness of (internal) management. External constraints are classified as economic, legal-political, sociological, and educational. These are aggregate variables.
4. *Managerial efficiency* or *managerial effectiveness*—defined as the degree of efficiency with which members of productive enterprises achieve their stated or given goals.

ASSUMPTIONS UNDERLYING THE APPROACH

A careful study of the Farmer-Richman model reveals that the authors make the following assumptions to develop their approach:

1. A firm or a productive enterprise attempts to operate as efficiently as possible in its environment in the sense of trying to achieve its goals with a minimum of resources.
2. Virtually all countries want more goods and services, and prefer higher level of per capita income to less. The managers' problem is to become increasingly efficient over time.
3. Efficiency gains are desired badly enough so that a culture (meaning a society), given probable trade-offs to get more efficiency, will opt for more efficiency.
4. Gains from urging changes in external constraints prove much larger than gains from improvements in internal management of productive enterprises.
5. Managerial effectiveness determines productive efficiency.
6. External constraints act on managers to inhibit or aid their effectiveness. Or, managerial effectiveness depends upon external constraints.

VARIABLES AND THEIR MEASURES

The variables in the Farmer-Richman model are all aggregate variables. Managerial effectiveness—measured in terms of a per capita income index, and a weighted value of the rate of economic growth—is the dependent variable. The argument here is that a specific act of a manager cannot be quantified; however, those of the entire system can be quantified. The independent variables are the external constraints. The relevant external constraints, that is, relevant to managerial effectiveness in an economy, are the four sets of variables identified by the authors as economic, legal-political, sociological, and educational constraints. Each of these sets is assigned a certain number of points. The economic constraint is assigned 200 points whereas the other three are assigned 100 points each, with a total maximum score of 500 points.

The Farmer-Richman approach is to give each of the external variables a numerical value suggesting its relative importance—relative to other countries. The scores given will be based upon a subjective criterion: How a constraint affects management. Thus, the higher the score of a variable the more favorable is its impact upon management. For example, if in a country A the variable "attitude toward education" scores 10 points, and if in country B the same variable scores 0 points, it means that A has an attitude favorable to management whereas B totally lacks such an attitude.

The purpose of giving numerical ranking, however, is to focus on the available subjective evaluation of a given variable. The authors, recognizing the highly subjective nature of this procedure, propose to improve it by using various techniques and by seeking the aid of experts in the respective countries.

STATED LIMITATIONS OF THE APPROACH AND THE USEFULNESS OF THE MATRIX

It is important to recognize and state the limitations of one's approach. Farmer and Richman accordingly recognize the following limitations of their model:

1. Many of the external constraints are interrelated.
2. Considering all the constraints which may appear to have some effect upon internal management is dangerous in that it may lead to a discussion of everything under the sun. Hence, one has to be selective.
3. Ranking of the constraints is desired only in managerial terms.
4. External variables are constantly changing over time, and it is impossible to pose questions in static terms.

The authors present data on the dependent and the independent variables in the form of a matrix. The usefulness of the matrix is stated as follows: Firstly, it has the virtue of allowing the investigator to ponder in his own mind the relative significance of various constraints affecting management. Secondly, the matrix is designed to provide a focus on difficulties which a country confronts. And, thirdly, this matrix might also be useful for American companies planning to establish branches overseas. Where weak points show up in a host country, the American firm could anticipate difficulties and plan accordingly. In essence, the matrix serves as a blueprint for remedial action.

MERITS OF THE MODEL

Developmental economics including economic programming as a field of study and research is relatively recent. Keen interest now has been evinced in these areas not only in the United States but also in other parts of the world. In contrast, ever since the pioneering international analysis of management by Frederick Harbison and Charles Myers,[3] little, if any, has been available in management literature in the area of comparative analysis of management systems. In the light of this intellectual paucity, the Farmer-Richman model deserves commendation. Parenthetically it should be noted that these two researchers have recently published a volume dealing with comparative management and economic development.

The cardinal concern of the Farmer-Richman model, if it can be restated, is perhaps twofold: one aspect is how to establish a functional relationship between aggregate managerial efficiency and a set of selected aggregate variables; the other aspect is how to represent this relationship in a manner which would pinpoint the problem areas for investigation. This model is noteworthy in two respects: one, the authors have endeavored to develop an approach for research in comparative management, and two, they have clearly identified the complex sets of variables which impinge upon a country's managerial effectiveness.

Their quantification procedure, although subjective, is on sound lines. They do recognize the need for improving it. Getting help from knowledgeable and informed persons in the respective countries entails considerable cooperation and teamwork which, this writer believes, is worthwhile.

The idea of presenting the functional relations between external variables and managerial effectiveness in the form of a matrix is novel, and has interesting possibilities in the application of matrix algebra.

Last but not least, this model has the value of generating interest, among both the academicians and managers engaged in inter-

[3] Frederick Harbison and Charles Myers, *Management in the Industrial World* (New York: McGraw-Hill Book Company, 1959).

national business operations, in the problems of comparative managerialism.[4]

DEMERITS OF THE MODEL

Since this is a descriptive methodological model, one literary criticism was considered apt. The comment is that the language of the model could certainly have been improved with a view to enabling the reader to comprehend, without confusion, what the authors were saying.[5]

There are sweeping generalizations in the Farmer-Richman essay, the validity of which is rather dubious. For example, note the following:

. . . most studies of management have taken place within a black box labeled *management* without concern for the external environment in which the firm may operate;

Management may be defined as the coordination of human effort and material resources toward the achievement of organizational objectives. The organizational objectives reflect the desire of people for useful goods and services;

Governments uninterested in development (economic) have been overthrown, to be replaced by those who are;

The English with their sparse university population appear weak in regard to formal education.

[4] The concept of "comparative managerialism" is elaborated in the "Conclusion" in this volume.

[5] For example, study the following statements made by Farmer and Richman: "Explorations of the management theory jungle reveal that virtually all theories approach the problem of management as an internal problem within a productive enterprise. External factors, if considered at all, are assumed constant in most formulations." A discerning reader, who recognizes the "management theory jungle" as the exposition of Professor Harold Koontz, is prone to raise these questions, not necessarily as a criticism but as point of fact or clarification: What are all these theories? Are they theories or approaches? Can the problem of management (meaning the manager or the managerial group) be anything but an internal problem? If something is an internal problem, is it not redundant to say, internal problem within an enterprise? What is the productive enterprise? Productive of what? Is the productive enterprise a large corporate form of organization as in the US or a small workshop as in India? What are external factors? Are they external to the firm? Are they internal to the country?

These and other generalizations with philosophical overtones to be found in their approach add very little, if any, to the approach. Even if one regards such generalizations as apropos, one should document them and then perhaps one could use them either as assumptions or as elements for developing a suitable frame of reference.

When one is attempting to develop and suggest an approach, it is essential that one ought carefully to define the terms one desires to employ. This is not simply a semantic requirement but a methodological prerequisite. For example, efficiency and effectiveness are used interchangeably. National efficiency, physical efficiency, managerial effectiveness, managerial efficiency are all used as synonyms. Similarly terms such as pressures, constraints, variables, all are used in the same sense. Lack of precise definitions in operational terms have rendered many of the valuable concepts nebulous.

Farmer and Richman identify external factors as external constraints but they have assumed that these are controllable variables. If, for instance, the comparative management matrix indicates that a country scores very low on the variable "view" (of managers, scientific method, wealth, etc.) it is hard to believe that this is a directly controllable variable. From a social science point of view, to construe that all of the so-called external variables are controllable is fallacious.

Despite the soundness of the comparative management matrix, and despite a clear indication of a high correlation between GNP-Growth Index and the constraint score index, it does not necessarily follow that the two measures are causally related. Since a model is supposed first to explain phenomena, explanations of phenomena may not be emanating from the comparative management matrix. That this situation exists and that it can be remedied is not recognized by the authors.

The criterion used for scoring the external variables is: how, or more precisely to what extent, a variable affects (meaning fosters or impedes) management in the country as a whole. Since there is no typology of management developed or adapted in the Farmer-Richman model, one can only surmise that the authors view management as though it were a uniform and comparable process in all countries. They are fully aware that it is not so, but nevertheless, it is unfortunate that they do not bring out the ramification of this fact which is, in the light of their own approach, crucial.

Nothing is said about a very important variable—size of the

population and its rate of increase—in the Farmer-Richman model. It is needless to say that people are human resources but too much of this resource, as has happened in most parts of the world, does become a serious constraint in the entire developmental process.

One logical implication which emerges from the Farmer-Richman model is that someone or a country's government or an agency should manipulate the variables, if possible, so as to facilitate the so-called managerial effectiveness. Since managerial effectiveness is measured in terms of per capita income and rate of economic growth, this may be tantamount to saying that centralized planning and programming are imminent. Also, there are arguments in favor of and against increased governmental role. Moreover, whether or not increased national effort is needed, for example, in elementary level education does not stem from an examination of the comparative management matrix alone.

CONCLUSION

The authors address themselves to a very important problem, that of improving macromanagerial effectiveness. Of course, no one can deny that a societal environment is a composite of multifarious variables. Some of these may be classified as internal to the production unit or external to it, or as economic, social, political, and so on. There is no doubt that many of the approaches initiated by investigators belonging to one discipline or school have had weaknesses. The approach which Farmer and Richman suggest deserves careful consideration by all those who may be interested in comparative management. Just as excessive concern with factors internal to the management of productive enterprises is dangerous, so too a concern with the so-called external variables. A realistic approach is to examine all the variables. Farmer and Richman certainly enlighten the problems involved in considering variables external to the productive enterprises.

Some of the criticisms levelled against their approach are done so in the fervent hope that methodological problems can be discussed [6] and solved before the design is used in empirical investigations of the problems of comparative management.

---

[6] Farmer and Richman further discuss the essence of their model in a communication in the *California Management Review*, Vol. IX No. 1 (Fall, 1966), pp. 93-95.

19

A Research Model to Determine the Applicability of American Management Know-How in Differing Cultures and/or Environments *

ANANT R. NEGANDHI
BERNARD D. ESTAFEN [1]

The perennial argument between those who believe that management is a science governed by universal principles and those who say that these principles are culture-bound will probably be intensified as a result of current cross-cultural research in management science. Particularly, the needs of developing countries for advanced technical and managerial know-how in their economic development efforts will compel us to ascertain which elements of American management know-how are transferable and which are not. It is indeed true that to date many management "process school" theorists believe that "management is management wherever prac-

* Reprinted with permission from the *Academy of Management Journal* (December, 1965).
[1] We wish to express our sincere thanks to Cyril O'Donnell, Harold Koontz, and Barry Richman for their help in clarifying and increasing our understanding of the various management concepts used in this model.

ticed, a universal profession whose principles can be applied in every organized form of human activity." [2] A mere glance at the existing textbooks on principles of management will validate this point. Harbison and Myers,[3] after studying management practices in twenty-three countries, came to the conclusion that "Organization building has its logic . . . which rests upon the development of management . . . and . . . there is a general logic of management development which has applicability both to advanced and industrializing countries in the modern world." [4]

CROSS-CULTURAL CHALLENGE

However, many cross-cultural studies of management practices have challenged this contention of the so-called universalists. Gonzalez and McMillan,[5] in their study of the applicability of the American management philosophy in Brazil, found that the management philosophy is culture-bound, and that "American philosophy of management is not universally applicable." [6]

Winston Oberg, in his study of "Cross-Cultural Perspectives on Management Principles," [7] argues that if the ground rules under which the manager operates are different in different cultures and/or countries, then it would be quite fruitless to search for a common set of strategies of management. From his overseas experience and empirical research in Brazil and the United States he concluded that "Cultural differences from one country to another are more significant than many writers (on management theory) now appear to recognize. . . . If management principles are to be truly universal . . . they must face up to the challenge of other cultures and other business climates. . . . [The universalist claim] is hardly

---

2 See Harwood F. Merrill, "Listening Post," *Management News,* XXXVI, No. 1 (January 1963).

3 Frederick Harbison and Charles Myers, *Management in the Industrial World* (New York: McGraw-Hill Book Company, 1959).

4 *Ibid.,* p. 117.

5 Richard F. Gonzalez and Claude McMillan, Jr., "The Universality of American Management Philosophy," *Academy of Management Journal* (April 1961), pp. 33-41.

6 *Ibid.,* p. 39.

7 Wiston Oberg, "Cross-Cultural Perspectives on Management Principles," *Academy of Management Journal* (June 1963), pp. 129-143.

warranted by either evidence or intuition at this stage in the development of management theory." [8]

Farmer and Richman, in their recent article, "A Model for Research in Comparative Management," [9] have also stressed the importance of external environmental factors on the efficiency of the manager. They argued that:

> Most studies of management have taken place within a "black box" labeled management, without much concern for the external environment in which the firm may operate. As long as this external environment is about the same for all firms, the approach is valid; however, in cases where the environment differs significantly, . . . as is the case between nations, present theory (of management) is inadequate to explain comparative differentials in efficiency.[10]

Based on these premises, they have offered a model to ascertain the influences of what they call external constraints on managerial efficiency.[11] The general classes of external constraints considered by them are:

1. Educational Characteristics
2. Sociological Characteristics
3. Political and Legal Characteristics
4. Economic Characteristics

To evaluate the managerial effectiveness in any country, they argue, one should take into consideration all the above factors. For judging relative effectiveness of managers in different countries they also have proposed a tentative ranking for the individual factors discussed above.

It is indeed true that external environmental factors do affect managerial performance. To this extent, Farmer and Richman's insightful analysis of external constraints may provide a sound basis for further theoretical developments in management. However, there is evidence that certain elements of American manage-

8 *Ibid.*, pp. 141-142.

9 Richard Farmer and Barry Richman, "A Model for Research in Comparative Management," Chapter 17 in this volume.

10 *Ibid.*

11 The detailed description of external managerial constraints listed by Farmer and Richman, *Ibid.*

ment know-how [12] are successfully applied in altogether different cultures and environments. Gonzalez and McMillan, who have argued that management philosophies are culture-bound, admit that "American management is most highly respected abroad . . . and American management know-how . . . has yielded great dividends for the host country." [13]

Besides, those of us who are familiar with the operations of the American and British companies in foreign countries (particularly in developing countries) are acquainted with some widely held opinions, for example the following:

1. American and British companies operating in foreign countries are more efficient than domestic companies.[14]
2. The higher efficiency of the American and British companies is not entirely due to their advanced technical know-how but also due to managerial know-how. Domestic firms using similar "hardware" and technical know-how have been proved to be less efficient as compared to the American and British companies.[15]
3. The domestic firms using the American managerial know-how are regarded as more efficient and "progressive" as compared to other domestic firms not using such managerial know-how.[16]

If there are differences among the firms operating in similar socioeconomic, legal, and political environments, then it could be argued that all the external environmental factors listed by Farmer and Richman may not necessarily be influential in changing the internal process of management [17] and/or managerial effectiveness. This is, however, not to deny the opinion and thesis of Farmer and Richman that external environmental factors influence management process and thereby its effectiveness. Some external environmental

[12] By American management know-how, we mean various techniques used by the manager in a large scale firm in the United States to carry out his basic functions of planning, organizing, staffing, directing, and controlling.

[13] Gonzales and McMillan, *op. cit.*, p. 39.

[14] National Planning Association case studies of US business firms abroad have shown this point to be true for many cases.

[15] *Ibid.*

[16] *Ibid.* In particular, see the case study of *Sears, Roebuck de Mexico, S.A.* (Washington, D.C.: National Planning Association, May 1953).

[17] Throughout this article, management process is understood as the way in which the manager carries out his five basic functions of planning, organizing, staffing, directing, and controlling.

factors do affect the way in which managers will carry out their functions.

However, in this case, we need to specify the particular external environmental factors affecting specific functions of the manager. This would enable us to ascertain the elements of American management know-how which are transferable and which are nontransferable into differing cultures and/or environments. The model presented below attempts to do so.

NEED FOR THREE DIMENSIONS

Managerial effectiveness [18] in a given industry with a given technical know-how is dependent upon the way in which the manager carries out the process of planning, organizing, staffing, directing, and controlling. However, the management process is dependent on both the external environmental factors and the management philosophy.[19]

Thus, there are three key variables in our model: management philosophy, management process, and management effectiveness.

To date, most of the "process school" theorists have recognized only two variables, management process and management effectiveness. In the main, they have studied the impact of management process upon managerial effectiveness. As Farmer and Richman pointed out, "most studies of management have taken place within a 'black box' labeled management, without much concern for the external environment in which the firm operates." [20]

Recently, Gonzalez and McMillan,[21] Oberg,[22] and Farmer and Richman,[23] among others, have recognized and emphasized the impact of culture and other external environmental factors on management process and effectiveness. However, they have not gone far

[18] This concept is defined and explained later in dealing with the third key variable.

[19] Managerial philosophy as used in this model is nothing more than what is commonly known as managerial policy of the firm concerning consumers, stockholders, suppliers, distributors, employee unions, community, local, state, and federal governments.

[20] Farmer and Richman, *op. cit.,* p. 56.

[21] Gonzales and McMillan, *op. cit.*

[22] Oberg, *op. cit.*

[23] Farmer and Richman, *op. cit.*

enough to indicate the way in which these influential external environmental factors might be ascertained. Besides, these researchers have considered management philosophy as "given," a product of the culture and environment. It is indeed true that management philosophy as understood in a broader sense is a product of a given culture and environment. However, certain elements of management philosophy can and have been "imported" successfully. In this model, therefore, we are concerned only with those elements of managerial philosophy that might be transferred into a differing culture and environment. Thus our definition of management philosophy is very restrictive and deals specifically with the policies of the firm across the six key interfaces shown in section (a) of the figure on page 266.

Management philosophy, used in even a very restrictive way, seems to have considerable impact on management process and effectiveness. Chowdhry and Pal,[24] for example, in their study of two textile mills in India, found that the company with a "quick profit" philosophy and changing manufacturing policy had low morale and efficiency as compared to another textile company having a "product conscious" and "long-range profit" philosophy. Both mills were using more or less the same "hardware" and technical know-how. Their differential philosophy, however, had an impact on employee morale, productivity (a measure of managerial effectiveness in our model), organization structure, delegation of authority, span of control, and communication patterns. Based on their findings and our own experiences with the operation of the domestic and foreign companies in India, we have introduced this third variable (philosophy) in our model.

THREE IMPORTANT VARIABLES AND THEIR ELEMENTS

The concepts used in our model (management philosophy, management process, and management effectiveness), have been used and understood differently by various researchers in management. Therefore, to facilitate understanding and exposition of our

[24] Kamla Chowdhry and A. K. Pal, "Production Planning and Organization Morale," in Albert Rubenstein and C. J. Haberstroh, eds., *Some Theories of Organization* (Homewood, Ill.: The Dorsey Press, Inc., 1960), pp. 185-196.

ideas, we will define these three concepts through the study of their elements.

Management Philosophy

The concept of management philosophy is understood in our model as the expressed and implied attitude or relationships of a firm with some of its external and internal agents such as:

1. Consumer
   (i.e., the company's attitude toward consumer, irrespective of market situation for a given product—does the company regard consumer loyalty important, or is it simply interested in quick profits?)
2. Company's involvement with the community
   a. Community welfare activities
   b. Educational institutions
3. Company's relationship with local, state, and federal governments
4. Company's attitude and relationship with unions and union leaders
5. Company's relationship with employees
6. Company's relationship with suppliers and distributors

Management Process

The management process is understood here as the way in which the manager carries out his functions of planning, organizing, directing, staffing, and controlling. The detailed description of the items which should be studied under each of these functions is as follows:

MANAGERIAL FUNCTION	DESCRIPTION OF ITEMS
Planning	a. Commitment period
	b. Location of planning authority
	c. Methodologies, techniques, and tools used in planning
Organization	a. Authority-responsibility relationships
	b. Organization charts

THE APPLICABILITY OF AMERICAN MANAGEMENT KNOW-HOW   263

    c. Degree of centralization and decentralization
    d. Span of control
    e. Degree of specialization
    f. The uses of informal organizations and management attitudes toward such groups
    g. Grouping of activities and departmentation
    h. Uses of specialist staff and its relationship with line executives

Staffing
    a. Methods used in appraising, selecting, and training personnel
    b. Promotion criteria used
    c. Management development practices used

Direction and Leadership
    a. The techniques used for motivating high-level manpower to cooperate in achieving organizational objectives and goals
    b. The methods and techniques used for motivating workers
    c. Communication techniques used
    d. Supervisory techniques used

Control
    a. Control techniques used for different areas, i.e., finance, production, marketing, etc.
    b. Types of control standards
    c. Information feedback systems and procedures for corrective actions

Managerial Effectiveness

The following elements or factors are suggested for ascertaining the degree of managerial effectiveness. It is admitted that this list of factors is not exhaustive; however, all the factors combined will give an overall idea of the effectiveness of the manager. These factors are:

1. Net and gross profits in the last five years.

2. The percentage increase in profits in the last five years (year by year).
3. Market share of the company in main product line and percent increase or decrease in market share in the last five years.
4. The market price of a company's stock and percent increase of decrease in prices in the last five years.
5. The percentage increase in sales during the last five years.
6. Employee morale and turnover.
7. Employees' evaluation of the company and ranking of the companies under study by the employees of each firm.
8. Overall evaluation of the company and ranking by the general public.
9. Evaluation of the company and ranking by the consumers.

SUGGESTED METHOD OF STUDY

To ascertain the impact of external environmental factors on management process and effectiveness, and to determine the specific external factors affecting particular functions of managers, we are suggesting the study of three variables, management process, management philosophy, and management effectiveness, through their elements listed above, in two companies (and three plants) in two countries. The aim of selecting two companies and three plants in two different countries is to keep management philosophy and external environmental factors constant for two of the plants. Let us assume that the three firms in the two countries selected are:

1. US company in the United States.
2. Subsidiary plant of the US company in India, pursuing the management philosophy of the parent company.
3. Indian company having same "hardware" and using similar technical know-how, but having a different managerial philosophy.

Thus, we will have an American company in the United States and in India having the same managerial philosophy but operating in different environments, and the Indian and American company in India having different philosophies but operating in the same evnironments. To facilitate exposition, these symbols will help:

Management Philosophy X
Management Process .... P
Management Effectiveness .... Z

Now let us assume that the US company in the United States has management philosophy X1, management process P1, and managerial effectiveness Z1; the subsidiary of this US company in India has the same managerial philosophy X1, but management process P2, and managerial effectiveness Z2; while the Indian company in India has managerial philosophy X3 (very different from that of the US company), management process P3, and managerial effectiveness Z3.

	MANAGEMENT PHILOSOPHY	MANAGEMENT PROCESS	MANAGEMENT EFFECTIVENESS
1. US company in the US	X1	P1	Z1
2. US company in India *	X1	P2	Z2
3. Indian company in India †	X3	P3	Z3

* No. 2 has same philosophy as No. 1, but different environment.
† No. 3 has different philosophy from No. 2, but same environment.

Now if our study of three companies in the United States and India indicates the differences in processes of management (or the way the manager carries out his functions) in the US company in the United States (P1), US company in India (P2), and Indian company in India (P3), then we can infer that the differences between P1 and P2 are due to the external environmental factors while the differences between P2 and P3 are due to management philosophy.

Again, if we find that the US company in India is more effective than the Indian company in India, then we can say that the management process used by the US company in India is more effective and the domestic companies aspiring to achieve the same effectiveness as the US company in India should "copy" the process P2. However, to use this process the domestic company may have to change its philosophy from X3 to X1. Also, we could ascertain the impact of external environmental factors on the management process by first describing the differences between process P1 and P2 and then relating these differences to the particular environmental factors. (This can be done by interviewing executives of the US company in India.)

SUMMARY

To facilitate understanding and exposition of our ideas, we have attempted to outline the entire model and its significance in graphic form.

a) MANAGEMENT PHILOSOPHY OR POLICY   ELEMENTS

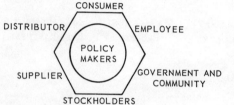

1. CONSUMER
2. EMPLOYEE
3. SUPPLIER
4. DISTRIBUTOR
5. GOVERNMENT AND COMMUNITY
6. STOCKHOLDERS

b) MANAGEMENT PROCESS   ELEMENTS

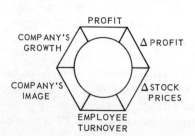

1. PLANNING
2. ORGANIZING
3. STAFFING
4. DIRECTING
5. CONTROLLING

c) MANAGEMENT EFFECTIVENESS   ELEMENTS

1. GROSS AND NET PROFIT
2. GROWTH IN PROFIT
3. GROWTH IN MARKET SHARE
4. GROWTH IN PRICE OF STOCK
5. EMPLOYEE TURNOVER
6. CONSUMER RANKING

Theoretical Rationale

Differences in processes P1 to P2 are due to the external environmental factors.

Differences in processes P2 to P3 are due to management philosophy.

Significance of Model

The model presented here will enable the ascertainment of the following:

1. The impact of specific external environmental factor(s) on the particular function(s) of the manager.
2. Provide an answer to our question of which elements of the American management know-how are transferable and which are nontransferable in differing cultures and environments.
3. Identify the most efficient process in a given socioeconomic, legal, and political environment, and suggest the means through which this process can be implemented.
4. Identify the strategic environmental factors which do affect the management process and thereby managerial efficiency.
5. Determine external factors which are controllable and those which are noncontrollable.
6. Indicate the upper limit to which we might transfer American management know-how in underdeveloped areas.

20

Conclusion: A Concept of
Comparative Managerialism

A concept of *comparative managerialism* as elucidated here can best be comprehended within a particular frame of reference. The following generalizations constitute the framework within which this concept—which had not yet entered the Encyclopedia of Management as of 1963—is distinguished from similar concepts which can be found in management and economic literature. Subsequently one can examine the approach of *comparative managerialism* in terms of its utility, and as a legitimate field of inquiry occupying a ground common both to industrial management and developmental economics.

A FRAME OF REFERENCE: ELEMENTS

1. There exists various degrees of economic development, and various patterns of industrial structures among countries. For example, Gottfried Haberler speaks of "semi-developed and wholly undeveloped countries; tropical and temperate zone agricultural countries. . . ."[1] Frederick Harbison and Charles Myers have developed a fourfold classification of countries on the basis of quantitative indicators of human resource development.[2]

[1] See Gottfried Haberler, "Integration and Growth of World Economy," *American Economic Review* (March 1964), p. 16.
[2] Frederick Harbison and Charles Myers, *Education, Manpower and Economic Growth* (New York: McGraw-Hill Book Company, 1964), pp. 32-36.

2. Industrialization is an important and an integral part—but no more than a part—of the much broader process of economic development and social change. All societies or national economies aspire to and formulate as their goal not only economic development but also social justice.[3]

3. All societies develop guiding philosophies and principles of developmental strategy. In implementing these principles they confront many problems. One of the major problems in implementing developmental strategies in developing nations is a combination of bureaucratic inefficiency and corruption.

4. There exist sets of continua, rather than dichotomies, of less-developed-advanced economies; internal-external constraints; and, traditional-modern managerialism, and so on. *Change is always taking place along these continua.*

5. Business behavior and industrial activity occur within a societal framework; they affect and are affected by the environment within which industrial organizations operate. Business administration or managerial principles are not absolute; they are relative to a given cultural setting. Culture consists of historically derived and selected ideas and their values.

6. Business organizations originate as owner-manager organizations. There occurs a transformation, not a regular one, of this form leading to a separation of ownership and management,[4] and eventually resulting in corporate form. It is at this stage that certain corporate managerial values (e.g., American top management philosophy) can be adopted although managerial techniques need to be adapted.

7. Rapid and deliberate change that constitutes the pattern of modernization has been associated with extreme nationalism.

[3] Social justice connoting protection and promotion of the interests of weaker sections of the population, narrowing of the disparities of income, prevention of concentration of economic power in the hands of a few, promotion of equality of opportunity in terms of education, employment, and so on.

[4] The original form of modern business organization was the small firm in which the owner was also the manager. The owner-manager was responsible to no one but himself for his business decisions. His interest as manager could not conflict with his interest as owner. That "the development of modern giant corporations has led to the separation of ownership and management" was first elaborated in the work of Adolph Berle and Gardiner Means. See their *The Modern Corporation and Private Property* (New York: The Macmillan Company, 1945).

This association is hardly coincidental, since nationalism provides a kind of nonrational focus of identification as well as a rationale for the disruption of the traditional order.

8. Adaptation of ideas and techniques are feasible along the continua; traditional-modern managerialism, and undeveloped-developed economic environment.

These eight elements by no means exhaust the frame of reference in which contemporary managerialism can be explored. But they permit a definition from a particular point of view. *Comparative managerialism* may be defined as the study and analysis of management as a process and a philosophy in all managerial situations and in all countries where further industrialization is pursued as an integral part of economic development. Before examining the question, Is comparative managerialism a cross-cultural or an intracultural phenomenon?, a distinction of this concept from other similar concepts is useful.

SOME DISTINCTIONS

Although the concept—comparative management—is aptly identified by Richard Farmer and Barry Richman [5] as dealing with the problems of management and managerial efficiency in various countries, the clarity of the concept—*comparative management*—can be enhanced by examining similar terms used in management and related literature. For purposes of illustration the following terms are chosen: International Business Management, International Management, Management in Foreign Environment, Management on an International Scale, and World Management.

International Business Management, as the term implies, is the management of international or multinational business firms. These firms are the ones engaged in global trade and production. The manager who is engaged in international business management is sometimes less aptly referred to as the "international execu-

[5] Richard Farmer and Barry Richman, "A Model for Research in Comparative Management," Ch. 17 in this volume. In their pioneering textbook Farmer and Richman begin their analysis by stating that "Comparative management deals with problems of managerial performance in various countries." See Richard Farmer and Barry Richman, *Comparative Management and Economic Progress* (Homewood, Ill.: Richard D. Irwin, Inc., 1965), p. 1.

tive." [6] There is as much internationalism attached to this term as there is to a "diplomat" or a "reporter" from a foreign country. Each plays his respective role, and in doing so has to behave in a social setting different from the one in which he grew up.[7]

Robinson suggests that the unifying purpose (or concept) in international business is to enhance the likelihood of mutually profitable international business transactions. This purpose is the basis upon which the practice of international business must rest in the long run.[8]

International Management, according to Sethi,[9] is a universal power-complex. It transcends the physical subsystems of authority which one finds in almost all cultural systems, and begins to create its own authority-process. It addresses itself to the welfare of the society both in terms of societal gain and individual gain. Sethi's is more of a philosophical conceptualization than a pragmatic one.

Management in the Foreign Environment, according to John Fayerweather,[10] means the development of policies and practices which permit successful international operation under those social, political, and economic conditions which differ from country to country. He also identifies management on an international scale as developing policies which are appropriate not only to individual countries but also to the variety of barriers and connections between foreign countries.

World Management implies making decisions on a global basis. According to Clee and de Scipio, "to adopt a world-wide management concept in all business affairs is to view the world as the company's market and to resolve all strategic business questions in the light of the opportunities in all of the world." [11]

These categorizations suggest some kind of global market orien-

---

[6] John Ewing and Frank Meissner, *International Business Management* (Belmont, Calif.: Wadsworth Publishing Company, 1964), p. v.

[7] The problems of adjustment of a foreign manager in a different SEC setting is explored by Keith Davis in his "Managing Productivity in Developing Countries," Ch. 11 in this volume.

[8] Richard Robinson, *International Business Policy* (New York: Holt, Rinehart and Winston, 1964), pp. ix-x.

[9] Narendra Sethi, "International Management," Ch. 16 in this volume.

[10] John Fayerweather, "Foreign Operations: A Guide for Top Management," *Harvard Business Review* (January-February 1957), p. 128.

[11] Gilbert Clee and Alfred de Scipio, "Creating a World Enterprise," *Harvard Business Review* (November-December 1959), p. 85.

tation. The term comparative managerialism has no such orientation. If it has an orientation then it ought to be growth-oriented. The term *managerialism* is used in preference to management because management is a concept which is generally associated with business management or industrial management in North America and Western Europe. Consider, for example, if one can appropriately say that there is management in an African country, except in a limited sense; but one can venture to say that there is managerialism, meaning that there exists a particular system of managing business enterprise, small scale and nonmanufacturing though it may be, in that country. The frame of reference as set forth in this chapter, and the distinctions made, lead to a question of central importance: *Is comparative managerialism a cross-cultural phenomenon or an intra-cultural phenomenon?*

By cross-cultural what is meant here is "among various socioeconomic-cultural settings" (SEC settings). The SEC setting constitutes the environment within which the managerial process including economic decision-making takes place. The SEC setting is dynamic. The cultural aspect of it may be more static than the social and economic aspects, yet the context as a whole is said to be changing. There is fragmentary evidence of managerial behavior in various SEC settings as brought to light by various authors in the previous chapters. Let us review some of them. For purposes of illustration the following managerial concepts are chosen: Attitudes, Communication, Decision-Making, Delegation of Authority, and Training and Development of Managerial Personnel.

Managerial Attitudes differ in various regions of the world. The attitude toward scientific method is extremely limited in the Latin American countries (McCann). In Europe, it is generally believed that the individual manager's "style" is decisive in terms of managerial success, failure, or mediocrity (Nowotny). German managers apparently tend to think of themselves not as professional managers but as engineers, lawyers, accountants, and so on (Frederick Harbison and Charles Myers). In smaller firms in African countries, foreign managers have shown a hostile attitude to the training and development of Africans (Vuerings). Soviet managers' attitudes and behavior are similar to the attitudes and behavior of American managers (Berliner). Even managers in the labor sector in Israel take similar attitudes as managers in other sectors (Derber).

Communications are largely neglected in Western Europe and Japan. With most of the strategic decisions concentrated at the top, there is a pronounced tendency not to communicate the reasoning behind decisions to those at lower management level (Nowotny). Sometimes social caste and rank interfere with team work and communication (Davis). Although decisions are generally reached rapidly in Japanese business, the democratization process requires that they be communicated slowly (Froomkin).

Decision-Making in Western Europe is still controlled by single individuals or at least by a smaller group of top executives than in the United States (Nowotny). The real problem in South America (Latin America) was that the supervisors had a father image in the "patriarchal" mill managers and were unable to make operational decisions without his approval (Davis). Decision-making is not very scientific in Latin America (McCann).

Delegation of Authority is avoided in many countries. Centralization of control or authority is characteristic of the French industrial enterprises as it is in the Italian or Indian enterprises (Harbison and Myers). There is a lack of application of the principle of delegation in enterprises in India (Prasad). The mill manager in South America tried to delegate decision-making authority to his supervisory personnel but neither he nor they were able to overcome the custom of deference to authority which existed in the culture (Davis).

Training and Development of Managerial Personnel is often neglected. European top executives try to save part of the time which their American counterparts spend on communication, though they do so somewhat at the expense of middle-management learning. An outdated convention still exists, namely, that a superior is not required to actively develop his subordinate's capacities (Nowotony). There is a general logic of management which has applicability both to advanced and industrializing countries of the world (Harbison and Myers). The superior-subordinate relationship among Indian managers is often a competitive relationship. This is in violation of one of the fundamental principles of effective management, namely, that it is a part of a manager's (superior's) job to train and improve the managerial skills of his subordinates (Prasad). Japanese workers (and managerial workers) are hired virtually for life and managerial promotions are mostly by seniority (Froomkin).

These few illustrations suggest that managerial practices, actions, and attitudes vary from one SEC context to the other,[12] and that an understanding of these variations and their repercussions constitutes one major aspect of comparative managerialism. The other is to find ways and means of improving management of business and industrial organizations via adaptation of successful techniques, methods, and philosophies. In this sense, comparative managerialism may be viewed as seeking results in the entire managerial system of the world, as though it were a large scale experiment. Failures are sometimes inevitable but improvements in design are possible.

This large scale experimentation is one of economic growth. Economic growth is commonly defined as a long-period increase in a country's national income in real terms. The theory of economic growth (or of economic development) is concerned with analyzing the process of economic growth, the forces responsible for it, and the accompanying structural changes. It is very well recognized that one of the major forces responsible for economic growth is "management." Evidence abounds to suggest that this recognition has taken place not only in managerial capitalistic countries but also in managerial socialistic countries.[13] The recent revival of interest in the Soviet bloc countries in terms of improved micromanagerialism underlines the recognition.

It is contended in this chapter that a study of management philosophy and process on a comparative basis will provide:

1. An insight into the problems of large-scale enterprises in public, private, or the labor sectors of a given country when comparisons between sectors are made.
2. A rationale for the organization and management of enterprises in such a manner as to minimize ineffectuality and maximize effectiveness.
3. A veritable source of information which may be extremely use-

---

[12] "That management philosophy is culture bound" is inferred in Richard F. Gonzalez and Claude McMillan, "The Universality of American Management Philosophy," *Academy of Management Journal* (April 1961), pp. 33-41; "that cultural differences are more significant than many writers appear to recognize" is stressed in Wiston Oberg, "Cross-Cultural Perspectives on Management Principles," *Academy of Management Journal* (June 1963), pp. 129-143.

[13] See Chapter 10 in this volume.

ful in adapting managerial techniques of one country in another SEC setting. This does not necessarily have to be an adaptation by a developing country of a technique from an advanced country.

4. An insight into the types of problems which may be common to many countries, and thereby foster increased internationally pooled efforts to solve these problems.

5. An opportunity to study the major aspects of one of the governing forces of economic growth.[14]

One may discern two related and mutually inclusive themes surrounding comparative management studies: international comparative studies such as those of McCann and Prasad (Ch. 2 and 3), Harbison and Myers (Ch. 5), Berliner (Ch. 9), and intranational comparative studies such as those proposed by Negandhi and Estafen (Ch. 19). The one major distinction between these two themes is that while in the former "environment" is a variable, in the latter it is a constant for research purposes. Comparative managerialism would include both of these themes.

In essence, comparative managerialism only broadens the scope of systematic study of entrepreneurship as a major element in the study of comparative economic systems. This field, a legitimate branch both of management and of developmental economics, is still in its infancy. However, it is encouraging to note that some graduate schools are offering courses in comparative management. It is hoped that this volume fulfills the objectives which were set forth at the beginning of the book.

[14] See the author's "Comparative Managerialism as an Approach to International Economic Growth," *The Quarterly Journal of A.I.E.S.E.C. International*, II, No. 3 (August, 1966).

Annotated Bibliography
of Selected Readings

ABEGGLEN, James C., *The Japanese Factory*. New York: The Free Press of Glencoe, 1958. Based upon the author's study of nineteen large and thirty-four small factories in a variety of industries in Japan, this book is concerned with "the aspects of social organization" of the Japanese enterprises. The social structure of Japanese factories is, according to the author, inconsistent with practices which American managers believe to be prerequisite for the efficient conduct of business concerns. One major conclusion stated in this book is that Japanese industrialization has been achieved within a social continuum which is much stabler than that of the West. The central point concerning the social organization of the Japanese factory is "life commitment" of members. Instead of causing a complete breakdown of traditional standards and creating virtually a new way of life, the Japanese factory has fitted quite well into the framework of a traditional society. This possibility bodes well for the underdeveloped countries which tend to look gloomily to Western experience to see what industrialization entails.

COCHRAN, Thomas C. and REINA, Ruben E., *Entrepreneurship in Argentine Culture*. Philadelphia: University of Pennsylvania Press, 1962. This book is neither a biography nor a business history in the conventional sense. It is a selection of the elements that appear historically and socially important in a case study of the introduction of mass production machinery into the "grain-and-cattle" economy of Argentina. The steps of the entrepreneurial career of Torcuato Di Tella, which the authors trace, provide useful insight into the general problems and attitudes arising from the process of industrialization. Di Tella and his family are studied as a part of the Latin American complex that operates differently from family-owned businesses in the United States.

EHRMANN, Henry W., *Organized Business in France*. Princeton, N.J.: Princeton University Press, 1957. The author presents a broad study of the French business lobby, its history, organization, modes of action, and postures on a variety of economic issues. Students of comparative management and of comparative political studies will find this volume of great interest for there has not been much in American writings about the issues which Ehrmann deals with. Methodologically, this is a conservative volume. The author tells of the extensive interviewing in his research but the results of interviews are not reported in the body of the text.

FARMER, Richard and RICHMAN, Barry, *Comparative Management and Economic Progress*. Homewood, Ill.: Richard D. Irwin, Inc., 1965. "Why do industrial managerial activity and the effectiveness of management relative to economic progress vary among different countries?" is the general question elucidated in this volume. The authors focus their analysis on industrial management. The stated aim of this book is to develop a general theory of comparative management. Since the authors view the book as a pioneering work in the newly emerging field of comparative management, much of it is highly suggestive of approaches and methods. This book may be the second strong link between management and economic development strategies.

FAYERWEATHER, John, *The Executive Overseas*. Syracuse: Syracuse University Press, 1959. This book explores administrative attitudes and relationships in a foreign culture, specifically the American manager in the culture of Mexico. The author examines executive relations and patterns of administrative action; individual work with respect to innovation, analysis, and action; and problems and possibilities of learning. Fayerweather's essential conclusion is that the major problems in relations between the US executives and those of other nations develop from differences in cultural attitudes which change slowly.

GRANICK, David, *Management of the Industrial Firm in the U.S.S.R.* New York: Columbia University Press, 1954. This substantial monograph is focussed on the plant directors who manage firms in Soviet heavy industry. The author has made a pioneering study of industrial administration in a totalitarian society, based upon inductive evidence from primary sources. His analysis will permit all those who are interested in planning and decision-making to add weight to the previous speculative abstractions concerning the Soviet system and its operations.

GRANICK, David, *The Red Executive*, and *The European Executive*. New

York: Doubleday & Company, Inc., 1960 and 1962. In *The Red Executive* Granick examines the role of the managerial group in Russia's rapid industrial development and their apparently paradoxical position. The author analyzes the red executive as a cog in the Soviet system and as an individual—his education in technical but rarely in administrative or management subjects, and his mode of living. A companion to *The Red Executive* is Granick's *The European Executive* in which the customs, class distinctions, traditions, and attitudes of different level managers in Great Britain, France, Belgium, and Germany are examined. The author emphasizes, throughout the book, national differences in management and labor patterns rather than similarities. This is a candid appraisal of the European manners and customs at the upper levels of managerial hierarchy.

HARBISON, Frederick and IBRAHIM, Ibrahim A., *Human Resources of Egyptian Enterprises*. New York: McGraw-Hill Book Company, Inc., 1958. This is an analysis of the human aspects of Egyptian industrialization. The authors chart the dimensions of the labor problems of industrialization in Egypt and suggest some general approaches toward the solutions. The book has three major sections: The Setting, Development of Manpower Resources, and Management of Labor Protest.

HARTMANN, Heinz, *Authority and Organization in German Management*. Princeton, N.J.: Princeton University Press, 1959. Devoted to an analysis of the system of authority as it is related to the internal organization of modern industrial enterprises in West Germany, the author suggests that German industry has evolved its own unique system of authority which is firmly rooted in the traditions and values of German culture. He also compares general administration, industrial relations, and management development in four case studies of patrimonial and professional management. Discussion of "codetermination" is also interesting. Hartmann's suggestion that the rationalization of management has limited the role of innovation and has encouraged the substitution of the concept of manager for that of the entrepreneur, can be seen in his "Managers and Entrepreneurs: A Useful Distinction?" *Administrative Science Quarterly*, III, No. 4 (March 1959), pp. 429-451.

LANGLEY, Kathleen M., *The Industrialization of Iraq*. Cambridge: Harvard University Press, 1962. The building of industrial plants may be of little benefit to a country unless people can run them and markets can be found for their products. The author, from her observations during a period of residence in Baghdad between 1953 and 1956, examines the above general theme within the context of Iraq. Chapters III and IV deal with the Iraqi industrial scene.

LAUTERBACH, Albert, *Enterprise in Latin America*. Ithaca, New York: Cornell University Press, 1966. Based upon personal interviews by the author, this study is an excellent investigation of the managerial attitudes toward economic development in Latin America. Policy implications both for Latin America and the United States are well brought out.

LEWIS, Roy, and STEWART, Rosemary, *The Managers*. New York: The New American Library, 1958. Lewis and Stewart make a penetrating examination of the philosophy and practice of the English, German, and American managers. An unendearing portrait of the manager is presented. This portrait makes the manager neither heroic nor lovable but efficient and a man of foresight. With perception and candor, the authors describe the qualifications, examine the problems, estimate the prospects, and consider the power and privileges of the English, German, and American managers.

MARTYN, Howe, *International Business*. New York: The Free Press of Glencoe, 1964. In this book the reader will find an analysis and description of international (multinational) enterprises along with an explanation of the various economic and social factors that lead international firms to establish overseas subsidiaries. The author, who has himself been intimately involved in the management of international business, offers useful guidelines to managers of international business.

McGREADY, Edward A., *The Americanization of Europe*. New York: Doubleday & Company, Inc., 1964. This is a study of the impact of Americans and American businessmen in Europe. Students of management may find Chapter 15, which is concerned with "Why top American managers are relatively rare in Europe," an insight into the international problems of American business firms.

MOSSON, T. M., *Management Education in Five European Countries*. Doctoral Dissertation, University of Manchester (England), 1963. This thesis sets out to trace the form of management education in Belgium, France, Italy, Spain, and the United Kingdom, and to show the forces which have shaped the institutions concerned. Throughout the study particular attention is paid to the role played in management education by the social sciences.

MYERS, Charles A., "Lessons from Abroad for American Management." *Journal of Business* (January 1960). The author examines recent trends in American managerialism in the light of studies of managerial structures and philosophies abroad, and raises the question if American management is as advanced as many believe.

NATIONAL PLANNING ASSOCIATION monographs: especially, *The Development of Latin American Private Enterprise* by Frank Brandenburg; *The General Electric Company in Brazil* by Theodore Geiger; *The Development of African Private Enterprise* by Theodore Geiger and Winifred Armstrong; and, *Aluminium Limited in India* by Subbiah Kannappan and Eugene Burgess.

NIEHOFF, Arthur, "Caste and Industrial Organization in North India." *Administrative Science Quarterly,* Vol. 3, Number 4 (March 1959), pp. 494-508. Anthropologist Niehoff, who spent a year in northern India as a Fulbright scholar, deals with the unique barrier to industrialization, namely, the caste-system. Throughout the paper it is shown that the social system and industrial organization interact upon each other. He also infers that the mixture of castes within the factories has presented few problems because of the unemployment problem, and the tremendous social distance between the worker and the manager.

RICHMAN, Barry M., *Soviet Management.* Englewood Cliffs, N.J.: Prentice-Hall, Inc., 1964. Dr. Richman deals at length with the organization of Soviet industrialization as a whole, including the changes of recent years, in order to show how this affects the manager's behavior. It is the organizational aspects of Soviet management in which the author is most interested. This book is valuable for the detailed manner in which it is presented, and for the comprehensive approach. As the sub-title implies, the reader will find a good picture of Soviet management with some significant comparisons with American management.

YUDELMAN, Montague, *Africans on the Land.* Cambridge: Harvard University Press, 1964. Convinced that Africans south of the Sahara must first expand their present exchange economy if they are to satisfy growing aspirations to industrialize, Yudelman concentrates on Southern Rhodesia whose developmental problems are similar to many other countries in the African continent. The author presents an analysis of the current situation and a strategy for development, taking into account the interrelated social, agricultural, economic, and political factors. This book gives an excellent account of the environment within which certain elements relevant from the point of view of management for industrialization can be identified.

WELLISZ, Stanislaw, *The Economics of the Soviet Bloc.* New York: McGraw-

Hill Book Company, 1964. This study is a primer of Soviet-type economics, and is designed for those who do not wish to acquire specialized knowledge, yet who would like to learn about the role of the consumers and of workers, and about the role of the party leaders and planners. This study aims to show, in a broad and general way, how the Soviet system works, and how Soviet management is an integral part of the Soviet system.

In addition to the above selected works which will be of great interest and usefulness for students and researchers, comprehensive bibliographies relevant to international/comparative management can be found in the following:

1. LINDFORS, Grace V., *Bibliography, Cases and Other Materials for the Teaching of Multinational Business*. Boston: Harvard University Graduate School of Business Administration, May 1964.
2. STEWART, Charles F., and SIMMONS, George, *A Bibliography in International Business*. New York: Columbia University Press, 1964.